At 12th & MARQUETTE

At 12th & MARQUETTE

A Story of Love, Faith, and Caregiving

A Memoir

Deborah – Thank you for buying my book. I hope you enjoy! ♡

by Marie Malicki

At 12th & MARQUETTE

© 2021 by Marie Malicki. All rights reserved.

All rights reserved. No part of this publication may be reproduced or transmitted in any form or by any means, electronic or mechanical, including photocopy, recording, or any information storage and retrieval system, without permission in writing from the publisher. Please contact publisher for permission to make copies of any part of this work.

Windy City Publishers
www.windycitypublishers.com

Published in the United States of America

ISBN:
978-1-953294-15-9

Library of Congress Control Number:
2021918448

Cover Design by Douglas Malicki

WINDY CITY PUBLISHERS
CHICAGO

This book is to honor those who have so enriched my life, particularly during Jim's illness.

To Jim, my beloved husband. Thank you for 40 years!

To My cherished children: Cheryl and Douglas, and son-in-law George.

To all those relatives, friends, and "the Hood," who sustained me with their prayers and support when life got tough. You know who you are. I would not have made it without you.

And to caregivers everywhere
who so unselfishly and mercifully give of themselves to serve the needs of others.

INTRODUCTION

From June 2006 through July 2007, I was spun into a quasi-transcendental state as my compassion and physical strength, which allowed me to nourish and support Jim, surpassed anything I imagined possible. When I try to identify its origins, I can only think there must have been some ad hoc coded instruction in our marriage's DNA.

Early in the course of Jim's illness, journaling, initially undertaken to log my observations and to keep track of the minutiae of his care, became a soothing friend. I lingered in those precious moments before bedtime. My companions were a cordial of amaretto and my journal; the perfect analgesic that broke the caregiving cycle to negotiate sleep. It's where I stashed away the day's story. Tumbling onto the blank pages in front of me were my appeals to God, my anger and fear, human kindnesses, and the joy and humor that left a mark on my day.

With this writing, I'd like to document the all-consuming role of caregiver, a role many of us will find ourselves in during our lifetime. Entwined with this, one of my goals is to bring awareness to the disease amyloidosis, and to reveal Jim for the remarkable man he was in his efforts to achieve renewed health, and his acceptance and peace with dying.

I reminisced with family members, friends and other relevant individuals as I gathered my thoughts for this memoir. I sensed that memories are malleable and their clarity is inconsistent. The passage of time will most often suppress or distort details.

My intention is to make this writing as accurate to my experience and memory as possible. It is based on my own specific memories and my personal interpretation of distant remembrances of the flow of my lifetime. Pertinent journal entries and medical records will be revisited and included in this writing.

Life is a pilgrimage on a meandering road. Undertaken in pursuit of happiness and the good life, the road ultimately takes us to our journey's end. We are given keys at a young age. We sit in the driver's seat of life. Barely able to maneuver through traffic, we map a course. Behind the wheel, the steady drone of the tires lulls us into complacency. Then, just when we're secure with the condition of the asphalt, the rules of the road change. Something unforeseen occurs which alters the journey. Finding ourselves at a critical point, or a crossroad we're not familiar with, we hit the brakes. We try to go back, we take a wrong turn, or we willingly sidetrack and steer a new direction.

There were times my life took a wrong turn; lost, I found myself on a dead-end street. Decisions were made as I backtracked and steered a new direction. The most relevant direction I took began at the intersection of 12th & Marquette.

PART ONE
THE ROAD TO 12TH & MARQUETTE

I did not write it.
God wrote it.
I merely did his dictation.

~Harriet Beecher Stowe

1
THIS PLACE

*One day I'll feel the depth of hugs once again,
and it's going to feel like home.*

~Nouf Alfadl

I'm sitting in Jim's maroon leather recliner that I bought him for Christmas many years ago. Its depth, brass nails and claw feet say "man chair." It's not comfortable for a woman my size, and I debated if I should sell it, but it's here with me. How could I sell it? Like his Chevelle, and the tools carefully systematized in his three and a half car garage, Jim loved his recliner. The recliner symbolized relaxation after a day's work, on occasion an evening drink, time to chat, read a book or watch TV. Occasionally, he did all that in one evening. The chair's functionality became a trusted friend. While he was sick, it took custody of Jim's safety and comfort; a haven of sorts, as our lives veered down the road to our last intersection together.

I'm not a pretty sight! Jim would be startled by my shattered appearance. I look how I feel. Battered emotionally, I look dreadful and unbecoming in gray, baggy sweats. My poor feet, cold since I arrived, are encased in two pairs of socks and my LL Bean sheepskin moccasins. The salty tears I've swallowed, fail to extinguish the fire of inner pain trying to unleash itself. I'm wiped out.

My mood forbids me from concentrating on TV, or anything else for that matter. A queasy feeling rises in my chest to the back of my throat. It makes a bid to overwhelm me when my mind wanders to thoughts of the last road we traveled together, and my helplessness to make Jim better.

I push myself to my feet, propelled as the recliner lurches forward with a thud. Cautiously, I maneuver around the boxes the movers have stacked in the middle of my sunroom. I have the sensation that I'm sleepwalking. My sensibilities return as I approach the frosty bare windows and wake up to the awareness of how cold I am. Even though the thermostat is set at seventy degrees and warm air is being forced into the room, it's a penetrating cold. Shivers run down my spine as I reach for the warmth and comfort of Jim's Marine Corps blanket, my security when I search for tenderness and warmth.

Woven in shades of red, white, blue and gold, adorned with a field of stars on a dark blue background, the Marine Corps emblem is heralded in the blanket's center. Jim had a penchant for nostalgia and he loved the Marine Corps. The blanket, a Valentine's gift from our daughter Cheryl and her husband George, was not only meant to keep his toes warm. As he drifted through the smoke of battle, the blanket and the Marine Corps NCO sword given to him from Douglas, Cheryl and George for his 63rd birthday, symbolized clarity to his fierce dedication to the mission assigned him. Surrender and retreat were not in his vocabulary.

My arms waste no time as they wend their way into the warm comfort of its fabric. I restlessly finger the fringe. In glum disbelief I scrutinize my new surroundings and landscape. Although I'm in Illinois, I somehow have the notion that I'm in a foreign land across many seas. The weather is blustery and snowy. A treeless, wind-whipped, snow-blanketed landscape peers at me from across the street. Lit up to the east is a four-lane highway. I'm not used to seeing so much light after dark. Street lights, retail lights and vehicle headlights; they annoy me.

The snow plow is persistent and offensive as its blade scrapes on the pavement. It grates on my last nerve. I'm hit with the queer grasp that my reality and universe have been permanently altered. It's January! I'm "up north," in the land of snow, sleet, ice and subzero temperatures. But more than this, there's a gnawing awareness that although my daughter and son-in-law live in the area and have given their all to soften the transition, this place is not a sanctuary for the anxieties that accompany deep loss. I wonder when, or if ever, healing will take place.

And there's the song. My brain won't release me from its bondage. Although it's a beautiful song that once raised my awareness to the certainty of the divine,

I wish I could make it go away. "Be Not Afraid" plays like a broken record; its repetition has left me exhausted. Ignorant to its verses, I'm trapped in its refrain.

My mind analyzes the mantra. I am afraid. Certainly, rest is sorely needed. Why am I astonished then to realize that the words precisely characterize my current temporal and spiritual anxieties?

I grapple for recollections of happier times and need to end this pity party. I decide to look into the rearview mirror, at the roads, stopovers and intersections that brought me to this place.

It's past the time for my daily phone call to check on Mom's day, so I dial her number. "Hello," Mom says. "Marie?"

"Yes, Mom, it's Marie."

"*Well*! How come you're calling so late?"

My stomach churns at the tone. I don't want to explain or ruminate about my evening. I fake cheerful elocution and tell her I was lost in thought, thinking about the "good ol' days." Most evenings she would have steered the conversation back to her daily activities or sketched in detail her new aches and pains, but I egg her on. I barrage her with probing questions about my birth. She yields. The story has changed a bit throughout the years; Mom's recollections are reconstructed with every telling. Today is no exception.

2
BIRTH

It was Sunday, May 16th, 1948. Harry S. Truman was president, and Dinah Shore was singing "Buttons and Bows." *The Original Amateur Hour* was on TV, and Gillette was touting "Look Sharp, Feel Sharp—Be Sharp." It was also the day, I the first of the four Jablonski kids, decided to make my debut.

Fate would have it that I was born in South Milwaukee, Wisconsin. Within the scope of Metropolitan Milwaukee, a place where beer, brats, and Friday night fish fries still rule, and where a water fountain is better known as a "bubbler," South Milwaukee thrived. Located on the western shore of the southern basin of Lake Michigan, South Milwaukee was the perfect Midwestern town to marry, raise a family, and live the American dream. Jobs were plentiful. Individuals were industrious. The U.S. was well on its way to becoming the richest country in the world.

In 1948, daily life in South Milwaukee's downtown played out like Norman Rockwell reality TV. A walkabout downtown had popular appeal. Milwaukee Avenue, its main street, had a business to suit anyone's needs. The street was especially busy, bustling with the new rhythm of life that tenaciously permeated towns across America following the end of World War II and the birth of the Baby Boom Generation.

Near where the city's water tower loomed tall and proud, the street included a Catholic book store, liquor store, tavern, and a drug store with a soda fountain. The pulse of the busy street was also complemented with a furniture store, shoemaker, photography studio, bakery, and South Milwaukee Hospital, the place of my birth.

As related by Mom, the epic tale of my birth is undistinguished in its histrionics. It was about 2:00 a.m. and I wanted out. With nervous exhilaration, Dad called a cab for the trip to the hospital.

A three-story structure, made from white clapboard, which had formerly been a single-family residence, the hospital had no elevators. Disquieting angst built when Mom realized she'd have to ascend two flights of stairs, but it didn't find a home for long. Nine months of pregnancy and her next labor pain persuaded her to come to terms with the stairs. Without hesitation, Dad shepherded Mom to the second floor. They entered the hospital's small maternity ward with trepidation.

Unlike today, a father's vigilance was preempted at the labor room door. Excluded from the particularities of childbirth, fathers were thought to be in the way. Accommodations for fathers-in-waiting were meager at best, so, urged on by Mom's nurse, my apprehensive father went home to wait out Mom's labor and the birth of their child. The nurse rationalized that a phone call and short cab ride to the hospital would have Dad back at the hospital in no time.

Prompted with the usual little smack on my inverted behind, I let out my first cry at 6:15 a.m. I weighed in at 7 pounds, 5 ounces, was bald as a cue ball, and named Marie Louise.

Minutes later, Dad was roused out of a sleepless stupor when an on-staff stranger called informing him everything went well. He was the father of a baby girl. Curious, I asked Mom why she didn't call Dad. Her simple answer: "There were no phones in patient rooms."

Straightaway, Dad called the cab company and made a beeline to the hospital. Cocky as he was, he had recklessly bet all his guy pals I would be a boy, but tickled to death when he saw his little girl, I'm told his captivated gaze beheld joy for my new life as part of his. Later, time with Dad had to be shared with two brothers and a sister, but throughout those hectic years, Dad's ardent joy that I was his daughter was open and loving. Paid without fail, the lifetime annuity of joy he expressed for me was truly the best gift he gave me.

As a child, when you're old enough to start assimilating knowledge about oneself, you wonder why you were given your particular name. I don't remember how old I was when I first heard the story. What I do remember is feeling a bit bewildered at Mom's indifference to where it came from. I've heard the "Marie Louise" story several times throughout the years. Here it is:

The rationale for naming me Marie Louise was twofold. First, Mom loved the name Marie and Dad wholeheartedly agreed. Second, as they were searching for a middle name, Dad hinted that Louise sounded pretty with Marie. What needs to be told is that following the D-Day invasion at Normandy Beach, while serving in the Army Air Corps during World War II, Dad was assigned to duty in France. He never spoke to us about his time in France or the war. One thing I did learn, however, is that he was an altar server at Mass in the church in the town of Sainte-Mère-Eglisé. This is the same church depicted in the D-Day movie *The Longest Day* where the paratrooper, John Steele, got hung up on the church spire while the battle continued to rage on. I don't know if it was in Sainte-Mère-Iglisé, or somewhere else in France, but in addition to serving his country, Dad apparently discovered the comforts of bonding while in a far-off place, and became enamored with a woman named Marie Louise. I've dubbed her Marie Louise France.

The war ended and it was time for Dad to return to the States. Honorably discharged at Fort Sheridan in Illinois on November 20th, 1945, he returned to his parents' home in South Milwaukee where he and Marie Louise France continued to bond via air-mail. Apparently, their bonding was not ardent enough to keep Dad from hanging out at Rawson Ballroom, which is where he met Mom the night of the Firemen's Ball.

Dad strutted his newly executed jitter bug steps with the young ladies, and downed a beer or two with his buddies, until, captivated by a brown-haired beauty across the ballroom, Dad strolled over to where Mom and her best friend were enjoying the company of friends. His sweetened advance—"Can I buy you girls a wine?"—yielded the intended results. Immediately attracted, Mom and Dad danced the night away. At the close of the evening, Dad asked

Mom if he could call. She said yes, and the rest is history. They married on September 7th, 1946, ten months after Dad was discharged.

As crazy as it sounds to give your daughter the name of a former heartthrob, Mom and Dad agreed that they loved the sound of the name, and that Marie Louise it should be.

I love my name and I've been delighted to be called Marie, but through the years I couldn't help but wonder how often Dad reminisced about my namesake in France. You know there had to be those moments in time when he spoke or heard my name that Marie Louise France tip-toed into his consciousness.

Hospital visiting hours came to a close. Never a rebel or one to challenge the rules, Dad left the hospital at the proscribed time. Ecstatic, he couldn't wait to share the details of the day with my grandparents, Frank and Johanna Jablonski.

To sum it up, I'd say, "What a day!" I came into this world, as did millions of other babies, as part of a demographic post World War II baby-boom. Although the early years of the Cold War were starting to wrap the nation in fear, it was a buoyant time in American history when opportunities were plentiful. America was an industrial power enabling many Americans, my family included, to enjoy a comfortable standard of living. When you add to this equation two solid, loving parents who provided a firm foundation for childhood and beyond, the start to my life journey couldn't have been scripted any better.

3
FAITH'S INFRASTRUCTURE

Adorned in a flowing, white christening gown, and held firm in the arms of my mother, I entered St. Adalbert Church for the first time on May 30th, 1948.

I let out a small cry when Father sprinkled my forehead with the living water of Baptism, representing life, death, cleansing, and growth. At the age of 15 days, my Baptism and initiation into the Catholic Church certainly was not a personal mountain-top experience. It was Mom and Dad's public stamp of promise that they would train me in the practice of Catholicism, and my childhood faith experience systematically unfolded to conform to their promise.

My parents and Godparents didn't have the vaguest idea St. Adalbert's would hold firm its attachment. Throughout my life I've zigzagged to and from its moorings. Most times it was habit or obligation that brought me there. At other times it was the Requiem Mass for the deceased. Its safe and stable religiosity sheltered both joy and sadness. It is a player in my story, and bears a bit of description.

4
ST. ADALBERT CHURCH

The decision was imposing. I took umbrage at the suggestion they'd even consider it. Why St. Adalbert's?

St. Adalbert Parish had not been my parish of worship for many years, but I took the news personally when I learned the four parishes of South Milwaukee were combining to become Divine Mercy Parish. St. Adalbert Church and its facilities would be put up for sale.

Veneration of St. Adalbert's courses through my veins. It's been a key stopping point on my life's journey. In my childhood, the school and parish were essential to my growth. As an adult, the observances venerating the beginning and closing stages of my love affair with Jim had the most impact. It is the one hallowed place where I have experienced the strongest of human emotions, from elation to heartbreak. Quiet power of all things worldly and otherworldly resides and holds memory at St. Adalbert's.

The ten stained glass windows were timeless in design. Scaled to dress approximately one-half of the side walls, their vibrant hues transformed the space. Their narration, whether illuminated with sunbeams, the warm and rich glow of day's transitional light, or low voltage incandescent light, encouraged a scriptural study of Jesus.

Cosmetic redecorating was completed in 1970 and 1992. Good fortune would have it that the church retained its ambience reminiscent of the period it was built. There were poor boxes and holy water fonts at the doorways, and true to its Polish heritage, enthroned on a side altar was an image of Our Lady of Czestochowa, declared "Queen of Poland" by King John Casimir in 1656.

The church interior took on different personas and moods depending on the observance. It could be elegant, cheery, serene, or somber, and sometimes mysterious. Smells and sounds were crucial to the experience.

As a child, it felt foreboding and ethereal to luxuriate in the aromatherapy of burning incense especially during evening services. The censer swayed back and forth, emitting an aromatic cloud of smoke symbolizing the rise of our prayers to heaven. Working a sort of effervescent magic, these rituals simultaneously roused a sense of sacredness and a feeling of holy detachment. Perplexed as I was about God, these glorious rituals fueled my puerile sense of Him as a bit bad-natured, a supreme patrolman of sorts. My notion was that his malevolent eyes were observing me from some secret vantage point ready to pounce at any sign of disrespect or misbehavior. Mindful of this, and Sister's vulture-like eyes honing in on those whose standard of devotion did not meet hers, my endeavor was piety. Piety: Remain motionless. Keep hands folded and head down. To avoid Sister's prizefighter knuckles, I stared chameleon-like at the spectacle, daring only to move the muscles on my face. My gaze shifted up, then down. Arched eyebrow right, arched eyebrow left. With no referee to temper the jabs hammered at her "opponent's" shoulder blade, those caught up in Sister's disapproval quickly learned you never wanted to go more than one round with her. To duck or weave guaranteed a second round, and if not in church, a lashing out for all those within ear shot.

St. Adalbert Church gave rise to songful incantation. Sounds distinctive to its Polish heritage aggrandized significant holydays and rituals. The children's choir, of which all students were a member at one time or another, learned hymns and Christmas Carols not only in English but in Polish. I can't remember the verses to "Be Not Afraid," but I'm proud to say I can still sing a bungled version of "Przybiezeli do Betlejem." We had no clue what we were singing when we practiced the Polish hymns. It was all a bunch of thick sounds, emphasized, re-emphasized and spit out by Sister, but we sang with vigor and pride, convinced that we knew Polish.

Also conspicuous was the prayerful buzz of the mostly chubby little old Polish *busias* (*Busia* is Polish for grandmother). They wore multi-colored house dresses and gaudy fringed babushkas to cover their over-permed gray hair, while their blue-veined and gnarled hands fingered the beads of the rosary. The expressions on their desiccated faces highlighted their hardened wrinkles.

Oblivious to the world around them, they whispered a monotone "*pshhh-pshhh-pshhh*" through pursed lips, an act which reinforced rote and mechanical meditation. It seemed odd. I wondered, *Why do they do that?* I thought these old women were permanent fixtures of the church. They were always in their assigned seats.

I'm sad to say that for all its aforementioned environment and history, St. Adalbert's has met a new reality. A victim to the priest shortage and financial woes of the Catholic Church, it has been sold and the church now serves as a mosque.

5
1950s CHILDHOOD, LIFE IN A BOX

A pessimist might look back on 1950s America and remember the fears of Communism, hydrogen bombs, and bomb shelters. However, optimism, rivaling all that was worrisome in the decade, is more likely to be remembered as people recount a patriotic, feel-good decade in America: The Fabulous Fifties.

The religious, financial, and social mores of the era dictated the protocols and statutes of the institutions and families that governed my life. Its combined force codified my family's canon for life and trained me to stay within the secure confines of the individual boxes. My reality was comfortable, practical, and controlled. At home and Catholic school, concepts of independent thinking, self-esteem, and self-confidence were subordinate to the broader constructs of obedience, guilt, self-discipline, and work.

Mom and Dad's undeniable zest for life in the 1950s was obvious to me. By 1954, their healthy Catholic marriage expanded the family to six. Five houses, one on 18th Avenue and four on streets beginning with an "M," were bought, decorated, landscaped, and sold. In 1952, the grandeur of the family's first automobile was ostentatiously displayed on Mackinac Avenue. Opulent in its bumper-to-bumper green glow, it had fat, white-wall tires and enough chrome to adorn three of today's cars.

During this period, my parents outwardly embraced cultural guidelines where gender roles were concerned in order to achieve a functional family.

Dad was the bread winner and took his parental duty to mean providing protection, shelter, and food. He strove in everything he did to improve his family's life.

I doubt Mom was as gleeful doing her chores as the ads for new appliances and cleaning products of the 1950s depicted, but I do know, sans the Donna

Reed pearls and high heels, she was a diligent housewife. She was a master at organization, a perfectionist and slave to cleanliness. Behavior and order were sacrosanct. I never asked, but I feel almost certain Mom and Dad felt judged by how they, the house and our family looked and behaved.

I can now appreciate the complexity of raising four children born in a six-year time span and their need for order. For the sake of raising good kids, there were many times they set aside some of that easy-going, spontaneity I had witnessed when it was just my brother and me. However, everything they did was wrapped in love with genuine concern for our futures.

ஐ

The Catholic school curriculum provided an environment that supported Mom's beliefs in the Catholic way as being the true and only way to heaven. I think this verse was Mom's motto:

Train a boy in the way he should go;
even when he is old, he will not swerve from it"

~Proverbs 22:6; New American Bible, Catholic Version

I attended St. John's school from grade one through the first semester of grade five. Time spent there was consistent with Mom and Dad's expectations and a lot more. My primary role was to learn from the nuns, not only the 3-Rs, but everything Catholic. Our lessons included living the liturgical calendar, memorizing the Baltimore Catechism's question and answer lessons of doctrine and morality, introduction to the sacraments, primarily confession and communion, litanies, novenas and benedictions, and the painful stories of those beset with the stigmata and the macabre events that made men and women martyrs. Regimentation and rules, sacrifice and reward seemed to be the theme.

We adopted Pagan Babies, those "poor, heathen" babies who were abandoned by their parents and left to die. An innocent baby's existence and soul hung suspended until we could collect enough money for the foreign missionaries to ransom and baptize a baby. Our lessons in sacrifice and reward, and Sister's promise that we could name the baby when the "official" Certificate of Adoption arrived on her desk, kept her jar filled with the coin crucial to saving a child.

School was a homogenized and patterned environment, a province of all white, middle-class kids and nuns. Each element was consistent no matter what grade you were in. Black slate chalkboards stretched across the front and one side of the room. There was enough chalk strategically lined up to write one hundred times, "I will not talk in church." Hardwood floors seemed to be installed to hurt your knees when forced to kneel, and the Palmer cursive alphabet was on display. Excessively anal, concise cursive was paramount to nuns. Any nun worth her salt would as soon remove your left hand than let you write with it.

☙

It took Dad about a year to design and draw up the specs and get the blueprints ready for what would be our next home, but it took only about four months to build. I was eleven when we moved to our new house in 1959. That was also when we left St. John's parish and school, and returned to St. Adalbert's.

It was the second semester of my fifth-grade year. Except for the harshness of the Felician nuns, life at St. Adalbert's was not unlike life at St. John's.

The nuns at St. John's could be described as firm, with a benevolent disposition. The nuns at St. Adalbert's were at times controlling, bristly, willful, and stern with an effusive firmness that was inflexible. Their tutelage affects me to this day.

To say I was uneasy and curious on my first day at St. Adalbert's is an understatement. That day, like all school days, started with Mass. You might think an assemblage of old women, nuns, and school children would be free of duress and physical force. Oh, not so! Sister must have considered the ringing of the joyful Sanctus bells her call to strike. Terrified, I watched as she pushed her agitated self toward several unsuspecting classmates. She bent over the pew back, clenched her knuckles and without hesitation vigorously applied them to the shoulder blade of one of my classmates. I couldn't imagine what behavior warranted this reprimand. I certainly didn't notice anything. Her penchant for corporal discipline was unrivaled by any other nun I ever had contact with. The incident absolutely got my attention. I vowed right then she would never have the opportunity to hone her skills on me.

My resolve was tested a few hours later as Sister guided the class through a language lesson. She snapped out a question calling on someone named "Yaboinske." Her haste for a response escalated. "Yaboinske," she shouted. "Answer me."

She grew visibly perturbed. I dismissed her outburst as one intended for someone sitting behind me. Frustration puffed her cheeks. Finally, her rankled gaze settled on me. I intended to avert her eyes, but she wouldn't give up the gaze. I bemoaned my fate. *Why me, why is she looking at me like that? My name's not "Yaboinske!*

Her temperament finally got the best of her, and frenetically, she jerked her body back to grab her wooden pointer. Rosary beads swayed left and right as she bumped and plunged her way straight toward me. She stopped directly at my desk where she drilled that darn pointer right into the floor!

Even as the spittle spewed from her furious mouth, her petulant tongue never missed a beat. "You! What's wrong? Your name! Don't you know it? Answer me!" Lambasted, I was scared and felt like the tears were about to flow. Visibly exasperated, she spun around and called attention to someone else. I don't remember the question or answer that started it all, but I do remember when someone finally did answer, she roared, "E-nun-ci-ate! You need to e-nun-ci-ate!"

All of this must have tired her out. She handed out an assignment, assigned a class monitor to squeal on us, took her teeth out, placed them on the desk, and fell asleep.

Within a few hours of being at my new school I grasped two things: the sternness of Sister's temperament, and that I had mysteriously metamorphosed from Jablonski to Yaboinske.

6
1960s TEENAGER, BREAKING OUT OF THE BOX

The year 1959, the same year Alaska and Hawaii were welcomed to the Union, was also the start of our country's transition to a decade of new cultural and political trends. Looking back, it seems to me that the nation's consciousness began to change in the early '60s. A shift in political and social precepts transformed the course of America. A social revolution that involved women's liberation, The Establishment, assassinations, counter-culture drug use, civil rights, urban unrest, and the Vietnam War with all its consequences, left no one untouched. Fortunately, the social revolution and political actions of the decade didn't interfere with the remarkable gains in technology, medicine and space exploration.

I was certainly aware of what was going on in the world, but navigating through my adolescent and teen years I focused on and utilized information that was important to "self," school, friends, what they were doing, what we were going to do together, hair, make-up, clothing styles, music, and boys.

Later in the decade it was all about dating, getting engaged, and married. Our daughter, Cheryl, who, like her dad, is a well-informed and fanatic devotee of history and trivia, considers the turbulent time and influential events of the '60s pivotal in U.S. and world history. I wholeheartedly agree. Cheryl can spout off a litany of cultural and social upheavals and trends that bolstered a rebirth of culture. Only as an afterthought might she throw in, "Oh by the way, Mom and Dad met and married in the '60s." My first recall of the era is the exact opposite. It's memories of high school, beer parties, dances, Bugsy, and marrying Jim. Buried beneath these memories are recollections of the era, and a thought that gee, we as a society, and I as a teenager, did survive it.

At 12th & MARQUETTE

It was 1962. Like all other 14-year-old girls I was naïve and immature, prone to infatuation and desperate for freedom. I accelerated from simple Catholic school girl to teen brain in no time. Even the chaos of the October 1962 Cuban Missile Crisis, which brought the world close to nuclear destruction, was of little importance to me. In my self-centered world, the only important news involved boys, the latest in music, school, and those extra-curricular social activities that come hell or high water, I couldn't miss.

A Summer Place, the theme for our Freshman Frolic, was the premier event of my ninth-grade year. I desperately wanted to get asked to the dance, by Jeff. Knowing that Jeff had still not asked anyone, when Jerry posed the question I put him off. What a little witch (some might spell it with a "b") I was. Jeff, in all honesty, probably didn't know I existed, but a girl can dream. When it comes to love and desire, 14-year-old girls are good at that! Dispirited that time was getting short and Jeff had not asked me, I stopped Jerry in the hallway and accepted his invitation to the Frolic.

Even though I wasn't with Jeff, it was a memorable and fun first dance, first date, and first kiss. I don't know if this was Jerry's first kiss, but before it was time for me to go into the house, he seemed to be putting out feelers about what to do next, until hurriedly, he went in for the kill. Shorter than me, he tottered on his toes and gave me a clumsy goodnight kiss. There was no magic in this kiss; it only remains memorable as the first. Jerry and I continued to exchange pleasantries at school, but we never dated again.

The middle '60s were spent at the senior high school, working in a grocery store bakery, and with my boyfriend, Bugsy. During these three years and the year following high school graduation, I blissfully tooled down the highway of life, believing that Bugsy and I would live happily ever after. Little did I know that toward the end of the decade this life would lose traction, that I'd take an off ramp and head full throttle down an unexpected avenue.

I was about to enter the senior high and I had long forgotten Jeff. My wanton and meandering eyes now prowled the Rawson school grounds and local dance floors for Bugsy. At the time, he most certainly was the cutest 15-year-old guy in town, possibly the planet.

About this time, partiality to touch dancing was starting to lose its momentum to whatever was the latest craze or novelty dance. We did The Monkey, The Mashed Potato, and danced to such songs as "Walking the Dog" and "The Bird is the Word."

Flirting took over at those dances. We were explicit in our pursuit of that one person we wanted to connect with. With a little luck, after some flirtation or prompting by a friend, the interaction might continue with the object of your flirtation asking you to dance, especially a slow dance which seemed to convey more of a romantic signal. Several rounds of open unabashed flirtation between Bugsy and me and we were dancing. We danced both fast and slow, and chatted easily. He asked to walk me home. This was the start of a four-year teenage affair of the heart, and the beginning of a significant time in my development to adulthood.

Thoughts of Bugsy come easy. In the vernacular of a 15-year-old, he was gorgeous. I remember his brown hair was combed from left to right. It swooped a bit down over his forehead, but a glide of fingers through his hair would easily set it back in place. His eyes cast a sleepy-soft gaze. He had full lips and a dimpled chin that set my 15-year-old hormonal fires burning. Bugsy was wholesome, generally easy going, unflappable, kindhearted; a person with no ragged edges.

Bugsy attended an all-boys Catholic high school. I admit I liked that. I didn't have to worry about girls at school focusing their efforts on him, and I was with him after school and on weekends, ready to squelch any attempts by anyone who thought they could horn in. My emotional immaturity was not yet ready to foster a sense of security in my young love infatuation, especially when I considered him mine.

With that in mind, lovesick and immature, I fought and lashed out against my parents when I discovered they were going to force me to go on vacation with my family for a week in Eagle River, Wisconsin. How could they ruin my summer like this? How dare they take me away from my friends and Bugsy? How would I keep him focused on me when I was up in the woods? My emotions were out of control!

It was eons before the use of cell phones or e-mail, and now I even wonder if there was a phone in the cottage we rented. An old-fashioned letter was the only way we had to stay in touch during that tortuous week.

Not knowing what time the mailman would follow through with his part in this deliberate and fatiguing melodrama I had created to remind my parents how cruel they were to force me to go on vacation, I trekked to the mailbox several times a day. Sure that some creature might prove threatening to my existence, this trek was not an easy walk in the woods for me. You couldn't see the road from the cottage. It was a long winding walk to the mailbox, and I thought I should at least be accommodated with some sort of shuttle service. That certainly was not going to happen. The recent tone and malevolence I had adopted toward my parents' harsh tyranny precluded any accommodations for trips to the mailbox.

The Marvelettes' 1961 hit "Please Mr. Postman" accompanied me on my trek as I anticipated my reward for having to endure time in Eagle River.

Finally, it had arrived. There was one envelope in the box and it was for me. I chuckled at the notation on the envelope: "Mrs. Jablonski, keep your paws off this letter." I slit it open with my finger and stood dead still to devour its contents, no matter what varmint might now threaten my existence. I don't have that letter anymore, and to be honest I don't remember if it was a "missing you," "thinking of you," or "what have you been doing" sort of letter.

Having reliable wheels represented a new freedom on the road to full adulthood, and like most guys he palled with, Bugsy was a car enthusiast. I don't know if his enthusiasm was innate and an extension of self, or merely in pursuit of owning a sharp-looking, high-performance, and reliable vehicle. Whatever the impetus, he labored hard on each car he drove (or sometimes pushed) into his garage, restoring its body, paint, interior, and mechanics enhancing it to become a four-wheeled vehicle of pride.

Wiling time away in Bugsy's garage was my introduction to "Car Restoration 101." My budding education included subordinate elements such as risking the grime of grease, breathing in choking fumes, and watching Bugsy sculpt body filler on a car with the longest tail fins you ever laid your eyes on, and later an old Ford Crown Victoria convertible. It wasn't all sweat and toil for Bugsy, and I personally didn't consider it drudge. It was easy to track us down, so friends randomly stopped by to assess progress, giving life to topics such as Bondo versus other auto body fillers, hemi powered versus big-block, Hurst shifters, school, who was dating who, and what was happening next weekend. If there wasn't much happening, after calling it a day in the garage, we might head to Gondek's, the closest food and drink establishment for some fries or onion rings. Fans of the witticism and spine-chilling horror stories of Dr. Cadaverino and his headless assistant Igor, we watched *Nightmare Theater* on Saturday nights.

Whatever we were up to, we always left early enough so we'd have enough time for a stop along the Oak Creek Parkway. We nestled in obscurity under the Pine Street Bridge, a quiet place where the only thing to disturb the rustle of the creek were our whispers and kisses.

Before Bugsy got his license and had a reliable vehicle, he would meet me after work at the grocery store to walk me home. I worked part-time in its bakery. In the Jablonski household the words "work" and "sixteen" were synonymous. It was more than expected that I get a part-time job when I turned sixteen—it was required.

I was now self-reliant when it came to the purchase of my clothing, entertainment, or anything else not considered essential by my parents. Bugsy did get his license and finally managed to have an operating vehicle. That addition to our lives made me feel more independent and even less inclined to listen to my parents or heed their warnings.

I consider myself fortunate that all those unheeded warnings didn't end up in disaster somewhere along the way. We weren't bad kids by any definition. We were teenagers, and teenagers take risks. Beer drinking was a commonplace past-time. To their dismay, my unsuspecting parents arrived home to stumble upon, or sometimes discern after the fact, that they were the unintentional proprietors of a facility that hosted an underage drinking party. Grant Park, obliging with its many hideaways, endured unrestrained teenage assaults at the larger quarter-barrel or class parties. Partygoers put down roots well past the last drop of the barrel, or until someone yelled out, "Cops!" Desperate not to get caught, stumbling partygoers scattered throughout the park.

At age eighteen, legal to drink beer in some of Milwaukee's adjoining counties, we jammed the accelerator to bars as far as 45 miles away, the car coming to a rest in the parking lot of Marty Zivko's in Hartford, or the Brat Stop in Kenosha. That there were no afflictions, collisions, or calamitous misadventures that set my life on a ruinous road I am grateful.

In our senior year, on occasion Bugsy and I double-dated with my friend Joan and her boyfriend Don. Excerpts from Joan and Don penned in my 1966 yearbook hint to the dimension of my relationship with Bugsy:

Joan Wrote: *"Remember the times we doubled? Boy, half the time we didn't even know what we were going to do, but we'd end up parking so it was okay then…take good care of Bugsy. Remember when you elope I'm your best woman."*

Don wrote: *"Marie, we sure had a ball doubling although you and Joan had to be along. (Just kidding). Good luck in the future and I hope you and Bugs are me and Joan's neighbors in a couple years."*

Graduation couldn't come soon enough. I was busy looking for a job, and my friend, Joan, was sometimes with me as we hit the pavement together. In the waning weeks of our senior year, we skipped school, were found out, and were suspended. We found that being suspended was okay. We used the free time to go uptown with the pretense of filling out some more job applications, which we did, but more to have fun.

Although one of the prominent teachers in the business department in school lauded my great typing and shorthand skills, her assessment was that I had a "less than professional business attitude" and "rancorous approach to things." It was her attitude that this would markedly diminish my ability to obtain a good position upon graduation. As a matter of fact, she asked me where I had applied for a job and told me I certainly would never be hired at any of those places. I passed all the employment tests with flying colors and received three good job offers. I accepted the one that was the easiest to get to (I still did not drive), and which, by the way, had the added bonus of good benefits and paid the most. I started my new job the Monday after graduation.

7
CROSSROADS

I was eighteen, had a job, and paid rent to live at home. Being the adult person I thought I was, I had no interest in anyone trying to run my life, especially my parents. One area where we clashed was their expectation that I continue to attend Mass on Sundays. Frankly, at that time the church held little interest to me.

It was also about this time that my friend Winnie and I started to spend more time together. Both St. Adalbert alums, we decided to "go to church" together—a late Mass, one we knew our parents never went to. I was all dressed for church when Winnie picked me up in her new black Mustang. We headed to "church"—which on many Sundays took us to the park, where we stopped at the beach and chatted away the hour until we were "let out of Mass." Following the February 1967 gas explosion that tore apart about 70 percent of the new addition adjacent to St. Adalbert Church, Winnie and I joked it wasn't a safe place to be. After all, the one time I stepped back into church for confirmation practice, it had exploded.

In the meantime, my life continued in the steady flow of traffic. Not much time had passed after high school graduation when my friend, Joan (of Joan and Don), needed a roommate to share apartment expenses. I jumped at the opportunity to finally taste full independence. Even though we didn't live together for a long time, life was good in the apartment with Joan. It was a freeing existence, which taught me how to budget more carefully and take responsibility for myself. Rice-A-Roni became my favorite meal. Because I wasn't the neatest at that time, and always in a hurry to get somewhere, there was always a dried up bit of rice sitting in a frying pan on the stove.

I had a fine job, but no way to get there except by bus. Winnie, who had a third shift factory position with a large Milwaukee employer, offered to stop by on her way home and chauffeur me to work. The rides to work were more like joy rides. We'd catch up with "friend" stuff and Winnie would inevitably carry on about her co-workers, people I had never met.

PART TWO
STEERING A NEW ROAD

*There is no such thing as chance;
and what seems to us merest accident
springs from the deepest source of destiny.*

~Johan Friedrich Von Schiller

8
PROVIDENTIAL MEETING

Winnie's new fixation was to enthusiastically jabber about the new guy she met at work; a mischievous romp intended to deliberately pique my curiosity. With impetuous vivacity, she gushed on about Jim; it was almost comical as she gleefully sprang up and down in the driver's seat. With more than a shiver of excitement she raved. "You should see the head on this guy! He is soooo cute, Rie. You'd love him. He's smart, mature, and sooo handsome! He was in the Marine Corps! He's got a girlfriend. I don't think he's too into her! She works with us. You've got to meet him!" On and on she sung the virtues of Jim. Although I was not at all interested in a new boyfriend, I have to admit that all the blather about the phenomenon that was Jim did bait my curiosity.

Thanks in part to Winnie's crafty plotting and adept driving skills, on a hot and muggy morning in late July, my world was opened to Jim Malicki.

The day started like any other. There were no tip-offs or premonitions about the spell that was about to be placed over my heart. Like every weekday morning, I stood at the curb awaiting Winnie's arrival. Half asleep, I prepared myself for our usual morning banter and her constant rave about the new guy at work.

Winnie's car seemed to gather speed as it roared toward me. I thought, *What the heck? Why is she going so fast?* She pulled to the curb at full tilt and motioned wildly as she pointed to the green blur that passed on the left. "Hurry, get in, there he goes," she screeched, as I gracelessly plopped into the passenger seat.

"What the heck's going on? What's the urgency?"

"Jim, the guy from work that I've been telling you about, that's him in the green Chevelle. We've been chasing each other since we left the lot at work."

She looked in her mirror, leaned on it, and there was no slowing that Mustang down until we were on Jim's tail. We got our break at 10th & Marquette. We pulled up directly behind Jim, foretelling a providential moment in time which was about to change my life.

Excitement buzzed as she laid on the horn, waved, and jerked her head out of the window until he looked back. His rakish grin acknowledged her high jinks. Jim turned right, and headed west under the trestle, and waited until Winnie pulled up next to him at 12th & Marquette.

☙

I didn't know the Divine was on call that day, ready to change my destiny. How else could you explain it? Divine care, with help from Winnie, wielded the gravitational pull that brought us together that fateful day in July 1967—a meeting which formed our destiny for forty years.

The three of us radiated lighthearted grins while Winnie exclaimed, in an overplayed tone, "Jim, this is Marie. Rie, this is Jim." My senses burst ajar. My inquisitive eyes eagerly took measure of Jim. Words were spoken, but my ears behaved as if paralyzed. The sparkle and voltage of the moment rattled and astounded me. The luminosity of his smile, his concentrated focus on me, and some magical indefinable quality I couldn't put my finger on, laid a trap. That first look, which ultimately claimed my world, notched a nick into my heart. As we pulled away from the intersection, I sensed that my life, which idled in contented neutral, was about to shift gears. The dynamic I had been thrown into had me wanting more. His non-verbal cues told me he felt the same.

The summer of 1967 became known as the "Summer of Love." Thousands of people were drawn to the Haight-Ashbury neighborhood of San Francisco to live the hippie experience of free love and free drugs.

However, the "Summer of Love" was more than be-ins and love-ins. There was the continued build-up of troops in Vietnam, and a summer that teemed with violent disturbances of racial unrest in many of America's cities. Milwaukee was not immune.

On July 30th, racial tensions escalated to a night noted for its lootings, beatings, snipers, tear gas, and the call out of the National Guard to regain control of the city. A curfew was put into place in Milwaukee and some of its suburbs, so those who worked third shift had to be there before the night's curfew was enforced. Cramped by these restrictions, Winnie and I hung out at the apartment on the phone with friends before she headed to work.

Impish in her desire to reframe my future, Winnie decided to call Jim. She delighted in her mischievous behavior as she scrutinized the phone book for Malicki listings. She got lucky on the first try, but it was his dad who answered and told her he was not home. Not one to abandon her matchmaking skills, she foraged for the numbers of co-workers she thought might know of his whereabouts, and coy, and with the help of some phone shenanigans, she learned of Jim's whereabouts and the number where he could be reached. It turned out, Jim and several others were at Sue's. Sue was the girl he recently met at work and had started to date. Undaunted, Winnie called. Sue and Winnie spoke for only a minute or so. Winnie, who must have pulled some shrewd ruse on Sue, was able to get Jim on the phone. Gleefully, she pranced in place when Jim said "hello," then forcefully pressed the phone into my hand. She averted my incredulous stare, well aware that her little caper to get us to speak had worked.

We didn't talk long. Although our tone radiated delight, our words were inconsequential, or at least that is what I thought. Catching up with Winnie at work that night, Jim quizzed her about me and asked if she thought I'd go out with him. "Yes," she responded, without consideration to my situation with Bugsy. The bald fact was it had been Winnie's not so covert aim to get us together, and Jim easily played into her hands. Flush with success, she called me during her lunch break. She paused all but a half second. "Okay, Rie, here's the deal. Jim's going to call and ask you out. I gave him your work number," she chortled. "Bye-byyyye, see you in the morning." *Click.*

To deny that Jim's arrival had upset my equilibrium and started to upend my life would be a lie. The dialogue in my head about him, as I decided whether to go out with him, opened a Pandora's box of conflicted emotions. Prior to our meeting, my life felt perfectly balanced. As I thought about Bugsy, my heart choked in the back of my throat. Bugsy had been my one and only boyfriend since I was 15. I knew it was a game of fantasy to think I could learn about Jim without turning my back on and hurting Bugsy. Up until I met Jim, I assumed our four-year relationship impenetrable. Meddlesome reasoning contrived to goad my heart. I couldn't help but wonder, *What if Bugsy is my once in a lifetime love? Am I about to consider something foolhardy all because of some energized voltage that's been sparked by a pair of genial eyes and the magnetism of a seductive smile? Were Jim and I meant to meet? Was this something that was written in the stars to happen before Bugsy and I did get engaged*? Bugsy and I had made no definitive commitment to a future together.

Jim didn't give me much time to stew over these emotions. Before I reached a decision, he called.

I picked up the phone and identified myself. Engagingly buoyant, Jim simply responded, "Hi, this is Jim." Then, in an airy and not-so-shy tone he straightforwardly stated, "I'd like to see *Grand Prix* on Sunday. Would you like to see it with me?"

Although my inner voice was loud with Bugsy guilt, I didn't waffle. To my own amazement, without a second's hesitation, I responded, "Sure!" When I hung up I thought I'd gone bonkers. I said to myself, *What have you done*?

Later that evening, I was keyed up and restless when Winnie popped in on her way to work. "Winnie..." I began, only to be interrupted.

"He cawhlled youuuu—didn't he, Rie?" Conspiratorially, she was eager to affirm what she wanted to hear. Her unplugged curiosity was about to get the best of her. She repeated, "He cawhlled didn't he? Did he cawlll, Rie?" My "yeah-yep" nod conveyed what she wanted to hear. Trusting her instincts, her mind and mouth leapt forward. "You're going out with him, right?! Rie, I knew it! I knew you wouldn't be able to resist." Unrestrained, she grinned from ear-to-ear. She relished her part in the scenes of the drama.

9
FIRST DATE

As the days moved toward our Sunday date, a guilt tape looped in my brain. I was a bundle of nerves. *Will Bugsy wonder why I won't be available on a Sunday afternoon? What should I wear? I can't wait to see Jim. What will he be like? Maybe I shouldn't be doing this. What shoes do I wear with that dress? Is all this worth it? What if I risk losing Bugsy and it turns out Jim's nothing but seductively attractive and I fall for it?*

Sunday, August 6th, 1967, dawned warm and humid. I realized a bad hair and makeup day could be in the making. Possessed by looking perfect, my mind zeroed in on creating the look. A good deal of time was absorbed as I applied blue eye shadow under the brow, gobs and gobs of black mascara, and black fluid eyeliner thickly traced to create a winged look beyond the outer edge of the eye.

I consulted the mirror methodically. Delighted the eyes were without flaw, I gauged the humidity as I started to tease my hair. Creating enough cushion to lift the crown and sculpt it to a soft swirl framing my face was a delicate process. Tease, sculpt, spray—tease, sculpt, spray. Done. A fixed stare at the mirror said, *So far so good.*

The guilt tape still on pause, I moved to the closet. Tucked safe in the back was my "short-notice" dress, the one I kept for that special occasion when I didn't have time to shop. Confidence about the dress helped to hijack my anxious brain cells to an easier place. The never-worn, cornflower blue, A-line minidress, more fun and flirty than haute couture, was the perfect dress for our first date. Hoop earrings and chunky heeled pumps completed the look. Satisfactorily accoutered, I lingered in front of the mirror. It would be my last consult. A deep, throaty hum burst through the open window. I gasped! To my amazement there he was, twenty minutes early, hotfooting to my door! My breathing constricted. I choked down the jitters and answered his knock.

No rehearsal could have prepared me for the enduring enchantment of our rendezvous. The magnetism of those initial moments surged like a potent drug coursing through my veins. Its side effects disoriented my thought process. As I delivered my "Hi, how are you, you're early, happy to see you" greeting in splintered phrases, Jim crossed the threshold into my apartment.

Deliberate and assuredly flirtatious, he didn't skip a beat. "You look pretty," he exclaimed. Flattered, my cheeks flushed warm. My eyes simultaneously surrendered all restraint to examine him. If I had ever idealized a handsome prince, Jim fit the bill. He was fairytale handsome. His sky-blue shirt sweetened his summer tan, which revealed an earthy sensuality. He looked hot!

As we headed out toward the car, three things stood out: One, his outstretched hand had long, slender, contoured fingers that were immaculately manicured. Two, his gait was fluid with an easy straight stride that he considerately measured to my pace as we walked down the stairs. Three, his car. He brandished a prideful swagger as he said, "I put glasspacks on her this week."

As he opened the passenger door, I thought it strange how he seemed to commune with his car. It resembled an introduction to a revered friend. My observation wasn't far off. I learned in a lifetime with Jim that it was his first true love—and as his guardian angel enhanced the spiritual side of his life, the Chevelle enriched the temporal. The Mountain Green, 1967 SS396, was a vehicle which coursed the landscape of our story and transported us to more than the places of our lives. In its early years it transported us to things both exciting and mundane. It was brought back to life twice, to shades of red. It showed itself off in later years, when it won many trophies for best paint and people's choice awards. This icon of the past also nourished life. The Chevelle attracted other "car people" to our lives, some who became car show acquaintances, Jim's best buddies, or our dearest friends. If matter held memories like the brain, the Chevelle would be the hippocampus. Memories live in it, skillfully and automatically brought to my conscious each time I gaze at it and ponder its virile attributes.

Even as The Doors anthem "Light My Fire" was playing on the radio, the silence between us set the guilt tape back on play. And, even as my eyes dazed out at the pine scent air freshener that dangled from the defroster lever, drop in images of Bugsy trespassed on my ability to relax.

Jim notched the radio down and asked, "Do you know what the movie's about?" I admitted the only thing I knew was that it was about auto racing. Jim filled in the details. As if he was the vice-president of publicity for MGM Studios, he explained that it was a story about Formula One auto racing that featured real life racing footage, and starred James Garner, Eva Marie Saint, and Yves Montand.

A mental image of Bugsy caught me off balance as we exited the car. I tried to decompress my nervous demeanor. I purposefully straggled, as I wanted to keep a little distance between us. It was only after we found our seats and James Garner appeared on the screen that the image ebbed.

The cinematic glaze was still in our eyes when he pronounced, "The movie was great!" He gesticulated with delight, and rhapsodized about race scenes we watched minutes before. While he pretended to steer a race car through the streets of Monaco his left hand boldly strayed from the wheel. I accepted the unrestrained gesture, and impulsively surrendered my waiting fingertips. The pleasurable tenderness of his hand was euphoric.

I didn't know what to expect as we drove into my parking lot. I realized a warm sensation was starting to percolate and spread within me in anticipation of what next. Again, it was Jim who made the first move. He turned fractionally toward me, shifting his gaze to meet my eyes. Smiling his words, he remarked, "There's a little time before I need to leave. Unless you're in a hurry to go in, maybe we could talk for a while." Sanguine, I shot him a crystal clear "I'd like that" smile. Spurred by an almost spell-like curiosity to learn more about each other, small talk effortlessly yielded to "get to know you" dialogue.

We fine-tuned our perceptions and soaked up everything we learned about each other. Curious to me at the time was how Jim boastfully recounted high school episodes. His bold candor surprised me. Evidently not at all concerned about the impression it made, he impulsively divulged that he graduated second from the bottom in scholastic average. He proclaimed his only goal in school was to graduate and get into the Marine Corps. He would have quit high school if it hadn't been a requirement to get into the Corps. Four years of fun and shenanigans occupied his time—that, and playing the snare drum in the Racine Kilties. To my consternation, in forty years he never did reveal what he wore or didn't wear under that darn kilt.

Almost giddy talking about it, his mouth curled in delight. Buoyantly he glossed over the details as he chronicled how he got kicked out of band. As I heard it from him, when a "hot" girl walked in late for practice, he broke into a rudimentary song and drum da-dah da-dah, da-dah da-dah version of "The Stripper." He not only embarrassed the girl, but on the spot, the astonished band director let loose a tongue-lashing and escorted Jim to the principal's office. Without hope for reprieve, the "humorless" principal kicked him out of band. The memory of his telling these stories is intact. I grin every time I reflect on those candid revelations spontaneously divulged on our first date.

In 1967 a set of connotations were ascribed to a person with tattoos—typically that of a rebellious biker, service in the military, or someone of anti-social persuasion. That being the norm, my quizzical "need to know" gaze to his forearms was easily read. As was his inclination, he took on a boastful posture. His voice crescendoed, "Once a Marine, always a Marine." He extended his left arm with pride. Admiringly, he traced the tattoo's design. Boiling down the detailed explanation—the snarling and helmeted bulldog on his arm was the "devil dog" mascot of the United States Marine Corps.

I then cocked my eye to the scripted "Jim" on his right forearm. Teasing I asked, "Are you afraid you might forget your name?" He answered as if a bit embarrassed. "It's about a night in Tijuana." Period. Dismissing my question, he rested his left hand over his name and said, "I'll save the Tijuana story for another time."

I learned that he was honorably discharged on October 14th, 1966. He served his last assignment at Marine Barracks, Rota, Spain, in the brig as a prisoner chaser and guard. His anecdotal comments revealed that he savored the years he served in Spain which afforded him the opportunity to travel throughout

Europe. He especially emphasized the opportunity he had to participate in the 20th anniversary celebration of the D-Day Invasion at Normandy Beach, where he played the snare drum with the Marine Barracks, Rota, Spain Drum & Bugle Corps.

He chuckled; I wondered why and asked. He said, "I loved the Marine Corps, but I hated to swim, and they could never take the fear of water out of me, and they sure tried."

"Why are you afraid of water," I quizzed.

"I don't know. I never liked it." He chuckled again. "Maybe I went down in another life on the Titanic. It started to sink on the same date as my birthday." Now it was my turn to chuckle. *What a kidder,* I thought.

ஐ

Jim dropped his gaze to the console clock, which indicated that our time before the curfew had ticked away. He pressed his hand around the door handle. Sighing, he said, "I guess it's time I leave. I'll walk you in before it gets too late." He stepped out into the early evening drizzle. I felt his fingertips as he waited for me to give him my hand. "I'd like to see you again," he said as we approached the stairs.

"I'd like that too." Leaning in he held fast to the back of my waist as we made our way up the stairs.

I couldn't breathe. I was a mess inside. Tipsy with anticipation, I thought, *If you think you want to kiss me, please do!* He must have felt my desire. Testing the waters, his hand roamed to my neckline. He stepped in, I felt his warm breath, and we kissed. A chemical cocktail shivered through me, opening the trap he set at our first meeting at 12th & Marquette.

He exhaled a flirtatious smile and turned to leave. "I'll be calling soon," he called back as he hurriedly descended the steps.

The touch of his fingers lingered. I scurried to the window and craned my neck. I caught a glimpse of him as he rounded the corner of the building, entered his car and drove into the damp haze. The evening's sequel started to play out.

Bugsy was not yet aware of the fissure I had scored in our relationship, but I was experiencing its tremors. The deep magnitude and sudden release of energy in our first kiss triggered the rupture. It was unmistakable. My post-kiss physiology, more importantly my gut feeling, led me to believe that something tangible, a kind of mystical communion, had started to unfold.

I was traversing a speedy slippery slope to a pit of gloom. The ties of four years, what I considered to be four wonderful, deeply affectionate, and tender years would have to be broken if I was to continue to explore a relationship with Jim. In doing so, I knew that even if it turned out that Jim and I were ultimately not meant for each other, my bond and relationship with Bugsy would be irretrievable. My heart dropped through me.

Contrary to what friends and others might have thought about my unalterable stance or perceived lack of emotion and caring, leaving Bugsy was hard to do. A personal, deep sadness about what the break-up could do to Bugsy, and my own loss of a treasured friend held tight for a long time. To this day I wish I could call him "friend."

10
BREAKUP WITH BUGSY

Bugsy was the last person who deserved to be hurt. He found out about Jim through a third party. That was wrong, and I rightfully claim blame for that. My temerity and over-analysis as I struggled to obviate the fall-out took too much time. When Bugsy and I next got together, he vilified Jim and me. He accused me of being a cheat, and asked if Jim got a "piece." I didn't expect the severe judgment. Bugsy's condemnation scorched. Impassioned as we were in that moment, I shouldn't have been surprised by the quick, sharp reproof.

I'm fuzzy on this, but I believe the last time Bugsy voiced comments regarding our break-up was at a drum and bugle corps competition. I was with a group of friends sitting on the sidelines in the grassy area at the junior high field stadium. Jim, who had recently started playing drums with a local rock band, was not with us.

Bugsy appeared out of nowhere. Boldfaced, he sat down on the grass next to me. The tension felt warped and unfamiliar. He muttered a cryptic dirge, pressing me about Jim. Rattled, I said little. What could I say? I stared at the grass. It was only a few minutes, but his drubbing managed to badger my emotions to the surface. Tears welled in the corners of my eyes. Exasperated, he finally ended the lopsided exchange. "I hope you're happy," he growled. He rose to his feet, turned, and walked away. It wasn't long after this I learned Bugsy was dating Joan's cousin. They later married.

Combing through my jewelry box I occasionally get caught up in "the old days." A tangible link that has journeyed with me through the changing phases of my life is a gift from Bugsy. It's a faceted round-cut, pendant made from red-brown garnet. It conjures up pleasant teenage images of high school, friends, dances, proms, homecomings, and my lovable high school sweetheart and best friend for four years. There is still a tender nub in a crevice of my heart and memory that belongs only to Bugsy.

11
MEETING THE FAMILIES

Jim met my parents early in the relationship. Operating on "Jim time," he arrived fifteen minutes early. I alerted my parents. "He'll be pulling into the driveway any second now." Dad looked at me quizzically. "It's his car. I can hear it," I responded. The same throaty, rapping roar that announced our first date now disturbed the neighborhood peace on Pine Street. Dad's head bobbed back; his eyelids scrunched in question. "Glasspacks," I simply responded.

I had already learned that Jim was fairly presumptuous about most things. However, he was anything but when it came to meeting my parents. Based on his own yardstick, when he compared his parent's lifestyle to my family's lifestyle and home, he sorted himself into a lower social class. To him, it appeared my parents were refined in a way his family wasn't. Simply put, he was afraid he wouldn't pass muster.

I rushed to the driveway to meet him. I wanted to calm his butterflies and bolster the bravura. "Don't worry; be yourself. They're going to like you," I assured him.

Jim squeezed my hand tightly. "I guess we'll soon find out."

After the few seconds it took to survey and eye each other up, the "pleased to meet you greetings" between Mom and Dad and Jim were dispensed of quickly. "I'm going to make Emily and myself a Manhattan. Would you like one, or a beer?" Dad asked. Although he was a beer guy, Jim accepted the Manhattan.

While Mom busied herself in the kitchen preparing the rest of the meal, Jim and I headed to the patio. We sat at the picnic table while Dad tended to the grill. Jim took a sip of the Manhattan. "This is good; thanks." He set his drink on the table. I believe that was his first Manhattan ever, and it remained on the table the whole evening. I don't believe he drank another drop.

Dad took the lead. "What makes your car so loud?"

He couldn't have asked a better question. My hardcore, hot-rodder exclaimed, "I love the strong sound. To get the over-the-top rumble I replaced the stock muffler with glasspacks."

Dad was not a car guy, but he listened intently, and moved the conversation to other topics. By dinner time, it was obvious my two favorite men were companionable. As eight o'clock approached, Jim became mindful of the time. "I've had a great evening, but it's about time I get a move on so I won't be late for work." Handshakes were extended all around. The evening was a success.

I knew from the moment he arrived he couldn't wait for the evening to end. He quickly passed through the garage and sought the safety of the Chevelle. Over the cadence of its rumbling idle, he mouthed, "I'll call tomorrow."

Almost every day for the next year, the families on Pine Street were treated to the robust rumble of Jim's Chevelle. His Chevelle broadcast at a frequency which transmitted, with precision, every time Jim and I left or returned home.

※

During this time, Jim was the drummer in a local rock band, the Try 'N Tymes.

Generally, the musicians rehearsed in Jim's sister's basement, so it happened she was the first of his family I met.

While the band rehearsed, Jim's sister, Verna, and I would inevitably end up together at the table in the small kitchen. In an atmosphere where gnarled cigarette butts, whorls of cigarette smoke, and the smell of black coffee permeated the room, Verna and I navigated Jablonski and Malicki family lore. Jim was the fourth child and baby of the family. I learned that Verna, fourteen years older than Jim, was a wonderful, but nervous, heavyhearted sister, who had shared a large stake in raising him. I sensed her motherly instincts. She observed, swallowed, and digested everything I said and did.

Verna's personality displayed anxiety over run-of-the-mill daily activities. One particular evening, not too long after we met, the room betrayed more than the usual pallor of thick smoke and everyday anxiety. She was drawn into herself—a bit detached. I could hardly bear the mood.

"Ahhhh, I need to tell you something," she finally said. Unloosed through the smoky haze, her words chafed with a bit of indignation. She recounted periods of hard times. "When Jim was little, we were left to take care of him."

She went on to tell me that during the week while Ma was working, Pa "found his manhood in a bottle." She talked about his bar-fly friends and how his drinking humiliated her. Bearing up to finish, she grabbed another cigarette. Antipathy, tempered with a respect for the Fifth Commandment, guided her dialogue. Paraphrasing Verna, "The truth is, we had to pick up his slack and cover his inadequacies. If we didn't react fast enough to his every demand, we'd catch hell."

Verna blamed Pa's drinking for their inability to live a better lifestyle, and why she and her husband had to pay the overdue property taxes on the 20 acres where Ma and Pa's house, the old diner, and a small rented ranch home that Verna and her husband had built stood. The resulting dispute about who owned the land was an issue Jim deliberately tried to steer clear of. I believe the rift, which sundered the family, lasted to 1991, the year Pa died. In the end, it didn't matter to me or Jim who owned the property.

I didn't want to say the wrong thing, so said nothing. There was no doubt that sharing this piece of family history clearly bothered her. I wondered why she felt she had to tell me her version. I told her Jim had already clued me in. What I didn't tell Verna was that Jim had laid open his embarrassment. To meet his parents was problematic for him—not me. He contrasted the newer and well-kept house my family lived in, to the old, rather run-down house his parents inhabited. I knew Jim loved his parents. He said as much. But the love for his father seemed buried beneath resentment and he didn't want to be like him. He told me his brother and sisters left home at their earliest opportunity. I passed no judgment and learned a lot about Jim during those discussions in Jim's sister's kitchen.

༄

The band was still rehearsing in Verna's basement. Tray, the lead singer, and self-proclaimed leader, was driven by an obsession for notoriety and local stardom. His egocentric personality quarterbacked the set list and costume schemes for the group. Tray asked Verna and I for our opinions regarding the members in their new Nehru jackets. We both agreed, as a unit, the band looked tremendous. Verna took a nicotine delayed breath when we reached the top of the stairs and grinned beneath a raised eyebrow. "When he wears that jacket, you better keep an eye on him. The women will swarm to him."

In his Nehru jacket, Jim was much more handsome than any of the Beatles or Monkees could hope to be in theirs. He was jaw-droppingly gorgeous in the fitted, single-breasted jacket; its design seemed to be custom made for him. Swaddled in the jacket, his vigorous sensual energy sent many a libidinous female following him to our table at break time. Some were disappointed his attention went to me and moved on. Others paraded by or tried to work their wiles when he'd walk to the restroom or the bar for a beer.

༄

We pulled into the driveway of his parents' home. Jim twisted his face and frostily repeated what he'd told me before. "When Pa did work, he made good money, but he pissed it all away. They have nothing and have to live in this old, run-down place. God, I hate it. I swear I'll never live this way."

My expectations prior to meeting Jim's parents were that of lifeless, old people. My expectations were turned on end. They were multi-layered; both intellectual in a country, earthy sense, clever, and sage. Not unlike Jim, his dad was quick-witted and generous of spirit. Entailments of time bent his back and nagged his legs. Jim's mom was spiritual and nuanced in the shadings of individuals and life, but she seemed worn with the hardscrabble existence of everyday life.

Pa was completely sober that day. In all the time I knew Pa, he was never in a state of what I would term "feeling no pain," and slightly tipsy certainly less than a handful of times. He treated me with utmost respect and an almost grandfatherly fondness. Although he was 62 at the time, in Pa, I saw where Jim got his good looks.

Near the road, three structures stood side by side on the twenty-acre parcel where Jim's parents lived. Jim's parents' home was in the center. Facing to the right was a tiny, two-bedroom ranch home, renter occupied, that Jim's sister and husband owned. To the left was a vacant diner. For several years in the mid 1950s, Jim's parents were its proprietors, prepping and serving such all-American fare as hamburgers, hot dogs, fries, and fountain favorites. Jim's mom showed me a picture of a pudgy-faced Jim. Bored at home, he was a frequent visitor to the diner. This, and stories about life at the diner piqued my curiosity about its interior.

&

Jim had intended that I meet his parents, spend as little time there as possible, and leave. Taking me to see the diner was not on his agenda. He warned me about the possibility of running into a snake in the tall grass and weeds. As afraid as I was (am) of snakes, my doggedness finally got the best of him. Grudgingly, he conceded: "Okay, let's go."

The sun hung above the horizon as we tramped our way to the diner. We reached the weathered front door. "You sure you still want to see this place?"

The notion that we turn back seemed silly. "Yeah, we're here. Let's go."

The door was a bit warped and a stuck hinge pin protested our entrance. Fortunately, with only a couple shoves, it fell open.

Burglar-like, we crept around the dusty and mildewed room and moved toward its' center.

"Euh!" I suddenly screeched.

A swath of cobweb caught across my forehead and my girly ick factor kicked into high gear. I instinctively swooshed my hands, tearing at the sticky mess. Jim laughed. He bounced in place and mimicked my hasty moves. "If you'll stand still, I'll get it for you," he grinned.

In no time he expertly disentangled the silk from my bangs. He wiped his fingers on the wall, but the stubborn, sticky residue was unyielding. In an automatic move, his hand went to his right rear pocket. Like a magician he shook open a perfectly pressed, white hanky, but instead of making a dove appear, he used it to clean his hands. I don't know if carrying a perfectly pressed, white hanky was a habit carried over from the Marine Corps. What I do know, is that most days of his life, he carried a white hanky in his right rear pocket. In the right front pocket, or attached to his belt in a pouch, was his pocket-knife.

I eyed the diner's perimeter. "What's all this brown stuff?" I asked, pointing to the floor.

"Mouse poop," Jim imparted. When I shot a glance around the room, I realized copious poopers had left their deposits scattered pretty much everywhere. I was also struck that the room's bones were held firm by a complex of fanciful twined cobwebs.

All this intermingled into a dusty smell that found passage through my nose hairs. I launched into a powerful succession of "*achoos.*" "Bless you, bless you again," Jim said as he slid from my side.

Slowly and deliberately, Jim set off to edge the diner's periphery. Halfway through his circle tour, he stopped in consideration of something; but what it was, I had no clue. His attention was drawn to something behind me—like he had seen a ghost. My hypothesis was not far off.

Twilight's complexion painted Jim's silhouette against the rich colors of the ebbing daylight. It seemed tailor made for what he was about to tell me. His candor was startling. It wasn't a ghost he saw. His hushed voice faltered, "I hope…I really hope you don't think I'm crazy. And I don't want you to be afraid," he said hesitantly. "My guardian angel is standing right behind you."

Although my eyebrows raised in question a huge *What?* Dumb-struck, I could not comment.

Although I am not prone to swear, I thought, *Shit, did I hear that right? He's got to be kidding.* Except it was obvious he wasn't. I knew he could spin a tale and prided himself on being a bit of a raconteur, but this was different. He was serious, and when he wasn't in a playful mood, he was a no B.S. kind of guy. I'm sure my face shouted confusion. I had to resist the temptation to ask, "Are you nuts?"

Even though every logical fiber of my being told me this was crazy, I had to take a look. I turned and flashed my eyes. Did I come face-to-face with his angel? Who knows? The space was certainly devoid of any spiritual presence I could sense. I shifted my gaze and threw my arm out as if to feel it or knock it off balance. A big nothing! Because I didn't know what to make of all this, I tried to shrug it off. I thought maybe his receptive field experienced an interrupted pattern of light, a rogue shadow of a bird, or something outside the window played tricks with his vision. But the question lingered and was tantalizing. *Why would he risk telling me there was an angel present, if it wasn't so? I didn't get it. And, what would his angel be guarding him from? Me?*

Jim's undisguised candor expected a response. My silence lingered. The longer I lingered, the more apparent his let down that I didn't see his angel. His face flushed. It was clear he was wrestling with something inside.

"I never should have told you," he said. "You must think I am crazy. It's not the first time someone thought I was only imagining my guardian angel."

I experienced a bit of the willies. I told him, "I don't think you're crazy. I just can't see it. I've never seen an angel. Where exactly is the angel? What does it look like?"

Obviously accustomed to seeing his angel, he pointed to my right. "He's standing behind your shoulder. He's short and stocky. I try to see his face, but it's always cleverly disguised, somewhat shadowlike, and almost formless."

His eyes avoided mine and his voice started to fade. "He's wearing a brown suit and hat. It's the same suit and hat that he's worn since the first time I saw him in grade school."

By now I could tell he wished he had never brought it up. He started to lock into himself and glossed over any further curiosity. "We should head to the car before it gets too dark," he prompted, as he motioned to the door.

As I stepped over the threshold, I took one last sidelong glance. There was no flash or movement—no wings! The cynic in me had a hard time reconciling what had unfolded. Yet to dismiss Jim's angel as pure fantasy didn't feel right either.

Throughout our years together, I would eventually grasp that Jim possessed a spiritual sense that to this day I can't fully fathom. Recurring sightings of his angel were sporadic throughout our years together. Later in life, I started to feel a bit jealous and cheated that I never saw my guardian angel. He once told me, "My angel is a presence I see and feel. Mostly, he comes to me in times of anxiety or when life is changing. He generally makes me feel good. I am always happy to see him."

Back in the car, Jim placed his hand over mine. "Well?" he finally said.

Well, what? I thought. *Do you expect a comment about your parents or the angel?*

Although talk of the etheric body lingered in the air, I chose to answer the "Well?" with a comment about his parents. He bobbed his head sideways and fastened his ears on my response. As direct and as warm as I could make it, I asserted, "It was great to meet your mom and dad. I like them both a lot."

My response seemed to relax some of the tension visible in his shoulders and neck. I also suspect the relief was as much from liking his parents, as it was for letting go of any further angel talk.

12
FORMING A NEW LIFE

Our new daily ritual spoke the language of love. At night, the Chevelle's periphery embraced our existence. No matter how the evening started, we found ourselves parked in the dark shadows of Jim's parents' driveway. It seemed each time we positioned ourselves in each other's arms we roamed deeper into regions of our hearts not yet explored. Our souls merged.

Devil-may-care confidence that we had a future together plunged us headlong into planning. Easily, we seemed to agree on everything. We started to talk about being married. We'd wait one year before we started a family. It would be two children; a boy and a girl would be great. If we didn't have a boy and girl after two, we'd go for three. Despite the fact that we rejected some Catholic Church teachings, especially with regards to birth control, we decided it was important to raise children knowing God. We discussed where we might want to live, and agreed that saving for a house would be a priority.

☙

It was Tuesday evening, May 14th, 1968. As we headed to the hospital to visit Pa, Jim's buoyancy epitomized happiness. His hands rhythmically bruised the steering wheel to the beat of The Human Beinz "Nobody but Me." He was not subtle about hiding his feelings. His lips curled to a wide smile, held it a bit, then pronounced, "There's something you need to get from the glove box."

It was then the prickly sensation started to build up my spine. It was two days before my birthday, and I expected the formal proposal at any time. The thought of being engaged and a diamond ring danced in my head. I pushed the button and the door fell open. Sure enough, there was the box, conspicuously exhibited right there on top of the 1967 Chevelle Owner's Manual. He already knew the answer, but asked anyway, "Will you marry me?"

Ahhh, the magic of a diamond. Its placement in the glove box and diamond size mattered—NOT! Set inside a modest white gold setting, my classic round, diminutive diamond was stunning and, to my eyes at least, appeared the size of the Hope Diamond. I slid it on my finger, held my hand out, and couldn't have loved it and what it represented more.

As we approached Lake Drive to turn toward the hospital, we passed Holy Sepulcher Cemetery. As I was trained by the nuns in grade school, minutes after I got engaged I mentally recited a short prayer for the "poor, pitiful" souls laid to rest there. We were taught when we die that our souls are still attached to our venial sins, and the dying must first suffer the misery of Purgatory until the debt for these sins is satisfied. Only then can a soul enter Heaven. The thought of Purgatory scared me more than Hell. I guess I figured I might commit a bunch of venial sins, but never anything that would send me to Hell. It became automatic to do this as I passed a cemetery, passed a funeral home, or watched the slow and solemn procession of cars trailing a hearse. The way I learned the prayer:

> *Eternal rest grant unto them, Oh Lord,*
> *and let perpetual light shine upon them.*
> *Eternal rest grant unto them, Oh Lord,*
> *and may they rest in peace. Amen.*

About two minutes later we arrived at the hospital. Too excited to wait for the elevator, we sprinted the stairs and bolted into Pa's room. It didn't take a second. I flung my hand in front of Pa, and then Ma standing next to him. Pa's arm slid out from under the sheet. He reached for my hand. As he mimicked surprise, he said, "Look, Helen. Jimmy's engaged."

It was then I noticed the tear that streamed down Pa's left cheek. I wish I could say it was caused by the glare reflected off the diamond's surface. It was the effects of his surgery to remove cancer from his face. The left side of his face caved in at the cheek where they had removed bone. For the rest of his life his left eye shed a steady stream of lazy, slow tears.

Ma echoed Pa's excitement. "I'm so happy," Ma said, elated. "Do you have a date?"

I told her I hadn't told my parents that it was official, but we hoped for a date in October, my favorite month.

Pa's shoulders curled forward, motioning me to come close. I threaded my way past Jim and his mom. We hugged. When I broke the embrace, Pa candidly said, "I knew when I met you, you'd be the one!" Inside my heart was singing. I couldn't have been happier. The hug was contagious and spread between the four of us. When I turned to wave goodbye, I noticed a tear in Pa's other eye, this time a real tear expressing real happiness.

A half hour or so later, we glowed as we walked into Mom and Dad's kitchen. "We're engaged," I exclaimed. Dad extended his hand to Jim, and welcomed him to the family.

Mom was equally excited. Like Jim's mom, she asked, "When?"

"October," I stated. Feigning meteorological aptitude, we speculated fall's optimum and best weather was likely to occur on Saturday, October 12th, 1968.

෴

The cheerful ditty bop I was doing to the Rascals "It's a Beautiful Morning" couldn't begin to explain my sparkle the next morning. Exhilarated, I burst into work. By 8:05, a flurry of congratulations energized the office, but for one individual the word "arousal" might be deemed more appropriate.

After things had settled down, I went to the back room to collate technical bulletins. The colleague who assigned this project joined me to make sure the packets were assembled correctly. I stretched toward an upper shelf of bulletins. That's when it happened. Brazenly, certainly faster than I could react or think, his arms went around me from behind. He grappled at my breasts while muttering something like, "Hmmm, they're nice. Jim is a lucky guy." My faculties went numb and dumb! Aghast, I responded with silence. To make things worse, he was the father of someone I went to high school with.

It wasn't until many years later that I even mentioned it, and it was in the context of a conversation with an individual who experienced something similar. Why did I let it go? Partially, I guess, is that sexual harassment was treated differently in the 1960s. Back then, sexual innuendo was the everyday norm, even at work. It boiled down to the fact that I lacked the confidence to upset a social pattern that was there long before I arrived. What he probably considered an innocent "compliment" has forever blemished the memory of the day.

ಸಿ

For it was not into my ear
You whispered
But into my heart
Twas not my lips you kissed
But my soul

~Judy Garland

And it came to pass! October 12th dawned brilliant. Iridescent dew enameled crusty leaves; clear fresh air and bird song greeted our day. Blessings of the celestial spun off the sun brightened sanctuary, and the breeze, as it wended its way past when we later stood at the altar and placed the Blessed Virgin's flowers at the foot of her statue, seemed a prophecy, for love that would last longer than a lifetime.

The clock ticked ever closer to 11:00. I viewed the final "package"—hair, makeup, dress, and veil. My thoughts recaptured a time thirteen years prior. It was not only because I once again was adorned in a beautiful white dress and veil. My first confession and first holy communion were the initial milestones where I felt a part of something "big," something tangible outside my immediate family. Once an observer, I was now a participant. The church's requirements for marriage preparation, which included attendance at Cana Conferences, had by nature done the same. I was prepared to become a part of something "big," something tangible—to commit my life to Jim through the Sacrament of Marriage.

The clock ticked slowly; still several minutes to wait. Flowers perfumed the vestibule. The florist handed off the boutonnieres to a helper, and motioned me to where she stood. "What do you think?" she asked. I was overjoyed with my bouquets, all three of them: the wedding bouquet, the toss bouquet, and the flowers I would lay at the foot of the Blessed Virgin statue.

The clock ticked 10:55. The stimuli and heightened awareness of what was about to take place made my heart race. Mom was escorted to her seat. The ushers met in front of the altar. As they unrolled the white aisle runner, the bridal party clustered in ceremonial formation. Anxious to take a peek at the full church, my eyes followed the runner's path. My senses were full. The smell of my rose bouquet, the altar bedecked in pink and white sprays of flowers, the crisp autumn light of the day, and the beauty that existed within the confines of St. Adalbert's fueled my love for Jim.

The clock ticked 11:00; my heart, his from the first moment we met, was about to vow "…from this day forward…until death do us part." Dad took my arm. I was atingle with happiness. It was our turn to walk the aisle.

I anxiously glimpsed the front of the church and caught Jim's eye. He was resplendent in his black tux with white bow tie and boutonniere. His face, tan from working outside, let out a smile as big as the sun itself. As Dad released my arm to Jim's, open windows carried gladsome autumn breezes from one side of the church to the other. The euphoric spirit in my heart soared. Jim bowed his head and pressed his arm hard to mine. It was at that precise moment I wholly transferred my life to Jim.

Our vows, the essential element that formed the covenant of our marriage, were said approximately thirty minutes later. A partnership was sealed for the entirety of life. Not only in love with each other, we were now "in life" with each other.

The euphoria as we formed the receiving line after the ceremony was heady with kisses, hugs, handshakes, and well wishes. I was there, but barely heard a thing, lost in the intoxicating force of my love for Jim.

The wedding announcement in the local paper read, in part:

> "The Rev. Raymond Mrozinski officiated at the 11 a.m. double ring rites which united Miss Marie Louise Jablonski and James Joseph Malicki in marriage.
>
> The bride, given in marriage by her father, chose an A-line wedding gown of delustered satin with a double row of lace at the hemline and edging the train. It was appliqued with lace. A tiara headpiece of crystal secured her shoulder length veil. Completing the bridal ensemble was a bouquet of white roses.
>
> Twenty-five guests attended the noon breakfast at Gondek's restaurant. The evening dinner and reception at The Patio was attended by 225 guests."

When the dancing and partying was about to end, we posed at The Patio's exit for a photograph. We turned away and disappeared to the Golden Key Motel in Hales Corners where the first thing we did was count gift money: three hundred and sixty dollars, enough to honeymoon a week in northern Wisconsin.

※

Little observances, unique to us, started that first year. Each year, on November 10th, Jim reminded me that it was the Marine Corps birthday. The first year we were married he surprised me with a box that held a small cake that read "Happy Birthday." It was to celebrate the Marine Corps birthday. That was the only Marine Corps cake we ever had, but each Veterans Day Eve he'd make mention of the Marine Corps birthday. If it happened that on the next day he had to go to work, he'd complain, especially when I was in banking and had the holiday off. He thought that unfair because after all, he was the veteran.

We also started to kitchen dance. Dancing felt easy with Jim. Coordinated to the rhythm it felt romantic and sensual to dance with him. Some of our most beautiful times were spent dancing. An unexpected dance could bolster, soften, and on occasion mend a day. The magnetism of the dance held power for us both, even forty years later.

Little annoyances made their way in as well: whiskers in the sink, the toilet seat left up, and I was disillusioned about all the laundry and the big dinner I thought I had to prepare each evening, but on a day-to-day basis, there weren't many edges we needed to smooth.

ଔ

A month and a half after our vows, Jim was suspended seven stories up on the monumental façade of Gimbels Department Store hanging Christmas decorations. Aglow in the vibrancy of the season, Jim shopped at Gimbels and bought me a little present every day he worked there. Typically, he surprised me with a special piece of bakery, some chocolate or another inexpensive item.

However, one day after work, I was taken aback when I discovered a short, gray, faux-leather skirt with suspenders and sweater laid out on the bed. "You're going to look great in this," he said. The skirt seemed a bit much. Not too sexy or anything; it just wasn't me. Faux-leather with suspenders! *A yodeling, lederhosen look! What was he thinking?* "Try it on," he urged. I put it on and glanced myself in the mirror. The Von Trapp family from the *Sound of Music* immediately came to mind. I could see he was thrilled to surprise me, and he loved the look, so I wore it to his next gig. He couldn't keep his eyes off me.

The best of Gimbels was saved for last. Jim placed the beautifully wrapped box under the tree a few days before Christmas Eve. The temptation to sneak a peek was intense. If I knew I could get the paper and bow back in order, I would have done just that. My inquisitiveness was relentless, but Jim held out. On Christmas Eve we decided to exchange our gifts before we headed off to his parents, and then mine. Dang it! Wouldn't you know, I drew the short straw. Jim got to open his gift first. Deliberately, he took his sweet time. He was thrilled when he discovered it was the Black and Decker electric drill he had hinted and hinted for.

I didn't have a clue then that the drill would be the first in a collection of tools that would eventually fill a three and a half car garage, and then some. His firm tapering hands deftly handled every manner of tool. He worked on cars, built a bonus room, screened porch, several decks, installed crown molding, remodeled a kitchen, and was able to fix almost anything that needed to be fixed. I look back and think it is amazing the thousands and thousands of dollars he saved us—and it all started with a Black and Decker drill.

Finally, he said, "Your turn." I didn't waste a second. I tore at the bow and paper. I lifted the lid. It was empty! He hunched his shoulders and breathed, "Hmmm?"

"Stay here," he smiled. He got up and headed to the bedroom. I strained my ears and heard the closet door open and close.

"Close your eyes."

I did as he said. He gently pulled my arm toward him. "Open your hand," he requested. I didn't wait to open my eyes. I watched as he placed a silver charm bracelet and Santa charm in my hand. I was tickled pink. The bracelet now holds twenty-five charms that tell a good portion of my story from December 1968 through the 1980s. I didn't realize then, how all these years later, the history held in each charm would be its own celebration of a piece of life with Jim.

In a flash it was October 1969. Family and friends gathered at our home to celebrate our first anniversary. There were red, long-stem roses, paper gifts, snacks, and drinks. The top layer of our wedding cake, which had been stored in Mom and Dad's freezer all year, was served for dessert. Jim raised a fork of cake to me, "Happy anniversary, honey. I love you."

Within seconds of the last guest leaving, we eased into each other's embrace. We kissed and sidled to the couch. For more than a year, we had been waiting for this moment. "We have a baby to make," Jim's voice whispered in my ear. The tenderness and love expressed that evening was palpable. Later, wrapped in the comfort of Jim's arms, I said, "I think we did it. I think we made a baby tonight." Jim's words echoed mine. We fell asleep, ending one of the simplest, yet most beautiful days of our marriage.

13
1970s – LIFE UPENDED

We were individuals, each with a set of rules encoded since birth. Our family experiences, temperaments, and attributes set a heart code and marriage DNA unique to us.

Dreams can and do come true, but within two years we learned that fairy-tale thinking does not make a marriage any less vulnerable. Self-limiting beliefs on the roads in life's new grid would take us where we had never expected to go.

It was a time of stagnant pessimism in America and it seemed to rub off on us. The upheaval that identified the '60s continued well into the '70s. Inflation was skyrocketing, and prime rates were in the double digits. An oil crisis, economic recession and events like the Kent State massacre in May 1970, put much of the American population into the doldrums. The now-common catch phrase, "Houston, we have a problem," was coined during the aborted mission of Apollo 13 in April 1970. Complex problems vexed the nation, and our home life as well.

Per Dictionary.com, the definition of *synthesis* is "the combining of separate elements or substances to form a coherent whole." If I conceived the night of our anniversary I'll never know, but forty-one weeks later, on July 26th, at 8:15 a.m., we celebrated the arrival of a beautiful baby girl, our Cheryl, who we called Sherry. I considered the remarkable existence of this coherent whole. The realization that this perfect baby was our creation, was hard to absorb.

Cheryl's birth was probably not much different than most, the exception being that nowadays, I don't believe the obstetrician would prescribe a strong, alcoholic drink to relax me when the frequency of contractions reached five minutes apart. The brandy Manhattan my dad prepared sat ready in a jar in the fridge. At around 10:00 p.m., I placed ice in a glass, poured the Manhattan on top, and sipped it down. When I finished, we headed to the hospital.

It was hot and foggy. As we neared the hospital, we passed Holy Sepulcher Cemetery. The souls laying beneath the weight of their tombstones, and the humidity carried on the air off Lake Michigan, invoked my automatic prayer for the dead: *Eternal rest grant unto them, Oh Lord…* Another contraction, however, quickly changed my prayer. *Please God, I pray my baby's okay and that this goes fast.*

As I ratchet back to those memories, I realize that even though I wanted a baby and worried about the health of my baby, I wasn't exactly prepared to have a baby. First, I was a lot more naïve about the birth process than women of today—and especially what was to come later.

When we arrived in the labor room, the nurse asked Jim to step into the hallway. She smiled gleefully. "Dear, we need to get your enema done." I was baffled by the nurse's comment. My obstetrician did not forewarn me about this, or maybe I hadn't listened. Gross! I had never had an enema before, and briefly considered objecting. Quivery obedience to authority won out.

I vowed long before I went to the hospital that I would not scream in childbirth. It wasn't going to happen! As it turns out, there was a woman at the opposite end of the room who let it all out. Her profanity grew in intensity with each contraction. She blasphemed her predicament—God, her husband, and everyone near her. It irritated me, but more than that, it scared the life out of me.

Jim was mostly quiet and nervous, and when I let him, he held my hand tight. He often repeated, "You're doing great, honey."

The pains were increasingly powerful. It seemed way too long that everyone had been telling me to not push. "Relax, it's not time yet. The doctor will be here soon." *What is he waiting for? Doesn't he know I'm having a baby?* I was horrified that he still hadn't arrived at the hospital.

Finally, Dr. Obstetrician arrived. Dressed in medium blue scrubs, I thought he looked like the Fisher Price Chubby Cub, a roly-poly, pull-toy. At 300 or more pounds, his side-to-side swivel was exaggerated while in the work mode. This is the same doctor that yelled at me and told me my husband would call me "lard ass" after I gave birth. He was upset I gained four pounds in my fifth month. As it ultimately turned out, I only gained nine and one-half pounds the entire pregnancy!

Dilation was slow but progressive. All the staring "down there" between blasts of pain added an element I found intimidating and nerve-racking. I don't know the exact time I was administered the epidural, or subsequently what type of anesthetic I received. However, I do remember the doctor telling me, "This is it. Push."

The maternity ward was packed to overload. I gave birth in a fog and was moved from the delivery room to a sidewall in the hallway. They lined me up behind several other moms. For them and the passing audience, I was still half drugged up. I didn't scream in childbirth, but now I was a blithering idiot, bawling my eyes out.

I can only imagine what people thought. As I laid there, I had mixed feelings. I was scared and apprehensive, and excited and happy all at the same time. I couldn't wait to see and hold Sherry.

I did have an early moment of sadness and it had to do with the fact that I did not have a boy first. Why? I thought Jim wanted a boy first, and as a little girl, and more importantly as an adolescent girl, I wished I had a big brother. I wanted that for my girl. Although I was protected, and capable of taking care of myself, the protective instincts I imagined an older brother would have had for me carried an idyllic quality. When it came to entering junior high and high school, I wished I had had a trusted source for peer advice. It now seems foolish, but because of this, before I even held her, I felt I had let her, and Jim, down.

I was finally moved to a room.

"Here we are, sweetie. It's time to meet your mom." The nurse was effervescent in her pronouncement, but I was suddenly near tears, again. When the nurse pressed forward to hand me Sherry, I was uncomfortable and restrained. Like she knew what I was thinking, the nurse said, "Here, let me help you get comfortable."

Sherry's eyes drew me in before I unwrapped the blanket. The short time I saw them open I noticed they were dark, almost a slate gray, and although they say newborns cannot see, I felt we simultaneously exchanged a look. It was as if we sized each other up. I noticed her hair next. Her hair was dolled up in an "updo," twisted and slicked up off her forehead to keep its fringes from touching her eyes. She was pretty pink, and her left hand was splayed open. I touched her palm. Her fingers clenched my finger in a mighty grip. It was at that moment she slipped open the gateway to my heart. I hoped I was in hers. The Carpenters' "Close to You" was the Billboard Hot Single that summer. When I hear the song's lyrics referring to the day someone is born, I'm back at the hospital in 1970 holding my beautiful Sherry.

In between sitz baths to soothe the episiotomy, classes in how to bathe my baby, and visitors to the hospital, the four days before we went home slid by quickly.

ഇ

We settled into a routine. Sherry's personality exhibited great independence and a sense of self from day one. She was not a cuddler. As long as she was fed and her diaper was changed, she was satisfied with life. She rarely cried. I can only remember one night when we took turns walking the floor. After about a week, she slept a six-hour stretch at night.

ഇ

When we moved to the little white house next to Jim's parents, we went to church right down the road at St. Matthew's. When we attended, Jim was happy to worship at the church he was baptized in and attended on occasion as a child. We were impressed with the young Father Bob and asked him to baptize Sherry. Although lukewarm practicing Catholics, there was never a question that she would be baptized Catholic. We would raise her the way we were raised. Whether her faith would grow beyond the cradle and keep within her, only time would tell.

14
A HARSH HELL

There is a place of the mind where the celebration of what should be the happiest days of life unfold against an ebbing black undercurrent, a flow I didn't understand or know how to restrain. I never dreamed something like this could happen to me, or anyone else for that matter. The climb out would be long and harsh!

Indifference started to settle in not long after we got home from the hospital, and it felt very strange. When Sherry was about three or four months old, I recognized there was something beyond my understanding that was holding hostage my every thought. From somewhere deep inside, an unidentifiable dark murky flow of emotions, words and feelings, screamed a vexing noise that sickened my mind. The bright, happy love marriage and children dreamscape portrait took on new hues of blue, gray, and black.

Like Alice, I tumbled further and further down a black hole. It affected daily functioning. Compulsive homicidal and suicidal thoughts incarcerated my mind. I couldn't connect with my true self. Bizarre delusions and auditory hallucinations prompted me to harm myself and Sherry. Visions of two bodies lying on the ground after a free-fall from a two, three, or four-story window hammered my thought process.

I was too terrified to tell anyone, even Jim. Even though by this time I started to feel somewhat detached from Sherry, I wanted her, and I was afraid someone would take action to remove me from our baby and lock me in an obscure mental ward somewhere.

The disharmony in our household grew in tandem with the speed of my fall down the dark hole. Jim struggled with the pressing requirements of work and home. Uncertain about my frame of mind, he'd call several times a day to check up on me. Some days he'd show up at home for lunch. The weight of this manifested in his behavior. He begged me to "please" come clean about what was going on with me. When he questioned me, the undisguised concern in his voice matched the tense muscles on his face. The stew pot of Jim's emotions made me cry and scream out, "I don't know what's wrong with me. I think I'm crazy. I'm having horrifying thoughts about Sherry and myself that won't go away." Afraid, I turned inward and wouldn't tell him any more.

There was no way to ignore the undisguised concern in his voice. His hazel eyes darkened. "Terrible thoughts? What do you mean? Tell me! I have to know!"

I was teetering on the edge and Jim knew it. It was tortuous for us both. It was the first time I couldn't confide in him. He changed his tack.

Decisive and firm, he demanded, "You need to see a doctor, now!"

Dr. Obstetrician was the only doctor we knew at the time.

I stared a hole through the phone. My fingers were numb. I could not dial the number. When Jim came home for lunch to check on us, his forceful tone torpedoed straight to the matter. "Did you make the appointment?"

"No," I responded. His derisive glance was cringe-worthy.

"Get the number and call it," he demanded. I dialed Dr. Obstetrician and made an appointment to "talk."

℘

It was my turn to see the doctor. Jim squeezed my hand and begged me one more time to tell him everything. He tried to put a brave face on things, but the worry lines crossing his forehead betrayed him. Tension carried in his whispered words. "I love you, honey. It will be okay."

My ankles felt as if they were chained to the chair. Dr. Obstetrician had a domineering, snap of the towel, locker room mentality when it came to women. I dreaded seeing him about this. Grudgingly, I trudged to the inviolable sanctum of his office. Sure he'd weigh in and judge me insane, I feared a major meltdown. *Dear God, I prayed, help me get through this! I don't want to be sent away.*

I choked and stammered as I circled my way around the outer edges of the topic. Dr. Obstetrician glanced at my file, and tapped it with his pen. Finally, he wrote something down. After an intimidating silence, he proclaimed, "It's a little late, but I think you may be suffering from a complication of childbirth. It's called, the baby blues." It wasn't until years later, when post-partum depression came out of the closet, so to speak, that Jim and I came to the realization that that was what the baby blues had actually been. "What's going on in your mind, and how long has this been happening?"

My infected brain was exhausted and I continued to step around the problem. "I'm scared you'll think I'm crazy if I tell you."

He stopped tapping. His wise-ass demeanor softened. "No, go ahead, tell me what's going on. I'll see if I can help."

Enervated, I sat clutching my purse. I could only cry, stripped of my responsibility to tell the truth about the depth and desperation of my problem.

He pitched his voice so I could hear through my sloppy sobs. He advised that I get out more and leave the baby with a babysitter, perhaps get a job. "I don't have my driver's license, I stammered."

"Then get it! Get off your butt and get a license," he insisted. "Maybe if you get out more you'll feel better and the crying will stop."

My teary binge left me tired and irritable. I was pissed that I had to go the doctor, pissed that I danced around the subject, and generally pissed at life.

His advice wasn't an original idea, but it was simple and made perfect sense. When we got home, we called Sears Driving School. Before we had even talked to the neighbor about babysitting, I was signed up for several classes. Within a month's time I got my license. The classes not only got me a license, it got me out of the house. It felt good to get away from it all. The focus on driving had given me a bit of respite from the debilitating and soul-crippling depression I was in.

There's no good time to lose your job.

It was about a month after I got my license. In the middle of the afternoon Jim burst through the apartment door, stormed to the kitchen, and pitched his keys toward the key box. Astounded, I thought *Why the hard knuckle demeanor?*

Sherry was banging a spoon on her high-chair tray. I lifted our playful baby out and put her in her crib, then I hurried back to the kitchen. With the distraction gone, I asked, "What's wrong?"

I didn't have to force an explanation. He talked as he faced the window. His words sunk under their weight. "I never saw it coming. On top of everything, now I don't even have a f***'n job."

I knew we were in huge trouble. Jim never used the "f" word. Our life was in complete disorder.

My "I-can-take-care-of-things" husband woke up Monday morning groggy and unrested. Unemployment, combined with my depression, challenged his resilience. As a husband and family man, unemployment stripped him of his manhood.

"I'm going to call Tom and talk to him about selling cars. He told me they always need salesmen," he said.

I was stunned to silence and wondered what was going on in his mind. I didn't believe he had it in him to negotiate deals, and the thought of living on commission was scary. The negative stigma attached to used car salesmen during the era was that of a shyster, something Jim was not. I wished he would have looked around a bit, but his mind was set. Panicked about our finances, the last thing he wanted was to be unemployed.

Within two or three days he had been hired to sell used cars.

Jim's hours changed. He was no longer home most evenings. That left me at loose ends. Several months slipped by, and we had to dip into the house fund to pay the rent, which drove us both crazy. We both understood something had to change.

It was a Sunday at Mom and Dad's. The discussion started as Mom and I prepared dinner and spilled over to the dinner table. We took our customary seats, while Mom and Dad continued to share the details of the duplex they considered buying. "If we buy it, would you like to live upstairs?" Dad asked. Who wouldn't? I had been in the lower unit with its leaded windows, wall sconce lighting, Spanish plaster and other amenities. Mom and Dad said the unit was fairly duplicated, except for the portion of the lower unit that had been added on in recent years. It didn't take much thought. The rent would be less than what we were paying, and decidedly, the space had an ambience that we could have never afforded anywhere else.

The timing was also good. With Jim working crazy hours, there was an added benefit: the sense of well-being that someone would always be around as I still struggled with the depression.

The paint was barely dry on the walls in our new apartment when we agreed to put the saved rent money into our house account, the balance of which had been squeezed to the dollars required to keep the account open. The money subject didn't end there. The earworm about getting a job was impossible to ignore, and at every opportunity he could summon up the daring, Jim alluded to the doctor's advice. "Honey, you need to listen to the doctor. I think it will do you good. It might help with the depression, and it will also help with our goal to buy a house."

At first blush I thought it impossible. One, from the beginning it was our plan that I be a stay-at-home mom, albeit a plan that was hatched in the steamy confines of the Chevelle when I was all of nineteen years old. Two, who would babysit? Three, how would I get Sherry to a babysitter and myself to work? Jim had a dealer car and we had the Chevelle. The Chevelle was his other "baby." It was passionately pampered and his pride and joy. As I thought about driving it, I became a basket-case. The car did not have power steering and I had to sit on the edge of the seat to engage the clutch, which was almost impossible. When I approached the subject of trading it for another equally "cool" car that had an automatic transmission and power steering, Jim bristled. Undisguised agitation formed his words, "Cool cars do not have automatic transmissions."

He continued to pooh-pooh my uneasiness and zigzag off-subject. It drove me crazy. *Get out more. Go to work. But how?*

I gulped at the sound of Jim coming up the steps. *Breathe, Marie,* I said to myself as I prepared to take the pot roast, one of his favorites, out of the oven. In recent days I had given a lot of consideration to both the doctor's advice, concerns about moving through the depression, and our future. My mind had gotten past the "stay at home mom" thing; I figured I'd be able to find a baby-sitter, but I was unglued regarding the car. The topic was volatile. A fire ignited in Jim every time I brought it up. Aware that getting behind the wheel of the Chevelle was a near spiritual experience for Jim, all day I strategized how I would once again bring up the subject of the car.

It was an easy and pleasant evening, almost like the pre-post-partum days. He kissed me on the cheek. "Supper was great," he said. We chatted while doing dishes, aligned ourselves on the couch and cuddled as we watched TV. Everything seemed almost perfect. I hesitated to bring the issue up, but as it approached bedtime, I knew it had to be done.

"Hon, before we go to bed we have to talk about the car."

His response was strong, almost harsh, "Not now. I don't want to talk about it. I thought we were going to bed."

I pushed, "We need to talk. I got my license, but still can't get out without worrying I'll have an accident."

I had no difficulty continuing, "We have to get this settled."

Firm in his resolve, he went to bed.

The atmosphere was cold the next morning. We said only what we had to, short and crisp.

When he left for work, I called my previous employer. Why I was nervous I don't know. I reasoned if they had an opening it didn't mean I'd get it or have to take it if offered. I didn't even have to tell Jim if I didn't want to.

It turned out there were fill-in jobs I'd be qualified for and was told to come and fill out an application. I wrangled with my thoughts all day. Ultimately, I speculated that maybe if he knew I could go back to work, even if only as a fill-in, he'd be happy about the prospect and reconsider about the car.

When he came home that evening our words trampled over each other. "You first," Jim said. I told him what I had done, and that I could work, at least for now, as a fill-in.

Resignation narrowed his voice. "I'm really sorry I've been so stubborn. You've been right about the car," Jim said. "We can't move on if you're not able to drive. I looked at a Pontiac Lemans GT sport coupe today." We went to look at it together and agreed we both liked it. I didn't say any more. Jim took care of the details.

❦

The money and title for the Chevelle were exchanged—then its lifeblood, the keys. Smiling a toothy grin, the buyer pressed the keys in his hand, thanked Jim, got in the car and turned the key. Through the throaty farewell of the glass-packs, Jim waved an admonitory finger. He couldn't have been more firm and direct. "Take good care of my car," he called out.

My heart ached for him. Paramours separated by a sales transaction. My first inclination was to try to placate his mood, but I didn't know how. He sat in silence staring at his tropical fish. His glazed look said audibly, "I need to be alone." After a bit of time, the gouramis, red-tail sharks and angelfish (the same angelfish that in Sherry's nightmares would get out of the tank and walk to her bedroom) tranquilized his mood.

I gradually worked myself into a full-time position. Setting my mind on something other than myself and Sherry helped to lift my post-partum depression. As it slowly tapered off, the stress we were under diminished proportionately. Although Jim was still selling cars, the assurance of my steady, bi-weekly paycheck was instrumental. It brought us back to a pattern that nourished our family life and time moved on nicely.

It was the 2011 holiday season. I got in line at the grocery store. I glanced at the magazines, then looked up. It was déjà vu. Facing me from the child seat in front of me was a remake of Sherry at about ten months old. She was all in pink and joyously smiled at me. When I smiled back, feelings and thoughts welled through the unexpected tears that formed in my eyes. I thought about post-partum depression and what it had robbed us of.

My depression resulted in a less than motherly response to Sherry when she was that age. Consequently, we both missed out on the warmth and cuddly interaction between mother and child, and all those years later the thought made me sad and angry.

I searched our current day relationship for any tell-tale signs of neglect, coldness and general lack of interest I displayed when she was a baby. I couldn't see any, and have been assured by Sherry that there are none.

Knowing what I know today, I marvel that we all made it through intact without anti-depressants and professional counseling. Sadly, I suffered through its hell mostly alone, ashamed at the time to reveal what was going on. Without Jim's love and support, a baby girl that was independent and happy on her own and, I realize now, the infusion of God's grace, this chapter of my story would have turned out different. Maybe horribly different. It might have been the last.

15
NEW HOME

In the early 1970s, in my neck of the woods, society's norm was to have two children. By the time Sherry reached two and a half, my family's meddlesome hints that it was time to try for a boy was annoying at best. Questioning whether post-partum depression was fully behind us, we struggled with the issue ourselves. The silence I had finally achieved in my head didn't want to be tampered with. It had taken such a long time for us to once again fall asleep and wake up happy!

Sherry was pure joy. She rejoiced in anything that involved a ball. She loved to talk and to sing. The melodic lyrics of Neil Diamond's "Song Sung Blue" were repeated over and over again. Her happiness spilled to us both. Jim was enthusiastic and dedicated to finding a different job. With the addition of my paycheck, our house savings sprung to new life. Basically, I was peaceful and happy with the way things were, happy to be rid of most of the intrusive thoughts, and simply happy to be with those I loved.

By the time Sherry turned four, the "it's time for another baby" advice was in full swing and irritating. Unsolicited baby comments were not welcome. What they didn't realize was our decision didn't have to do with the usual questions about finances, daycare/work game plan, etc. For us it was all about depression. We were certain we could work out the rest.

The answer seemed to come with the third bedroom. More and more, as we looked at houses, the third bedroom became the "baby's room."

So, it was decided in the summer of 1974 that we would hit the reset button, abandon birth control, and see what would happen. If it was meant to be, then so be it. By sometime in September I was pregnant, and in October Jim started working second shift at a new job on the assembly line at the local GM plant.

Our dream of owning a home came true less than a year later. The older, three-bedroom Dutch Colonial was a bit of a fixer-upper. Undaunted, Jim was certain some do-it-yourself renovation was all it needed. Personally, I was thrilled we finally had our own home. Almost immediately we had a new furnace and central air installed. The itty-bitty kitchen was cosmetically improved. Jim installed new basement steps, redid the fireplace mantel, and we transformed Sherry's room into a pink and green girly paradise, girlier than her tomboy, ball-playing self. And, optimistically, we decorated the "baby's room" with accents of blue.

~

It was a Saturday night about the time I started my third trimester. Following a day of errands and house projects, we put Sherry to bed. Soon enough there was the smell of wood burning.

We settled in by the fireplace, wonderfully cozy in the crackling warmth of the fire. Smiles danced on the flickering flames. Concerns about the potential for another round of post-partum depression were set aside. We talked about baby names, maybe Matthew or Joshua for a boy, and girl names that I no longer remember, and although we had barely moved into our first home, we talked about bang for the buck renovations that would make the house more easily saleable when we decided to move up.

16
COMMUNICATE EQUALS COMPLICATE

*Even good marriages fail. One minute you're standing on solid ground,
the next minute, you're not. And there's always two versions–yours and theirs.
Both versions start the same way though;
both start with two people falling in love.*

~*Grey's Anatomy,* Season 8 Episode 1: "Free Falling"

I'm coming upon the part of the book where I tell the story of our divorce. For many reasons it will be hard to write. I will not share all the details. You see, Jim and I made a vow to each other to never reveal or discuss with anyone the *initial* issue that started us down the road to divorce. Even after death, we are inseparably connected and bound to this vow. Except for what will be revealed here, I consider the issue buried.

Many people have speculated and they're sure they know. With respect to the original issue for our fall-out, I say this with confidence; they don't. What I will say is that the road to divorce was about three and a half years in the making. Infidelities come in many forms, not always sexual. What was often visible didn't offer the whole truth. From 1975 to 1980, life's events had a way of smashing and bumping into each other like no other time in our marriage.

The embers of the fires continued to warm our evening, until a startling utterance began its destruction. Splat! Out there! So quickly it was said! Briefly it hung in the air. Burdened with its mighty weight, the words eventually sunk to the deepest level of our marriage, and they could never be pulled back.

The evening ended without nastiness. It was the stupefied numbness that called the end of the day. Sooner than planned, we went to bed. What would happen or be said next required our faculties to be intact. I laid motionless as I studied the light rimming the pulled shade; the distress in the air was palpable. Jim laid there as well, quiet, but awake.

The next morning felt extreme in its wordless quiet. The baby was due in a few months. Our efforts had been so tied in doing whatever we needed to avoid another round of post-partum depression, I think, at least on my part, we didn't want to take the matter on. We did decide to go to church, and although we were zoned for St. John's, we went to St. Adalbert's.

By the afternoon we were as actors. We carried on as if it was business as usual, but it wasn't. Life marched along, but at times, words would scrape the scabbed surface, only for it to fester and scab over again. It became a bad habit. Not at all a good way to effect a cure.

೫୭

I wasn't comfortable and couldn't sleep, and decided to get out of bed to move about a bit. The trickle of warm, amniotic fluid moved down my legs. I woke Jim. We wasted no time in getting to the hospital. I was more than two weeks overdue; the plan was to induce me early the next morning.

We took the familiar ride up Lake Drive, passing Holy Sepulcher Cemetery. By the time I finished murmuring my prayer for the deceased, we had pulled into the hospital's parking lot.

I was at the pushing stage. Nurse Nice asked a few questions. "Sweetie," she mildly intoned, "We're taking you directly to the delivery room. Your baby is ready to come." *Hallelujah,* I thought, *no smiling enema nurse.*

Jim pulled in close to me, but seemed to be more engrossed with the activity that surrounded my bed. Everyone was talking at once. I felt like shouting,

Hellooooo, everyone, I'm the one having the baby, but as usual, my passive self said nothing.

"The baby's head is exceptionally large," Dr. Obstetrician finally spoke. "Let's get going with the epidural," I heard him say to his team, "We'll need to do an episiotomy."

Stem to stern the incision was made. The doctor averted his eyes sideways and said parenthetically to the nurse, "Forceps, please."

I didn't say a word through the whole process. I let it happen.

Douglas came to life boisterous and loud. Also, he was not a beautiful baby in the same sense of the word Sherry was.

Considerable force was placed on the forceps to grab and maneuver his head from the birth canal. My heart palpitated in my throat when I first saw him. Even though I had been assured by the doctor and nurses that his flat head would round out, and his body would grow into his head size, his large, misshapen head and flat nose were troubling. I don't remember how long it took for him to grow into his head size. Until then, so that I could get his shirts on, I slit them at the neck.

Once assured about his head's size and shape, it was the bruising on his temples that troubled me the most. He looked sore, as if he had been in a fist fight. I sought information and comfort from a nurse. I feared Douglas was suffering pain, and although it was too late, I wondered if his birth could have been handled differently. I was assured he was suffering no pain, and that it was a "common occurrence" to use forceps at birth.

֍

When Douglas was two to three weeks old, using the stairs and holding him became problematic. My knees worked like rusted hinges, and my right elbow became rigid and inflexible, stuck in what I termed the "baby holding position."

I was referred to a rheumatologist. Efficient in his task, Dr. Rheumatologist touched and pressed every joint from the top of my body to the last toe. He hesitated when considering a joint that felt warm, or when I expressed an area that felt tender to his touch. His main concern was my right elbow. I thought it strange when he asked me to put my coat on, then take it off. It was a test to see if I could successfully achieve getting my coat on and off without a struggle. I struggled. He informed me there was no definitive test for rheumatoid arthritis, but he was fairly certain that's what I had. With quiet, doctorly authority, he explained the rheumatoid factor, anti-bodies, how stress can exacerbate RA, and possible treatments. Blood tests were done, X-rays taken.

Several days later I went back for the results and received my first cortisone injection. It was a shot into my right elbow joint. The anti-inflammatory did its job. In no time my elbow was pain free and normal function restored. Daily aspirin therapy to decrease inflammation caused tinnitus. Naprosyn (now sold as Aleve) was substituted and coaxed my knees and left elbow into relief.

Sporadically, I've dealt with this all my adult life. I consider myself fortunate that I've always had great doctors and I've been able to handle the flare-ups quite easily, but sometimes wonder if the RA diagnosis was the right one. I know individuals who suffer tremendously from RA and I've never experienced their type of pain, so I occasionally wonder if I deal with something else. Besides Naprosyn, I've been on Methotrexate, Plaquenil, and Celebrex. There were times I considered Cortisone my friend.

∞

Life events continued to bump and smash into each other.

Our existence was pressurized. The aches and pains of my joint issues, the everyday rigors of going back to work, the incessant picking at the scab of our wounded marriage, and the challenges Doug presented, frazzled our last nerves.

∞

Doug tended to wake up every hour and a half or so screaming. It wasn't until he was about two and a half when he finally started sleeping a three- to four-hour stretch. Sometimes rocking would help. There were nights it seemed Doug and I were engaged in a contest of who could last longer. Most nights, he won.

Sherry was frustrated as well. She came out of her bedroom, and arms akimbo, she stood in Doug's doorway. As if scolding me, she shouted, "Can't you keep him quiet for a while?"

❦

It was a Sunday morning. My turn with Doug came at about 3:00 a.m. I was tired and thirsty and searched for a 7-Up. I ransacked the fridge from front to rear. No 7-Up. I turned and cursed the case full of empty bottles. Milk and beer were my choices. I debated. Beer won. I set the open bottle next to the rocker, picked up Doug, laid his head in the crook of my left elbow, took a sip and started rocking.

The rocking motion was intended to soothe us both, but Doug could not be pacified. He squirmed and screamed; his agitation was visible. The tension vein in my poor baby's neck and the muscles in his jaw grew rigid. I dissolved into tears. My beer breath pouring into his nose, I cradled him close. "I'm sorry I don't know how to help you. I'm sorry I can't make you happy so you don't cry. Please don't cry, my Doug. Mama's here. I love you." Our sobs undulated across the room.

When Doug finally did settle down, I finished my beer. I sat the empty bottle next to the rocker, put Doug in his crib and fell into bed exhausted. The next morning Jim looked at me with bewildered eyes, his shoulders shrugging. The empty beer bottle was in his hand. I didn't answer. He put the empty bottle in the case. I believe a desire for a peaceful morning and the mute stoicism we were becoming good at kept him from commenting further.

❦

Doug was about five months old at the time. This particular evening, his turmoil went beyond my ability to cope. His prolonged thrashing, then rigidity, and his cry that sounded like a rabbit in distress, could not be calmed. The way he held his breath was the scariest. Doug had no control over his convulsing little body, and neither did I. I was a basket-case of emotions, and physically my arms were worn out trying to carry and rock him into some sort of peace.

Pandemonium wretched at my emotions. *Is he suffering pain, intense pain? Is he having a seizure or expressing frustration? Is he experiencing sensations or something going on in his head? Should I take him to the hospital, what should I do? I need to know what to do.*

I would have taken him to the emergency room, but a few days earlier his pediatrician told us not to worry about this type of aberrant behavior. "Babies do this."

I laid a blanket on the living room floor, recited a Hail Mary and placed Doug face down on the blanket. At the summit of his screaming, his face raged redder and redder. A second Hail Mary ended with, *Please don't let him turn blue again.*

Although I was taught differently, I've questioned on and off for years whether praying to the saints and the Blessed Virgin to petition God is a "legitimate" endeavor, but when it comes to Doug, I always turn to the Blessed Virgin. Her earthly life was mother of a son. After all these years, it's still what I do.

I was utterly helpless to soothe him. Jim was at work. I bolted to the kitchen to call Mom and Dad. By the time I got back to the living room, Doug had expended sufficient energy to squiggle himself to the slate in front of the fireplace. He screamed and banged his head up and down on the hard surface! I was horrified.

Mom and Dad lived close by and rushed to my aid. Dad extended his arms. "Here, let me take him." I eagerly handed Doug off to Dad, my elbow aching as if it was going to break. I don't know what it was—grandfatherly repose, the snugness he felt in Grandpa's arms—but within several minutes, Doug's skirmish with himself ended.

Jim managed to get a pediatric appointment the next day. I had to go to work, but asked Jim to talk to the doctor once again about the forceps birth. Motherly instinct was telling me some damage, maybe nerve damage, occurred at birth where he had been bruised. I had already talked to the doctor several times about it, but he made nothing of it. He said, "Babies get angry, frustrated, and turn blue. Don't worry, when that happens he'll catch his breath and everything will be fine." According to Jim, in a strong and curt voice, the doctor repeated what he told us before. "If it gets to be too much to handle, I'll write a prescription for tranquilizers for Douglas." Using the same strong and curt approach the doctor took, Jim told the doctor, "No thank you."

A few weeks later we tried another pediatrician. He assured us that for some babies this was normal behavior. Like his primary pediatrician, he offered no specific advice. He was certain that the forceps had nothing to do with Doug's behavior. I didn't buy it, and never have!

Doug's head banging started to taper off after he was about two years old. It stopped completely when he was a little over three. During major growth spurts he complained about generalized pain in his limbs and occasionally complained that "I don't feel good," or "I feel weird," none of which I made much of; I figured it was growing pains.

However, during puberty other symptoms occurred besides the typical acne, clumsiness due to his feet growing faster than the rest of his body, and an increased appetite. Sensory symptoms played with his body. One half of his head would feel a bit numb and he'd be slightly thrown off balance. He occasionally had trouble finding words, and when he did he'd trip over them, sometimes with a bit of a stutter. During these episodes his ability to concentrate was compromised as well. We took him to neurologists in both Wisconsin and Tennessee. Each one asked if he had ever experienced head trauma. I always mentioned the bruising from the forceps. How they processed that bit of information, I don't know. One neurologist told us it was "all in his head" and he needed psychiatric help. We didn't buy it. We took it as an insult. Life went on with no diagnosis.

It was many years later, after Doug moved to New York City, when he saw another neurologist. He said, "It was one of the best days of my life. I think I finally found out what I've been dealing with."

Although he's never had a specific diagnosis, what he deals with is, or is something akin to, complex migraines, the same type of migraine the on-air reporter, Serene Branson, suffered in February 2011 while reporting at the Grammys. Viewers thought she was having a stroke. Doug used the terminology "like a thunderstorm in the nervous system" to describe his episodes.

Although our moods were getting into each other's way, we became adept at operating on the safe fringes of our marriage when we were with others.

The façade was most prevalent when, in the midst of all the emotional turmoil, we made a decision to look for a ranch style house.

I felt energized house hunting. I think Jim did too. It was a huge diversion and something we both loved to do. Once again, Sundays were spent riding around town looking at houses in our price range. Most properties were given a fleeting glance. However, there was a duplex that caught Jim's attention. We called the number on the sign.

The lower unit was abandoned by the owners. The upstairs tenants, whose habit it was to throw empty beer cans out the window, were still there. The good news, however, was that the property was substantially underpriced for the market, but the low valuation bore a big caveat: It needed a huge amount of interior work in both units and the basement. The upstairs tenants would have to be evicted.

Lickety-split my excitement waned. Instead of envisioning paint colors and how our furniture would work in the house, I envisioned hours and hours of hard labor. Jim, always ready to fix or build anything, was certain he could tackle it all. I wasn't so sure. The second time we looked at it, he bounded happily through each room. His toothy smile articulated his delight, a smile that left me less than ignited. He had a plan. He reasoned the physical effort and time spent would pay off in the long run.

I did love the layout, the yard, and was not averse to having tenants overhead. Ahh, but the work! Stupidly, I bit my tongue. What a huge mistake I made. We bought "The House of Danes."

Great Danes! I don't recall the number of dogs kenneled in the basement. As evidenced by the stained and smelly carpeting, gnawed windowsills, punched out screens and other damage scattered throughout the house, at times they must have been left to roam the main living quarters. Not until Jim tore out the kennels and scrubbed the basement with bleach and whatever other chemicals he was using was I able to make myself go down there.

We tore out all the carpeting and scrubbed the subfloors. The stench was obnoxious. Everything in the kitchen and bathrooms was scrubbed. The rooms would still need remodeling and paint, but at least they were clean on moving day. Walls, baseboards, doors and windows were scoured in the kids' rooms; new paint and carpeting was installed within a few days of moving in.

A notice of eviction was served on the upstairs tenants. They left in about ten days. They also left scads of dirt, minor damage and trash.

I was overwhelmed by moving day; I wanted an easier life. But there was no rest. Financial concerns required that we make the tenant unit rentable. Doug was still waking every couple of hours. The head banging continued and my elbow was acting up again. Jim worked second shift. Harmony and balance were gone. We had taken on too much. Our marriage and attitude toward each other deteriorated daily. Instead of talking we were blowing fog, adding murkiness to our situation as neither of us wanted to engage in conversation.

ಸಿ

About this time, Jim's mom became ill. A history of cardiovascular disease vexed both sides of Jim's family. It wasn't uncommon to hear that one or another aunt or uncle suffered a heart attack or stroke.

As told to me, Ma had been to her internist to find out about the mid-upper abdominal pain she was having. She related the family history, but was told not to worry about her heart, that it was gall bladder spasms. The doctor gave her medication and told her to come back if it acted up again.

Several weeks later, we stopped by for our usual once a week visit. Ma was curled up in her chair. It was evident she was in pain. She could barely speak and was a bit nauseous. Jim leaned in over her from the side. He didn't disguise his concern. "Ma," he said, trying to coax her from her chair, "I'm going to take you to the ER." Never recalcitrant, she was that day and shooed him away. "No," she spit back. She told us she would take the pills from the doctor, and have Jim's sister take her in the morning if she wasn't better. Pa also protested. I don't remember his exact words, but his inference was that she exaggerated pain for attention, and to get out of some work. The words I do remember struck me as plain ridiculous. "She doesn't want to help with the pickling," he stated. The muscles in Jim's jaw tensed. He searched my eyes for support. I too suggested we go to the emergency room. Unwilling, Ma whispered an exasperated "no."

When she finally did get back to the doctor, they determined she had had a heart attack and needed bypass surgery. It was 1976, probably the last week in August when she had the surgery. We were thrilled to hear she made it through without any complications. The doctor predicted she'd have a speedy recovery and be home in no time.

However, a week or so later, the downward spiral that took her life spun out of control. She experienced extreme exhaustion, loss of appetite, and a feebleness that was not present, even in the first days after surgery. The doctors and staff essentially told us there was nothing wrong with her that some exercise and time wouldn't take care of.

Unfortunately for Ma, Pa listened to the medical staff and not his wife. While Ma felt utter helplessness, Pa's cringe-worthy comments about her getting home to take care of those darn pickles riled my disposition toward him. Then one evening, there was the acerbic, cold-eyed nurse who rebuked Jim and me for placating Ma instead of admonishing her for her lethargy. *Couldn't they see her lifeless eyes were telling another story,* I thought?

That was it. Jim had it with the nurse. Bulls-eye perfect he glared at her. His blast of anger was something to be reckoned with. As a result of this, and pestering by the rest of the family, they ran a few tests. "It's hepatitis, the result of a tainted transfusion," the doctor informed us. Ma was "born to eternal life" on September 9th, 1976.

For a period after the funeral, the emotional pulse of our marriage went limp. It was a dispassionate atmosphere. Jim was in a place he had never been before, grieving the loss of someone so dear to him, his heart broken, and he was angry at the health care system that allowed a tainted blood transfusion to kill his mother.

℘

I cursed my luck. My left front tire was flat. I retreated to the house, blaming the glacial winter and cheap tires we had put on the car.

Bewildered in his half sleep, Jim groaned, "Another flat?" Grim resignation spurred him out of bed.

It seemed to take forever for the tire to get changed. Never understated when speaking her mind, Sherry was relentless in her carping. "Tell Dad to hurry up. I don't want to be late!"

Swaddled in his polar apparel, Doug began to pull at his clothes. "Hot," he whimpered. I shed his outer apparel. As long as he was undressed, I asked, "Doug, do you have to go potty?" He shook his head "no."

The tire was finally changed. For the second time that morning I dressed Doug. Sweater on, check. Scarf on, check. Snow pants on, check. Boots on, check. Jacket on, check. Mittens on, check. Hat on—"Mommy, go potty!"

The pause was weighty, enough to balance the pros and cons of taking him potty or heading to school. We left. Doug had on training pants. The worst outcome, I'd have to change his pants at daycare.

The potty dialogue continued all winter. Doug always made it to daycare without an accident, and mysteriously to me, when we got there he didn't have to go!

∞

Lest we get complacent, winter's contempt whacked us one more time. My gloved hands struggled to unlock the door. The second we bounded into the warmth of the hallway I knew something was wrong.

"Shush," I motioned to the kids. *Phh-plop, phh-plop.* What was I hearing? *Phh-plop, phh-plop. The sound of rain?* I thought. It took a few seconds to register the sound was coming from the basement. "Stay where you're at," I instructed as I advanced to the bottom step. "Shit," I cursed under my breath. Water was raining from the basement ceiling, enough to form a shallow pond.

Jim was at work. Perplexed, in my haste to call the fire department, I slipped and slammed to the floor. The only damage sustained was to my heavy wool coat, wet from the water on the kitchen floor that was streaming its way through to the basement.

Bewildered eyes surveyed the rest of the house. Water penetrated to several rooms.

The fire department arrived. The first to enter made tracks to the basement. The second split through the kitchen and darted to the bedrooms in the back. I would find out later their big, wet, dirty boots carried a mess to the farthest corners of the house. The water wended its way through ceiling and light fixtures. The master bedroom and Sherry's room were spared. The firefighters met back in the hallway, then instinctively, sprinted the stairs to the upper unit. The first hollered back, "It must be a broken pipe on the second floor." I followed close behind, drawing in near the attic door to size up what they were talking about. A pipe had burst. Insulating the pipes was on the "to do" list, but unfortunately, it was several line items down. The water was turned off at the main. Their job was done, while ours had just begun.

Jim was finally located at work and came home. Once again, Mom and Dad responded to my plea for help. That night we tore out Doug's carpet and hauled it outside. We moved individual items out of harm's way, soaked up what we could and went to stay with Mom and Dad. Professionals were hired to come in for the rest of the clean-up. Jim and I worked the overlap. After all the elbow grease it took to clean, paint, and repair the house when we moved in, to have to do some of it again about threw me over the edge. I began to hate living there. Instead of feeling good when I walked through the door, I was resentful. Every time I tried to talk to Jim about living there, he'd loudly sigh, roll his eyes and stare me into dropping the topic.

Resentment penetrated our marriage as well. Vexed on both sides, we were exhausted hashing out our situation, cleaning and repairing the house, and staying up with Doug half the night, but we continued on, zombie-like.

༄

Spring eventually arrived and turned into summer.

By the time Elvis died in August 1977, we couldn't stand each other. While trying to live our own truth about the issue, belittling sarcasm became the norm. Jim became controlling. His self-centered and exaggerated sense that he was the only one right about the issue chewed at my innards. He became rigidly domineering. He was sure he knew what was on my mind, and insisted he knew what was best for me. He had no clue.

In fairness to Jim, this is how I perceived his feelings then, in those moments. I realize now that we could have handled the situation in so many different ways. If Jim were to read the previous paragraph, I wonder if he would take umbrage at the "controller/self-centered" reference. I do know at the time, he didn't see himself that way. Reflecting back all these years, I believe his aim was to take control, to end the whole messy situation his way, with us intact.

I had nothing left to deflect the pain. It was about this time we started to play a high-level game of one-upmanship. Going our separate ways, we both completely undid our marriage.

Emotionally, I was done with it, but agreed to do one more thing. We'd see a marriage counselor.

Neither of us were resolute about what we were about to embark upon when we arrived at the Pentecostal Church. Our demeanor was skeptical.

A well-tailored, fortyish looking gentleman answered the door. He extended his hand, an air of pleasure hinting on his thin smile. He introduced himself as pastor and counselor and directed us to sit.

The "get-to-know-you" session turned into an "I-need-to-know-if-you-attend-church" session. I was skeptical before we left the house. Disclosing the dark palette of our marriage to a counselor/pastor of a religious domination I was not familiar with was distressing. I wondered, *Would he look down on us? Would he try to dig into areas I didn't want to talk about?*

Counseling widened the gulf between us. Splinters of anger, blistering words, contrary moments of oppressive silence and back to the never-ending argument about what started it all accomplished one thing: it made us both particularly miserable. The counselor didn't think this was unusual. He believed we needed to go through this in order to exit safely on the other side.

Each visit he pestered about religion. Personally, I felt my relationship with God, or anyone else for that matter, was private. As a couple, we did admit we had become semi-occasional Catholics. The admission seemed to give license to his pursuit that his church was the pathway to saving our marriage.

In the spirit of counseling, we agreed to attend a worship service at his church. To say the worship was different from what we were used to is an understatement. Anonymity was our goal, so we found seats next to the door. We wanted to leave as soon as the service ended so as not to mingle with the parishioners.

The pastor cleared his throat as he vigorously strode to the front of church. His diction was perfect, even as he smiled broadly while introducing the Malicki family to the congregants. Those around us extended their hands in greeting, happy to have us worship with them.

Lit with energy, his voice incited the worshipers. Spiritual expressions unheard of in a Catholic church saw arms raise spontaneously upwards. Shouts of "Amen" were lifted to heaven.

Inspired by the end of the service, the women were brought together at the front of the church for a "special" prayer. I did not participate. With arms raised skyward, they rambled utterances I could not understand.

The pastor pressed one hand to his forehead; the other hand moved to the top of the head of each of the individual women. Rapt in some sort of divine mystery, some of the women fell to the floor, overtaken by something I couldn't understand.

Even Jim, who still on occasion claimed to see his guardian angel, was baffled. Neither of us had witnessed this kind of behavior in worship. Jim nodded toward the door, and we made our get-away. It was the only thing we had agreed upon in a long time. We never went back.

☙

We were good at meeting the skills of everyday living, but this edged the drama on far too long. Our marriage was not docile or manageable. Jim's moods kept getting in my way so that I couldn't think straight. We had browbeaten each other and the situation too many times. I hired an attorney. The blistering words and power struggle unintentionally launched almost three years earlier needed to stop. I knew of no other way.

Teary eyed, my trembling voice let it fly. I extolled the soundness of a decision I had made, then: "I've filed for divorce. You'll be served soon." Although I said them, and meant them, the words rang strange in my head. I felt nauseous and dizzy. He stared at me in complete astonishment, as if I hadn't told him over and over again that if we couldn't get it together, I would do this. His response was that I didn't have the guts to file. Sweat beads were forming on his forehead.

His immediate silence felt aggressive. I knew his emotions needed an outlet and wondered when it would happen.

I backed away when he tried to kiss me. "Divorce is not the answer," his brittle voice coaxed.

My heart quickened. "I don't want to talk about it anymore! I sobbed. "I'm done living this way."

He took a deep breath and blew it out through pursed lips. It was then the caustic ramblings started in again. I was a nervous wreck. I avoided his eyes. It seemed I was seeing and hearing another human, not my Jim.

Not much after I filed for divorce, pieces of us broke away. The house was sold. The kids and I moved to an apartment, and Jim rented the upper unit of a duplex a block from St. Adalbert's.

&

I accepted a position as administrative assistant to an elite member of the city's "CEO Club"—a cadre of white professionals that ran the city, and many of its institutions and corporations. Initially, I was the secretary for a vice president of the corporation. When Mr. A, the president and CEO of the corporation, needed a new assistant, I was approached to take her place. The executive vice president outlined the salary and offered a cursory review of the position. I thought it a bit strange there was no interview with Mr. A, but not strange enough to decline.

I was in seventh heaven. Something good was happening. The pay was greater than I hoped for, and the benefits were among the best in the market. Working in a premier building with imposing views of the city, its offices decorated in dignified traditional furnishings, was the icing on the cake.

Why I didn't know about this, I don't know. Mr. A, a buttoned-up, generous, brilliant man, had a drinking problem. The executive vice president did not mention it when we talked about the position. Maybe he thought I knew what I was getting into. His lunch-hour drinking pattern, or swigs from a hidden bottle when he didn't leave for lunch, turned him from Dr. Jekyll in the morning to Mr. Hyde in the afternoon. It was commonplace for Mr. A to come back from lunch with a buzz on, and his habit was to sleep it off on his couch. I was the alarm clock. "Wake me at 3:00," he'd say, or, alternatively, he would call me into his office to "work."

However, his focus wasn't always on work. It was during those interminable hours that I learned the world through the eyes of Mr. A. He rambled about "life."

On one particular day, his words drowned in boozy slather, he stated, "Marie, you dress so nice. One of these days I'll take you shopping."

Another afternoon, his head supported on his right fist, and his lids bloated with sleepiness, he inquired, "If you could drive any car you wanted, what would it be?"

Stupefied, I wondered where he was going with this. At that point I was wishing he'd take a nap! "A red Mercedes Benz convertible," I answered.

Swallowed in a big yawn, he said, "Let's go look."

"At cars!?"

Another yawn, "Yes," he responded.

"No, I'm not going anywhere," I announced. "If you need me for some dictation or other work, we need to do it now. I am leaving at 5:00."

Next to his hunting gear, binoculars were his favorite toy. Gazing out his window onto the city and toward the lake kept him busy for great lengths of time.

While I gathered papers strewn on a table near the window, he approached from behind, binoculars in hand, and he put his arms around me. I felt the forward press of his body as he tried to point something out in the city. I didn't like it, or invite it, and refused to be caught in the same position I was in 1968. I ducked down and out. My words carried malice. "Mr. A, don't you ever do that again." It was reprehensible and repulsive, and my anger even caught me off-guard.

Sobering up between 4:00 and 5:00 was the norm. That's when he wanted to get to the real work. One by one, that's also when the office started to empty out. Some would be there longer, but knew to never interrupt when his door was closed, and when he worked he always insisted the door be closed. It made me a nervous wreck. I knew the situation was headed for disaster one way or another. In a short time, I had grown tired of being his door goalie and playing defense for him. I started to look for a new job.

I had also grown tired of being his personal assistant, something I found demeaning. At his request I picked up his laundry and ran to various places to retrieve items he constantly left behind on airplanes or in various restaurants. It was not uncommon for him to leave his brief case on the floor next to the chair where he ate lunch. He even asked me to go and buy a birthday gift for his wife, a woman I had not even met. "Find a pretty silk scarf and send her flowers," he directed.

It was winter, 1979. Milwaukee was slammed and pretty much shut down due to a major snowstorm. I managed to dig out and get the kids to a sitter. I headed to work. Strong gale force winds and reduced visibility made it difficult to drive over the bridge along Milwaukee's lakefront. The winds were so high on the bridge, my heart sank to the ground as my car slid from one lane to the next. Drifts piled to eight feet in parts of the city and its surroundings.

One other woman made it to the office. She lived nearby. We got in touch with an executive of the company. He said, "Lock up and go home. The roads are dangerous, and no one else will be able to make it in." He further commented, "I believe Mr. A's flight made it out before the airport closed this morning."

We locked up as instructed. I took the elevator down to the gallery. Lo and behold, wouldn't you know it, Mr. A was walking right toward me. I found out later his flight did make it out, but due to weather conditions he was late for the flight.

"Where are you going?" he asked, as he approached me.

"Home. Mr. B told Mary and I to lock up the office and go home."

"We have work to do," he replied.

By this time, I was so suspicious of his motives and worried about the drive back home that I simply repeated, "I am going home." My heart was beating hard and fast. I knew I had angered him. I think too, a bit of it was that I had never stood up to authority that way. My training to be subordinate and obedient to nuns, priests, parents, and adults in general, carried over to my adult life when it came to bosses.

It was to be my demise. About three weeks later, when opening and sorting his mail, I came upon a copy of a letter addressed to Ms. CLM congratulating her upon accepting the position of administrative assistant to Mr. A. I remember thinking, *What the heck, that's my job!* It communicated her starting date, salary, and specifics. I was angry.

Mr. A was out of the office for a couple days. I took my anger to the executive vice president. He told me Mr. A had decided he needed someone else in my position. He offered me two weeks' pay. I told him I needed to think over the offer. I talked with several friends who encouraged me to go for it, to ask for six months' pay and to indicate I was ready to hire an attorney. I agreed with the advice that I had nothing to lose. Besides that, the sexual harassment, discrepancies I noted on expense reports that I was not to question, the drinking, and other information I was to hold close to the vest emboldened me.

I went back to Mr. B. I explained my position and inclination to hire an attorney if my request for severance was not met. To my satisfaction, he capitulated.

I thought I might not see Mr. A again, but as in the gallery the day of the snow storm, unexpectedly there he was walking toward me. He didn't say a word. Then, as if it was business as usual, I asked about his trip. He never looked at me. I could tell he was weighing his next words. Finally, he responded, "I am sorry things didn't work out. You're not flexible enough."

He was right. I wasn't flexible enough, not enough to have him put his arms around me, be his goalie at the door when he slept, to put in hours after 5:00 p.m. because he was sleeping off his lunch all afternoon. I knew he didn't fire me because I couldn't handle the work. As a matter of fact, he complimented me often on the quality of my work. On several occasions after I had scheduled his flight and lodging, and prepared and put in order materials needed for a business trip, I'd find a hand-written note on my desk complimenting me for a job well done. I had every one of those notes with me the second time I met with Mr. B when we discussed my severance.

I went on to interview for several positions. It wasn't long when I was hired as an administrative assistant for the chairman and CEO of a savings and loan that later changed its charter to a bank. I eventually became the bank's corporate secretary. I worked hard, but enjoyed every minute of the eleven years I was there. That job ranks as one of two wonderful banking positions I held almost to retirement.

17
DIVORCE

It was December 14th, 1978. We were escorted to a counseling room at the courthouse as a last-ditch effort of the court to see if there was any hope for reconciliation.

Emotional stench colored our surroundings as we sat waiting for our case to come before the judge. I believe it was the court clerk that called us forward. The judge, rightly, sermonized the sanctity of family and our responsibilities as parents. Maligned, I felt droplets of perspiration forming on my forehead. When finished the judge pronounced: "The petitioner is entitled to Judgement of Divorce."

The decree reads: *First. The bonds of matrimony heretofore subsisting between the petitioner, Marie L. Malicki, and the respondent, James J. Malicki, be and the same are hereby dissolved immediately and they are forever freed from the obligations thereof.* I left the court house feeling sad and hollow.

I read those words many times, recently and back then. Somehow, they never did ring true. If it starts with true love, it never ever ends that simply. Marriages all have cracks. I think it's sad that when it all started, we didn't have the ability and emotional maturity to patch it and pull it back. It was hard to live out of step with my religion, and family and friends who didn't understand. Also, a funny thing that sometimes got in my way when I addressed him, I sometimes still addressed him as "honey." Old habits die hard!

☙

It was the Chevelle that was to keep Jim going. Whether he owned it or not, he mused over its existence and the care it was being given. In the months leading to our separation, he bemoaned the fact that years before he had to sell it, and he set his mind to getting it back. I thought it impossible, but urged him on. Maybe it would give him something to concentrate on besides brow beating our situation to death. Luck was on his side. He researched the VIN and located the registration address.

He asked, and I agreed that the kids and I would take a ride with him to Elkhorn. He wanted to see where it was, and to hopefully catch a glimpse of it. There was no sign of the car from the street, but he spotted a garage behind the house. Jim skirted the alley counting the houses to the specific garage he was looking for. He stopped. The pull was larger than he could handle. He got out of the car, walked to the door, and rubbed a patch of dirt off its window. Like a voyeur, he stole a secret view of his first love. Aroused, he tilted his head waving for me to come and take a look. I peered into the dark and dreary space. There it was, neglected and diseased, a discard of society; a far cry from the robust condition it was in when he sold it. He had mixed feelings. He was elated he found it, but upset at its deplorable condition. "I'm sorry," his moist eyes conveyed as he stared at it. I believe a promise to an old friend was made at that moment. On the way home, he talked as if he had already bought it back. His plans to dissect its anatomy piece by piece were well underway.

He didn't waste any time digging up the owner's phone number. I listened as they conversed. Jim never did mention to him that he had peered into his garage. He merely told him he was interested in seeing his old car. "Sure, come on out," the man said. The mask disguising his eagerness fell. Excitedly, he told the guy he could come out any time. "Will tomorrow work?" They arranged a time, they talked, made a deal, and the Chevelle was his again.

Keyed up, he recounted when he first bought it. He knew the exact date he made the deal, July 6th, 1967 (July 6th, a date that would become significant 40 years later). He took possession a day later, after signing the loan documents. The cash sale and delivered price was $3,622.75.

For me, it was an innocuous transaction. It wasn't until many years later that I realized what holding the title to the Chevelle would mean.

※

I had no choice but to move along with the complexity of everyday living. I didn't have much time to think about anything else. However, I recall the curious mood I felt when I heard all the news about the nuclear meltdown at Three Mile Island in Pennsylvania in March 1979. Although the accident didn't happen close to home, it rattled me. It served as an admonition that bad events beyond our control occur in life. What if disaster occurred in my life? Safety for me and the kids had always been in Jim. Even when we were at our worst, I always felt he would protect me. I think it was this feeling that always left a piece of me open to him.

PART THREE
WELL WORTH THE JOURNEY

*Failure is the opportunity to begin again,
this time more intelligently.*

~Henry Ford

18
THE 1980s

Unlike the earthquakes and eventual eruptions of Mount St. Helens in 1980, the busyness of accommodating the kids' schedules and jobs eventually weaned our emotional turbulence to a tolerable level. Like a game of dominoes, the acerbic tones, pointed looks and frosty conversations collapsed under the weight of it all. Wrought out, we avoided conflict at all cost.

I went to pick up the kids. I don't remember the date, but I remember Jim's greeting. "Can you sit and hear me out about something?" Jim motioned to the chair. "Please listen, and then you can let me know what you think. You don't even have to answer me today." I knotted my brows as I shot him a side-long glance. *He doesn't seem angry,* I thought, and plainly he was non-confrontational. My curiosity was piqued. "I can stay a few minutes." As I sat down, I asked, "What do you want to talk about?" It was not explicit, but I sensed a lilt in his voice, something I had not heard for a long time. I thought, *What on earth? What is he up to?*

"You know I don't like the kids living in an apartment, and I don't think you do either. I've been thinking that maybe we should buy a house together, a duplex."

I was taken aback, my reaction hung-up in mute suspicion. *What was he suggesting? For me to live in one unit and he the other?* Finally, I spoke, "Exactly what are you proposing?"

He responded. "We could pool our resources to buy a duplex. You and the kids can live in one unit, and you could collect the rent from the other unit to help pay the mortgage. That way, the kids would be in a house and we'd both have an investment in property."

Initially uncomfortable about the proposal and not ready to start something, it was good I needed to leave. "I'll think about it," I said, as I gathered the kids toward the stairs.

I did think and pray about it, but more or less concluded there was no way we could make it work. Jim remained tenacious. He steadied himself and pitched his proposition every time we saw each other. In my mind there were too many questions, especially the legal ones. Although it hadn't been mentioned in weeks, the initial reason that set us to divorce remained ghostlike in the background. It was hard to imagine being in agreement on most anything, let alone something as hefty as this proposal seemed to be. Also, I didn't want the responsibility for yard work or home maintenance.

Jim had an answer for everything. He offered to take care of the yard on a set schedule. He'd do fix-up, maintenance type work we both considered necessary, and we'd share the cost, and on he went, but the towering question was what if one of us wanted out. In my mind these answers seemed too complex, but the more Jim pushed, the more I started to think that maybe we could make something work, especially for the sake of the kids. We saw an attorney, to talk it over.

Well, as you can imagine, the attorney looked at us cross-eyed, but agreed to work with us. Legalities were discussed that addressed concerns we both had regarding the whole process, from making an offer, to purchase and beyond. It took time, but we eventually had a solid document. We hovered over the attorney's desk before signing. He pointed out the few minor changes he had made since our last meeting. Jim eagerly signed first. Convinced, sort of, that there was no covert separate agenda, and the whole thing would be null and void if we didn't find a house we agreed upon, I paused, took the pen and signed. Our parameters set on paper, we were out house hunting.

Once again, we were together on Sundays, circling real estate ads and driving through neighborhoods. On those days we usually had dinner as a family, even if it was McDonald's. I observed Jim closely during that time. He seemed more relaxed than he had been in years about what brought us to the divorce and the devastation we had seeded and fertilized over the past several years.

The agenda was to find a house, and it was fun. I thought it a bit risky to ponder, but it seemed a tinge of affection had returned between us. The feeling was peculiar to our circumstances. I wondered if Jim felt it as well. He seemed to.

We wholeheartedly agreed upon a 1930s duplex. It needed work, but was a substantial house, abundant with character. Its Spanish plaster, coved ceilings and stained-glass piano windows were among its many decorative amenities. It was close to where I worked. Another benefit was the close proximity of the Catholic church and school where the kids would eventually be enrolled.

We were good together house-hunting, but we continued to live our separate lives. True to his word, Jim took care of the yard and used a good part of his weekends as he fixed and updated things he considered necessary to maintain a solid home. He scrutinized the house, as he looked for excuses to come and "fix" something.

He had returned to a non-critical good mood, and then it started. Every time he saw me, he asked the same question. "Want to get married?" My response: "Nope, I don't think so." I was surprised and questioned myself when the "I don't think so" first popped out. I asked myself, *Why didn't I simply say, "no?"* I certainly didn't want to mislead Jim, but like a misfired missile, those words found their way to and out of my mouth.

It was spring of 1980 when I started to think around the fringes of his proposals. What had started us down the path to ruin was still there, but as I mentioned previously, ghostlike in the background. It was no longer mentioned. We were getting along well. Great at times. I thought, *Dare we try again?*

We reached a turning point in June 1980. For most of a week I had been gone, attending a banking clinic in Oshkosh. Jim was eager to watch the kids and to terrace with railroad ties the mess that was our backyard. My car, on its last legs, could be problematic for the drive so I made arrangements to ride with someone from work. At the last minute my ride cancelled. Jim, who treated his Trans Am almost as well as he did the Chevelle, offered me the use of his car. I was beyond flabbergasted.

I didn't want to go to a bar every evening with the others, so I spent a good deal of my free-time in my dorm room. I rehashed our life together and prayed a lot. Jim's proposal was there, marinating in my consciousness. When I laid in bed, a vision of happiness as family passed through my heart as I continued the search for peace in my life. The beautiful hymn, "Let There be Peace on Earth," hitched a ride with me to Oshkosh. Its words were a great comfort. It was Christmas, 1978, when I borrowed a hymnal from St. Adalbert's, and sang it until I had it memorized. Its words became a comfort and distracted me at the clinic. Its easy formula for peace played louder than the speaker who was there to help me with my career.

It speaks of walking with your brother in perfect harmony. In Oshkosh, "brother" changed to "Jim."

All the way home Jim appeared in my peripheral vision. *Please, Lord, give me a sign*, I begged. *What do you want for my life and the lives of our children?* What was weird, was the more I drove, the more I felt the need to be in his arms, hold his hand and to dance.

By the time I turned into my alley I was almost giddy with joy. He became visible. Shirtless, dirty, there he was, a Greek god terracing my back yard.

I said to myself, *Thank you, Lord. You just gave me my answer.* Jim's gladdened smile called out to me as I walked to where he was standing. My heart opened its gates, as it had thirteen years earlier at 12th & Marquette. He planted a kiss on my cheek. "It's good to have you home." I wanted to blurt out, "Yes, I'll marry you," but I waited, wanting to surprise him with a "yes" the next time he asked.

I asked, "Are you going to stay for supper?"

"Sure," he responded.

I crafted a sly wink and uttered, "Take a shower and then you can help me get it ready."

It wasn't long until I heard him come down the stairs and enter the kitchen. I turned. The glint in his eyes could not betray what he was going to say next. My heart cheered. He extended his arms and hugged me as never before. He softly whispered in my ear, "I love you; will you marry me?" My earnest "yes" held no hesitation. Startled, it took him a second or two to digest my robust response. We froze in place, and held a long and loving kiss I'll never forget.

After the kids went to bed the conversation started. I was about breathless when he twined his fingers in mine. Gosh, how I had missed the touch of his hands. Finally, able to see through the air between us, we opened our hearts and ears. We talked and listened into the late hours of the night. There was restorative work to do. It was important, we agreed, to banish judgments and break the pre-divorce patterns of presumptions and reactions that sabotaged our marriage, to hold no debt to the past, and to celebrate our togetherness often. It became our finest hour when we deliberately chose not to go back and re-litigate the issues that got us to this point. We wanted a new, clean start to our future.

Our smiles beamed in the gloaming light of the room. After we toasted the future, Jim stood. Lovingly he offered his hand. We held ourselves in dance, our lips met, our heartbeats once again swayed as one. Later that night, his restful snoring was music to my ears.

The next morning Jim insisted we shop for rings. I told him I still had my rings, but he wouldn't hear about it. He reasoned a "new start requires new rings." I wasn't going to argue. I found out on our way to the jeweler that he flung his first ring as far as he could toss it, somewhere outside the courthouse the day we got divorced.

It so happens my favorite spot on earth is in Door County. Given our new status, I had to will myself to take a previously scheduled vacation there with a friend, her kids and mine. Jim had never been to Door County and decided to drive up on Thursday evening so we could spend Friday together before heading home on Saturday. I was so excited. I wanted him to love Door County as much as I learned to love it during our separation, and love it he did.

19
TILL DEATH AND BEYOND

Reno, "The Biggest Little City in the World," was our wedding destination. The Chapel's bulbs blinked to reveal a worn-out, tarnished aura. "Weddings," the ostentatious sign hawked, "Always a Value." As we were still married in the eyes of the church, we simply needed to make it legal, so we made an appointment for the next day.

Although we stood under a certifiably garish arbor embellished with plastic roses, we were certifiably in love and eager to make our union legal. The marriage record reads in part, *"A Minister of the Gospel, did on the 9th day of August A.D., 1980, at The Chapel, Reno, Nevada, join in lawful wedlock James J. Malicki and Marie L. Malicki."*

We toasted our remarriage at the MGM Grand. An energized impersonation of the King of Rock and Roll bounded to the stage amidst the blare of horns and a clash of cymbals. The wavelike swell of the drums encouraged the audience to their feet. It was great fun. You would almost swear it was the King himself; his vitality, the hair, the hip movements and the sexy snarl in his grin ignited swoons and screams from the crowd. Admirers stretched as far as their bodies would allow to touch their fake idol. When he bent to graze their hands, I anticipated a fan might faint.

Neither of us were frenzied fans and had never purchased any of his music. Our feelings changed that night.

Like the words to "Hawaiian Wedding Song," our hearts were "singing." However, it was the lesser played Elvis ballad, "I'll Remember You," that we sentimentalized. Its words call forth an enduring promise; togetherness for all eternity. It became a kitchen dance standard. It's not near as morbid as it may sound, but as we swayed to its melodic rhythm, we avowed the song would be played at the memorial service of the first to die.

The honeymoon continued for ten days. We called it the "circle tour"—Reno to Carson City, Lake Tahoe, San Jose, San Francisco and back through the Sierra Nevada Mountain Range to visit my aunt and uncle. Charms were added to my bracelet in San Francisco and from the Empire Mine in Grass Valley.

In our attempt to put our mistakes behind us, we decided to never go back or reprocess the time we spent apart. October 12th, our original wedding date, once again became the date we celebrated our marriage. In October 1980, two months after we married in Reno, we went to Door County to celebrate our twelfth wedding anniversary.

20

GLADSOME TIMES

Our rescued relationship would not be enough. Adversaries for so long, we realized healing needed to extend beyond the two of us. The kids needed connectedness as family, and we once again strived to become a parenting unit that our kids could hopefully emulate someday.

We were the typical '80s family. In the years since we had Sherry, two working parents became the norm. I continued working at the bank in a job I loved. Jim continued at GM, reticent to leave a job he despised due to its pay and generous benefits. The kids were absorbed in school activities, Scouts, and athletic activities that kept us all hopping.

We remodeled the kitchen which provided the perfect spot for a TV. News was on most evenings while I cooked and Jim snacked on potato chips. TV journalists at the beginning of the decade were thick-mustached men and women with big hair and power suits with broad shoulders. They informed us about such things as AIDS, the Space Shuttle Challenger disaster, and the fall of the Berlin Wall. Ronald Reagan's rosy cheeks seemed to beam at us nightly, while his wife, Nancy, consulted astrologers and supported a "Just Say No" campaign against the use of drugs.

Pac-Man became Doug's babysitter. Its sounds were happy, but at times drove me crazy. I can only imagine Pac-Man's chomping *waaka waaka* must play as tinnitus in Doug's ears today.

A diverse "society" populated our home in the '80s. Frieda's stinky basset hound odor permeated the air no matter how much she was bathed. She slept at the foot of Doug's bed. How he could tolerate it, I don't know. The kids took every other week to clean up after her. When Sherry got a bit older and had a bit of earning power, she paid Doug $1.00 a week to take over her duties. I thought he deserved more, but decided not to interfere with their negotiating.

Dickie Jefferson, Sherry's Cabbage Patch Doll, found a little space of his own in her messy room. Posters of Michael Jackson, James Dean, Corey Hart, and others covered the wallpaper. Doug's contribution to the population was about one hundred GI Joes and their war vehicles. Their rules of engagement persistently had them marching through the living room and under the dining room table. Transformers, Bumblebee, and Starscream, added to the mix.

Mini weekend trips and cross-country vacations were a part of '80s life. I'll always hear the *swoosh, swoosh* burner blasts of the hot air balloons at Dell Boo, and the waves hitting the shores in Door County, Wisconsin.

Our trips to Yellowstone and parts in between in 1984, and to California in the spring of 1982, are truly memorable.

While in California, we toured Alcatraz. I still have a bit of a dull panic when I think about the prison and how it makes me think of Purgatory. I can't bring to mind one of these places without relating it to the other.

Gray sheets of rain were falling the day we scheduled our Alcatraz tour, but we weren't deterred. We bought striped plastic rain jackets at the pier and were ferried across the rough waters of San Francisco Bay. I was hit with a sense of dread the second we stepped off the boat. It was like no other place I had ever been. As if hung out to dry in the cold mist of the day, the wind seemed to harken a soulful torture to the spirits remaining there. I could feel them, but not see them. I wondered if the other tourists had the same case of the willies I was experiencing. In row after row of cells, trepidation laid over me a disturbing heaviness I found hard to shake. I wondered if this compared to the torment and punishment of Purgatory. Souls waiting to get pardoned for their sins, or planning an escape, but to where? Cold waters, harsh currents, and armed guards, making it impossible to leave, were the barriers surrounding Alcatraz. Call it prison, or call it Purgatory, it's a place of tension and anxiety; it seems to me the damaged side of both life and death.

I have to admit Jim's car club activities were excessive at times. Jim was president of his club. During warm weather, we attended numerous car shows, swap meets, road rallies, and anything else that had to do with cars. Right behind myself and the kids, Jim was passionate about muscle cars, especially his Chevelle.

My career at the bank was personally fulfilling. It was in 1987 or 1988 I was voted on as corporation secretary. I was so proud of myself. I never thought my career as a secretary would take me that far. The only female in the room, I sat in at all board meetings, received a board fee, and traveled with the board to all planning functions. Though Jim had the "working man blues" confined to an assembly line all day, he encouraged my career and felt good for me. He told me this often. However, it did become a concern when we started to talk about moving—out of state.

21
TENNESSEE

Jim called me every day after he got home from work. One particular day, his voice seemed exceptionally purposeful and excited. "How would you like to move to Tennessee?"

"Sure, okay," I responded.

"I'll tell you about it when you get home," Jim said.

A moment later, as I tried to concentrate on my work, I thought, *Hmmm? Move to Tennessee?* Maybe I should have checked out the details before I responded. When I got home, he couldn't contain himself; pleasure showed in his eyes as he spoke expansively. I knew he had done his homework. GM was creating "a different kind of company" to compete against the foreign small car market. Its nameplate was Saturn. The company's new organizational structure was non-traditional GM, as was its UAW Memorandum of Agreement. Everyone was to be a stakeholder. "Old World" was out, "New World" was in. Jim desperately wanted to be a part of this.

Later that evening, we discussed the possibility. We talked about my salary and career. We knew it would be nearly impossible for me to find a similar position in Tennessee. How the pay cut would impact not only our current life, but our future, was an unknown. We didn't make a decision that evening. What we did agree was that Jim would garner information and stay abreast of Saturn's development. Based upon what we would learn, we'd decide if we wanted to take the next step.

I don't remember the date. A group representing Saturn came to Oak Creek to tout Saturn and provide information regarding recruitment and selection. I left work early to attend with Jim. I hadn't said anything to my employer about this, as we were still in the "decide what we should do mode." TV crews from all the local stations were there. I laugh at it now, because I spent most of the meeting ducking TV cameras so I wouldn't be spotted on the local news casts.

We got home and couldn't stop talking. We were ready for a new adventure. Jim would submit an application, and once again we decided we'd figure things out if and when he was called.

It was late 1989. His grin was uncontrollably huge. Jubilant, he punched the air with an envelope. "I got it!" It was his invitation to head to Tennessee for testing and interviews to take place in 1990. What an exciting day!

Jim loved his snow blower, but hated winter. It couldn't have been more apropos that it was a bitter, cold day when we headed to Tennessee with the hopeful prospect of moving south.

Doug was with us. His voice sounded troubled as he talked to Sherry from our motel room. He exclaimed: "There's nothing here but a school and gas station!" Dolefully Jim and I looked at each other. I thought, *Oh my, if this goes the way we want, I pray Doug will be able to adjust.* The process moved forward. Every step of the way we took pains to include the kids where we could.

Jim's interviews went well. On February 16th, 1990, we received the letter we were waiting for. It stated: *Please consider this letter as your formal invitation to join the Saturn team. If you accept, you are scheduled to begin employment on September 4th, 1990.* My head whirled as we jumped for joy. However, there still was the concern about cutting our combined income to less than half, at least temporarily. We talked and talked some more. We couldn't help ourselves. We decided to move, and from that moment we owned the commitment.

All in all, it seemed a bit provocative as I imagined a new start to our lives in a different state.

It's amazing how things slipped into place. Sherry joined us for our house-hunting expedition. She had her mind set on the house we should buy and dubbed it "Homer's Home" due to the name of one of the developers. Every house we looked at afterward never met her expectations, or ours. On May 15th, we made an offer on "Homer's Home" in Thompson's Station, Tennessee. It was accepted the next day. On our way back to Wisconsin, the drummer in Jim couldn't help but pound a happy beat to just about every song he heard. I thought he'd wear out the steering wheel. It was only a couple weeks later we accepted an offer on our home in Wisconsin. The buyer didn't want occupancy until August. Perfect!

Mom, Dad, Jim, Doug, our dog, and I pulled out of Mom and Dad's driveway on the morning of July 26th, 1990. After the hugs and goodbyes, Sherry was left in the driveway, alone. In a few weeks, she'd be headed to the University of Wisconsin in Madison. It was also her twentieth birthday that day. It was a struggle to say goodbye. Although I knew better, leaving her alone in the driveway had the feeling of abandonment. They were some of the hardest tears I ever had to choke back.

It was a long day getting to Thompson's Station. I laugh now, as I often think of it as a one-horse town, not because of the homes or people, but the one horse that was housed on the southwest corner of the main highway. He was there the day we arrived, and remained there, lonely, for many years.

We proudly took Mom and Dad on a tour of the house and set up for overnight. The delivery of our household items was scheduled for the next morning. Jim and I slept on an air mattress at the house, and Mom and Dad and Doug at the motel in Spring Hill.

It was a beautiful, hot and sunny morning. The van lines pulled up as scheduled. The Chevelle came off the truck first, and was set out of harm's way. Systematically our household goods and belongings were transferred from truck to house.

Three days later, Jim and Dad returned to Wisconsin. Jim had three weeks to complete at A-C Spark Plug before he could officially move. Mom and Doug and I stayed and set things up.

22
TENNESSEE FRIENDSHIPS

Ding dong! It was our doorbell the day after we moved. *Who could that be?* Two teenagers, Diana and Jason, stood on the porch wondering if they could introduce themselves to the teenage boy they observed moving in the day before. It was our first meeting with a member of the Shauck and Kosiba families. Within a short time, we would meet the Penders and Dickersons. Even though we all arrived in Tennessee within weeks of each other, and came from Wisconsin, Ohio, Georgia, and Michigan, we had a lot in common. All the guys worked at Saturn, were into cars, had teenagers Doug's age, and each family was establishing new roots.

Through time, I amassed the utmost respect for my group of Tennessee friends, dubbed the Hood. Caring and integrity strongly mark our interpersonal bonds. We shared the novelty of our new surroundings together and remain fixed as family today. In the many years we have known each other, these bonds have deepened and have served to carry each other through the best of times, and the worst of tragedies and sadness. Time may have changed our residences, but we have always remained true to the friendships. It's a cliché, but I truly can't express the deep love I have for them all!

Later, through my employment, we were blessed with the friendships of both the Moody and Battle families. Again, remarkable people who exemplify "Southern hospitality" and are treasured for their true sense of caring.

Somewhere along the way I found this quote. It is so absolutely true:

Each friend represents a world in us, a world possibly not born until they arrive, and it is only by this meeting that a new world is born.

~Anais Nin

23
THE 1990s

"How's life in Tennessee?"

Representative of my response were words like, "Wonderful! We're fortunate; we're living the good life."

Not too long after we moved to Tennessee, Saddam Hussein made good on his threats and ordered Iraqi troops to cross into Kuwait. Later in the year, East and West Germany formally reunited as one country. It wasn't that we didn't care about those world events, but in the honeymoon of our new adventure, we were busy settling in, making new friends, and in our spare time, driving throughout the beautiful countryside. It's also when Jim started pulling over to the shoulder of the road, to talk to cows. Truly excited to be in his new environment, Jim grinned wide as he leaned over the fence.

"Hi, Mr. Cow," he laughed. "You have a nice place here."

Chuckling, I said, "Have you gone crazy? I think you mean Mrs. Cow."

He responded airily to my look; once again he talked to the cow. "Okay. Mrs. Cow, you have a nice place here."

Early 1991 brought with it the death of Jim's dad. Jim flew to Milwaukee with his sister, who happened to be visiting with us, for the funeral. Due to pre-surgery testing for a hysterectomy, I was not able to go. We were saddened Jim's dad was never able to make the trip to Tennessee. We would have loved it.

Jim really enjoyed working at Saturn, and after my surgery, I too went to work at Saturn. I was an administrative assistant to the quality engineering manager.

After a year of temp work, I found myself back in a familiar position, banking. It's where I met the Moodys and Battles, made lasting friendships, met many of the citizenry of Franklin, and, through my office window, observed life on The Square. Lovers kissed, some argued, the fire department or police responded to various minor incidents (although not all of them were so minor, like the day a despondent man yielding a gun was walking The Square.) Homecoming parades and busloads of tourists were especially fun. There was also one special, eccentric woman. I'll call her Abby. A day without Abby on The Square could be considered a bit dull. Marked with painted cheeks and eyes, quirky hair, and sometimes garish costumes, she was adept at catching one's attention. She positioned herself as if she was a swan on her bike, danced in front of bank windows and was seen on numerous occasions exercising in front of the doors of the Catholic church or courthouse stairs. As a child, I learned to keep my behavior in check. It bred inhibition. I chuckled often when I saw her, but I was secretly a bit envious that she was able to give herself the permission to express herself in such a liberated way. I'll never know that feeling.

In April 1994, we headed to Wisconsin for Jim's sister's funeral. He was so saddened. It was hard for him to comprehend that she too had died. For several weeks he ambled about, his demeanor sad. Then the anger stage of grief took hold. He was terribly angry with her. She had been a heavy smoker, and died a terrible cancer death. For him, acceptance was a long time coming.

The whole OJ mess in 1994 certainly caught our attention, but most news was so secondary to what we were about, and what we were doing. Jim centered most of his attention on the Chevelle, readying it for the 1994 Saturn Homecoming. I thought the car looked great and told him so. "It's dated," he moaned. As if to prepare me for the redo, he repeated, "Dated!" every single time I walked into the garage or the car was mentioned. Dated or not, he cleaned, shined and buffed every square inch inside and out. The tiniest details were not overlooked. You could eat off its air filter!

Heat and hot sun, rain, and humidity plagued Middle Tennessee during Saturn's Homecoming Weekend. No matter; between cloudbursts and rain drenched fields, the "Automotive Woodstock," as some called it, went on in fine fashion. Over 35,000 owners and families attended. "Red ball" Saturns (with red balls set atop their antennas) clogged the highway in front of our subdivision. BeBe and CeCe Winans and Wynona Judd were the scheduled frontline entertainment.

Bands, singers, jugglers, fireworks, and tents scattered throughout the site entertained and hosted a variety of events. The Classic Car tent was particularly huge. Beautiful classic muscle cars, hot rods, collectibles, and antique autos were lined up in the tent for the public's viewing. "Please Look, But Please Don't Touch" placards were posted on most windshields.

Most of the Hood was there, showing their cars and having a joyous time. As Saturn owners and their families roamed through the aisles, we delighted in speaking with them. We learned where they were from, and most raved about their Saturns and Homecoming.

It was later in the afternoon, on Saturday. I said to Jim, "It looks like it might be getting dark out." We exited the tent. In the west, heavy, grey clouds looked as if they were ready to boil over.

"It'll hit before we have time to get home," Jim said. Never anticipating the force of what was about to hit us, we resigned ourselves to waiting it out. The ridge of anger heading toward us hit fast. Torrents of wind and rain whipped against the tent. As the roof bulged inward, its supports were breached. The wind and weight of the rain were too much.

"Stay here," Jim yelled. Before I knew what he was doing, he had raced toward the tent's opening to assess the storm. I was way too nervous and couldn't stand still. Six to eight feet away there was a break between two pieces of canvas. *Whoosh*! The moment I pressed the canvas apart a down-rush of water and gale force wind gusts caved the ceiling in. Steel wire and wood posts swung wildly in the air; stakes holding the guy wire pulled from their holes. Jim didn't make it outside and barely had time to dive to the ground before the tent blew away. As he laid there, the car tilted on two wheels. Afterward, he told me, "I thought I was a goner." Fortunately, it settled back. Completely exposed to weather, through the remainder of the storm, Jim and I, and our neighbors Beth and Don, sheltered in the Chevelle. A dozen or so people were injured, none seriously. The tent? It was in a heap on the ground, down field from where it originally stood.

The Chevelle sustained a good deal of damage. It lost a rearview mirror and there was a broken window and a big dent where a wood pole dragged across the entire top of the car. The inside was trashed with rain and mud. There were numerous other scratches and small dents.

It seems crazy how he had talked about "updating" the car. As it turned out, insurance money enabled Jim to restore his cherished Chevelle to its original vigor and soundness. Rehabilitated, the Chevelle carried home numerous trophies, and once again transported us to friends and good times.

ಸಿ

We were merrily rolling along. Many of our proudest days as parents were in the '90s. Sherry walked the stage and received her diploma from the University of Wisconsin in 1992. Before continuing her education, she sold cars at Saturn of Madison. That's where she met George.

The sun glinted hot that August day when we welcomed George to our family. Friends and family gathered in the assembly chamber at the Wisconsin State Capitol for the ceremony. Jim's audible gasp when he caught sight of Sherry turned heads to the back of the room. He was bloated with love and pride. When George's mom and George danced to Etta James' "At Last," I couldn't help but say one of those silent "mom prayers." It certainly was one of the finest days we celebrated as a family.

Doug graduated from Middle Tennessee State University in 1999. Little did we know that his senior year art trip to New York City would set his mind in that direction. He didn't sit on his plan. In September, equipped with a promise for temporary housing secured through a friend of a friend and a job at the Metropolitan Museum of Art, but not knowing a soul in the city, he packed two suitcases and a backpack and headed to the Big Apple.

We were at the Nashville Airport. Opposite us on the concourse, a group of twenty or so Muslims were bent over in prayer. I don't know what they were praying for, but once again I prayed a "mom prayer," for my son's safety and happiness. Although my heart ached knowing I would miss him, I was bursting with pride. He had the guts to lead his life and drive it to where he wanted it to go, a thing I held back on when steered away from college while in high school.

My body worked to breathe as he walked to a new existence, step-by-step up the ramp, until I could no longer see him. I didn't breathe easily until I knew his new roommate, Eric, had met him at the Bohemian Hall and Beer Garden in Queens, and later, that he was safe at Eric's apartment.

We were finally starting to see our way past tuition payments. It was time to start living our dreams. What Jim said we needed was a retirement house with space for a big detached garage. Over and over through the years he'd say, "I'd like to build another car, but I'd need another garage. Do you think we'll ever have a place where I can build a garage? I don't want to wait until I'm ready to die before I get a garage." I said, "Let's go look!"

Doing what we liked best, it took about six months to find exactly what we were looking for, a house we liked with enough land to accommodate a separate garage. As an added benefit, the yard abutted the woods and was naturally and amazingly beautiful. It was as if the house sat in Grant Park, but without Lake Michigan, although I often imagined the lake to be right there behind the woods. Jim built the deck first. It extended the full length of the back of the house: our own private piece of heaven.

As I could have predicted, Jim needed a new garden tractor, something with more muscle, for the two acres. So as not to cause any complications in his plans to acquire said lawn tractor, he was solicitous and encouraged I purchase anything I felt we needed for our retirement home. He didn't tell me that he'd also need a bagger, dump cart, aerator, de-thatcher, spreader, and a shed to house it all. It brought him so much happiness to work in the yard. What would tire me, rejuvenated him. His satisfaction was pure nature-fed contentment.

One day when he came in after mowing, I teasingly asked, "Does your guardian angel like it here?" He put his arms around me and turned me to face the windows. "Look out there if you're looking for the sacred," he answered.

"My angel loves it here." I thought back through the years when he first told me about his angel, and other "sightings," as I called them. Once again, I said nothing; I was envious he could see his angel and I couldn't see mine.

Reflecting on the '80s and '90s has been a joy. My only regret is those years went by way too fast!

24
2000–2005

Y2K, The Millenium Bug: worldwide, people feared that computers operating power grids, banks, airports, law enforcement, and about everything else in the world may fail. Apocalyptic predictions were made. Yet, the world was prepared. 1999 passed the torch to the year 2000 and the world did not come to a standstill.

Neither did my dad's illness. I doubt he realized or cared that the calendar now said "2000."

☙

The Saturday before Thanksgiving 1999, Jim and I made the trek through the drab brown states of Kentucky, Illinois and southern Wisconsin to go home for Thanksgiving.

Home sweet home! The plan was to have a relaxing week with Mom and Dad. Dad hadn't been feeling well, so I was hoping a bit of diversion might take his mind off the doctor's appointment he had scheduled for right after Thanksgiving. Sunday morning mass at St. Adalbert's, breakfast at Marquette Plaza, and a drive through Grant Park couldn't have felt more like home. Over dinner that night, Mom and Dad mentioned several errands for Monday. We decided we'd help out. Afterward, we'd all stop at Holy Sepulcher Cemetery, where visiting the gravesites of various family members was the ritual, and when we stopped by to clean up around Jim's parents' headstone.

Dad certainly wasn't himself that morning, but he still seemed eager to get on with the plan. The first stop was the UPS Store, then Piggly Wiggly. Mom needed to run in for celery and then we could be on our way. She was barely out of sight when Dad started to come unglued. He clutched his abdomen, then, slam! The horrible pain struck with a fierce determination. A powerful gasp, like I imagined the last gasp before death, struck my eardrums. "I need to go to the bathroom, I need to go to the bathroom, now!" Dad screamed sharply. Faster than lickety-split, Jim pulled the car from the parking lot to the fire lane in front of the store. Dad's demeanor signaled something bad.

Jim jumped out and sprinted to Dad's side to support him to the bathroom. Just as fast, Dad changed his mind. The cramping bent him over. He screamed again, this time, "Get me home; get me home! Where's Emily? Where's Emily?"

I followed Jim out of the car and ran to find Mom. She was already checking out. She was befuddled by the urgency I placed on her getting back to the car. I grabbed the celery and rushed her as best I could. We couldn't get home fast enough. Dad's cramping and retching moans made my heart pound. I remember thinking, *Does he need to throw up? Does he need to have a bowel movement? What's happening?*

Jim was immediately at Dad's side and helped him to bed, clothes, shoes and all. "I'm going to call 911," I said.

"No," Dad hollered. "Give me some Pepto-Bismol."

I raced for the Pepto on the vanity. Pink spewed back at us and made a mess of him and the bed. "Enough, I'm calling 911," I said. Mom seemed ready to collapse as she watched from the side of the bedroom, horrified. I reached for the phone and called 911.

The response was quick. When the EMTs questioned him about the pain, we all answered at once. Firm and direct, the EMT commented, "I asked the patient."

"Go away, he hollered," to us and the EMTs. There was no way we could "go away." He continued to writhe and twist in pain, and yet formidably resisted going to the hospital. He wanted to be left alone and did not want anyone to touch him. Finally, after a lot of panicked coaxing on our part, his attitude subsided and he was taken to the ER. As they put him on the stretcher, I noticed how quickly his skin had turned sallow. His eyes were glazed over and he looked terribly frightened. I prayed, *God, please take care of my dad.*

We followed in the car. By the time we got to the hospital they had taken him back and we were told to stay in the waiting room. I kept asking the ER clerk standing guard at the desk outside the ER when we could go back and see Dad. I told her Mom needed to see her husband. Each time I inquired I was told, "No, we'll let you know when there is any news and you are allowed to go back." I was ready to scream right there!

I'm not brave, I hate drama, and I hate to get loud and ugly, but it had been several hours since we arrived. I wanted to get past that locked door to Dad's side. I believed we had the right to be with him, to find out what was going on. I spewed forth a transfusion of verbal energy I didn't know I had in me. Finally, the "guard" went back to talk to someone and we were allowed to see Dad.

I was dumbfounded and horrified at the same time. First, it was ice cold back there. He still had his street clothes on, was on a gurney, and had no blanket. He had been alone the whole time! He was not hooked to anything, not given anything for pain. We learned a call had been put in to a gastrointestinal doctor who had not as yet arrived. The nurse, afraid to divulge much of anything before the doctor arrived, didn't want to speculate or offer a clue.

We were able to get him some warm blankets and tried to comfort him as best we could. Finally, the doctor arrived and several tests were ordered. He suspected peritonitis. "What's peritonitis?" I asked.

The tests revealed Dad had a perforated colon. His inability to pass sufficient stool exerted pressure on the colon due to a cancerous tumor in the rectum. A surgeon was called and Dad was operated on, if I remember correctly, about eight or nine hours after he arrived.

Post-surgery he was pumped full of antibiotics and fluids that expanded his body considerably, so much so, that during the process his wrinkles disappeared. Although he was 80 at the time, when I looked at him he reminded me of the man who walked me down the aisle at the age of 49. He now had a colostomy bag.

We made many trips to Wisconsin that winter. Snow, sleet, ice: we drove through it all to visit, or when we'd get the call that the doctor thought his time may be nearing the end.

I remember one trip in particular. We were on the road in Kentucky, and it was still a bit dark. We were awestruck at the reddish, humongous, full moon sitting directly on the road ahead of us, as if it was waiting to block us from moving forward. When talking about it at the hospital with an aide, I learned the size was merely an illusion when the moon appears on the horizon. Nonetheless, it was a magnificent sight, and emphasized the awe of life and God's creation.

Dad's face opened into a faint smile when he heard my voice. "Can you rub my feet?" he asked. Lying in the bubbling sand bed that prevented bed sores, he drew great comfort when family visited, and especially when they rubbed his feet. The ten or so hours on the road seemed worth it to bring him that pleasure. As he was finding some relaxation from the massage, a nurse approached. It was time to change the colostomy bag. In a tender, yet businesslike way, she said, "When he leaves the hospital, his caregiver will have to do this for him."

I stepped wide, but she motioned me closer. "You need to see how this is done," she said. I reluctantly moved in closer and hunched silently. I watched as her hands deftly changed the pouch and cleaned Dad's wound. Praise nurses! Alarm flooded my head. I thought to myself, *How on earth will Mom be able to handle this if this becomes her job? And, the bathing, the feeding, and everything else?* I had no answers. *One day at a time*, I told myself.

It was January, and freezing rain, ice, and snow were our detested companions on the way home. It was harrowing at times. The wipers could not handle the build-up. Jim's driving visibility narrowed to a few inches at the bottom of the windshield. We stopped on the shoulder of I-39. It was still dark and not at all safe, but neither was driving. Jim scraped the ice off the lights and watched as the flashers glinted through the freezing rain/snow. It was an hour or so later when, beyond the loam of clouds and storm, we could finally make out daylight. It was time to move on. We stood on the truck's bumpers and scraped until I felt my arm would fall off. It was a long road home.

That was to be the last time I saw my beloved Dad alive. He died January 22nd, 2000. It's weird, I don't remember the weather that trip, the trip that took us home for his funeral. What I do remember is delivering the eulogy at St. Adalbert's, and praying the one prayer always prayed at Holy Sepulcher Cemetery, *Eternal rest grant unto him, Oh, Lord, and let perpetual light shine upon him.* It was his 81st birthday.

The value I put in his love for me was immense. Beforehand, I couldn't have imagined how I would miss him. Great sadness overtook me at times in the early months after he died, especially as I thought about his great physical suffering. I had never experienced loss at this short distance, and the pain was surprisingly piercing at times. I often wondered the meaning of the one life that was my dad's life. *Was it to create me? What's this all about?* I heard myself say over and over.

It was spring, 2000. We were relaxing on the deck before dinner. There was no conversation. Heck, Jim didn't even seem to know I was there. His full concentration was centered on the grassy spot reserved for the garage. Ever the cynic, once again he quipped, "I don't want to wait until I'm ready to die to build my garage."

"I know, I know," I responded. Having been put in charge of family finances many years prior, I told him I'd go over things to figure out the best way to "get 'er done."

Several days later we were back at our favorite spots on the deck. "I figured it out," I said.

"The garage!?" he replied.

"The way to realize your dream, and my dream."

"Garage and Italy?"

"Yes, garage and Italy," I commented breezily.

He beamed. "Really?!"

"Yes, really."

After dinner he worked on the design, something he'd done many times since we bought the property. It had to be absolutely perfect.

On June 6th, 2000, the building permit was secured to build a brick, three-and-a-half car garage. Jim contracted with three brothers. Their drawls, slow, low, and slurred, were hard to understand. The lead brother's name was Daryl, and fairly soon into the project we referred to them as Daryl, Daryl, and the other brother Daryl. However, much we laughed, they did a superb job building Jim's dream.

∽

The morning of September 11th, 2001: "Good morning, this is Marie speaking."

"Have you heard what's happened in New York?" Rick, my boss inquired.

"No, what?"

"An airplane has hit one of the twin towers." My first thought was that their sheer height was amazing to me, maybe a small airplane ran into trouble and boom, the tower got in its way. "I'll be in a little late, I want to watch some of the continuing coverage."

Oh my gosh, has Doug heard about this, I thought? I quickly called. The phone rang and rang. No answer. I later learned he was on the subway when the first tower was struck.

I walked to the window and watched the early morning hustle on Franklin's square. I wondered if they'd heard and knew this was not to be an ordinary day. Sentiment beckoned me back to a day and place three months prior. One of the most wonderful days ever with my adult kids was the day we traversed the pedestrian walkway of the Brooklyn Bridge. Lower Manhattan, the Statue of Liberty, and the river views were beyond spectacular. I deliberately took pictures so the World Trade Center towers would show in the background.

The second time Rick called his words were startling and cryptic. "Hey, Marie. An airplane has flown into the side of the other tower. It was deliberate."

I needed to comprehend this. "Deliberate, terrorists?" I asked.

"That's what it looks like."

Dizziness punctuated my anxiety and fear. New York City was under attack. I desperately needed to talk to Doug.

I hit his number on speed dial. *Burrmp, burrmp, burrmp!* The call didn't go through. Damn it! Angry and nervous, I hung up and jammed my finger hard at his number. *Burrmp, burrmp, burrmp!!* On the fourth try or so, thank God, the pounding yielded a ring. Doug answered with the same words he always used. "Mom, what's going on?" He added, "What's happening? What do you hear?"

He was at work. I spit it out, "Doug, the country is under attack." My comment ended with a silent bump. His attention drifted to the people surrounding him in the Great Hall at the Met Museum. Uncertainty hung in the air about what was happening. His voice was uneasy. "When I got off the subway, I saw the smoke from the first tower. Now people are saying the second tower has been hit. I'm going to find out what's going on. I'll call later. I love you, Mom."

"Love you, Doug!" *Click.*

Doug called back shortly after the Pentagon had been struck. The museum was being evacuated. "Doug, I need to know exactly where you are going to be." I was horrified that if the city was further attacked, I wanted an address where he was last at. In case I didn't hear from him, I'd at least have a starting point to look for him in the aftermath. I had a morbid feeling in the pit of my stomach. I didn't get an exact address, but found out he was going with a co-worker to her mother's apartment near 96th St. and Lexington. They watched TV and listened as the fighter jets patrolled the New York skies.

Later that day, Doug made it safely back home. I was relieved, but only a smidgen. "The vanishing point," as Doug termed it after the attacks, was nothing but the smoldering gray-black smoke as seen from his neighborhood in Queens.

∞

I closed my umbrella as I entered the service door to Jim's garage. I wanted to see what he had been working on and to let him know it was time to call it a day. Regardless of the hat hair, greasy hands, and coveralls, my heart leapt. It was one of those ordinary moments that make up life, and while in it, I thought, *Gosh, I love this man.* "Hon," I repeated several times. He was so engrossed in what he was doing, it took a bit before my voice crept into his world.

There were always improvements being made to the Chevelle; however, on this day, he was working on a tractor. He purchased a beat-up, barely running, 1951 Ford N-series tractor. Excited when he found it, he took me to look at it before the purchase. I couldn't imagine he'd even want to buy it, but then his name was Jim, and Jim could fix anything. The plan to clean it up a bit, and flip it to earn extra cash for the eventual purchase of another classic car had been on his mind for a while. He couldn't stop at a bit. He needed to go all the way with it. Jim could never do anything without completing a job to perfection. Before I could blink, there was a shelf on the bookcase filled with tractor books, and tractor parts spread across half his garage.

The yard and the garage augmented an already good life. Jim craved more of this, but there was hesitation. "You hear that people die soon after they retire. Do you think that's true?"

"Nah," I answered. "Those people were probably sick already. You're healthy!" So it was. When GM offered a generous buyout after 30 years of service, he jumped at it. He retired October 2004.

The 4:15 alarm was no more. I was now the first one out of bed and I missed my coffee. My server was still hugging the pillow. Although he was barely up when I was ready to leave, we'd hug, kiss, and say, "I love you, have a great day." This was Jim's cue to ready himself for his three- and-a-half mile walk at the mall.

We lived a contented life in Columbia. Even though Jim teemed with anxiety when he'd think of neither of us working, he would surprise me. "Just quit," he'd say. He was aware of my commitment to the mortgage company, so we decided I wouldn't retire until the fall of 2005. That way I'd have given the mortgage company two full years, plus we could finance several trips, and put aside money for the big one, Italy.

Jim wasn't a fan of New York City. I was. We had already seen all the tourist sites on previous trips, so to placate Jim, we timed our 2005 trip to coincide with the New York Auto Show, and a tour of the Intrepid Sea, Air & Space Museum. It also happened to be Easter. What could be better than to go to St. Patrick's Cathedral for Easter Mass? As we stood in line to enter St. Patrick's, we were entertained by the bizarre and eccentric processionists in full regalia on 5th Avenue. Based on the "Easter Parade" song extolling bonnets with frills upon them, I thought everyone would be in their Sunday finest. Wow! Was I wrong! The frills were outlandish flowers, painted eggs, and rabbits—lots of rabbits! Afterward, Doug, Jim, and I walked through the city and stopped for brunch. Except for when the kids got their Easter baskets when they were young, Easter 2005 is my favorite.

Door County was also on our agenda in 2005. Knowing we'd probably never be able to do it again in such fine fashion, we rented a five-bedroom house on the bay side of Door County. Doug didn't have to sleep on a couch, which was important! Everyone had their own rooms. The amenities were appreciable and we took full advantage of them. The back of the house was mostly windowed and looked out over the bay. It was astonishing, especially at sunset. The time our family, including Mom, spent together that summer certainly ranks at the top of family memories.

I retired November 2005. I couldn't believe how relaxed the holidays were that year. Not having to hurry back home from Wisconsin and Illinois for work, and casually picking travel days, was exhilarating. Freedom to come and go as we wished! A true luxury! We decided our next trip to visit with the kids would be in June 2006, and we were planning our Italy trip for summer, 2007. As our first step in preparation for Italy, we acquired passports and bought an Italy travel guide. Evenings, when we sipped our cocktail in the living room or on the deck, our planning and thoughts were on Italy. Yet, through all these good times, I couldn't shake the feeling that something was going wrong or about to happen.

About six months after Jim retired, a prophetic sense of doom, which descended as a great weight upon my soul, overwhelmed me at times, especially when I was alone. I couldn't put my finger on it. I'd try to talk it away, telling myself it was anxiety about our changing lifestyle. *Don't look for storm clouds where there aren't any,* I'd repeat over and over. *The tempo of our world is changing just as we planned!* Yet for all the reasoning, the winds continued restless, a gloom I couldn't comprehend or shake.

It wasn't long before I'd learn that our next journey would not be Italy. It would turn out to be grievous and hurt so bad.

PART FOUR
STEADFAST UNDER TRIAL

Not forever does the bulbul sing
In balmy shades of bowers,
Not forever lasts the spring
Nor ever blossom the flowers.
Not forever reigneth joy,
Sets the sun on days of bliss,
Friendships not forever last,
They know not life, who know not this.

~Khushwant Singh

25
JANUARY 2006–JULY 2006

Retirement meant togetherness. We went everywhere together. If Jim wanted to run and get a tractor part, he'd ask me to ride along. We did the grocery shopping, and most every other errand that had to be done, together. Every ten days or so, we went to a movie in the middle of the afternoon and typically had a light dinner out afterward. It felt like playing hooky.

Jim worked in the garage and spent hours and hours working in the yard, while I made quilts. One place I didn't go with him was the mall for his morning walk. I tried, but going around in circles was not my cup of tea, and newly retired, I wanted to sleep in. He also walked fast, straight, and erect, breezily passing other walkers with a "hi" as he passed by. Besides, he made a lot of friends there, and it was great he could have a cup of coffee and chat with the guys before coming home without me by his side.

My idea of a great morning was a cup of coffee with an issue of *Southern Living* to pore over. Its tendency to include articles featuring incredible screened decks or other outdoor space would make me salivate. I often shared the pictures with Jim. "That would be easy to build," he'd sometimes comment. Other times he'd say, "That'd be way too much for us to tackle."

Nudged by the pest he was married to, after the holidays Jim decided it was time to get going on the screened porch, and toward the end of March we headed to our favorite shopping destination, Lowe's. For me, heading to Lowe's together was like going on a date with the hottest handyman in town. The date wasn't exactly cheap; we scoured the aisles for exactly what we needed for hours. We spent thousands of dollars at the Columbia Lowe's.

We started the build in April: measure, measure again, saw, hammer, stain. Most days, we worked until Jim determined a natural stopping place, or until he was tired. Although I noticed our quitting time was coming a little earlier every day, I thought it was because Jim had five or six World War II books sitting on a shelf that he wanted to read. Since he was an avid reader, I assumed that in between all the spring yard work and building, he also wanted a little recliner time.

We were coming to a close on the project, with the exception of the final touches, but they'd have to wait. On June 11th, we headed out to visit the kids, Mom, and the rest of the family. When you put Jim and George together, I daresay they could compete with the *Property Brothers*. However, they sometimes talked and acted like the other brothers of *Car Talk* fame, Click and Clack. They enjoyed being together and admired each other for their talents and skills, but they were also a little competitive.

During our stay, George had to prepare for a business event that required him to set up displays, including a ramp to exhibit a Saturn. Jim who was normally always ready to jump in and help, hesitated. His pause was weighty and his expression pained. "I'm feeling worn out." He was more tired than usual, but as we were prone to do, we chalked it up to aging.

"Come on, Jim. Come and hang around," George urged.

"Go on," I coerced.

So he went. Later that night when we settled into bed, he said, "The work today with George was almost physically more than I could take."

"Why did you do so much?" I asked.

He put it so simply, "Because George needed the help."

Jim had a fitful night. Fortifying himself to get out of bed in the morning, he sat a moment. "I feel wiped out, and the day hasn't even started." I handed him a shirt and noticed his eyelids were partially black and blue, as if he had put on a thick band of eyeliner. "Look in the mirror," I prompted.

"What the hell?" he intoned. Puzzled, we talked about it, but blew it off to his fitful night and overzealous eye rubbing.

Jim was anxious to get home. Concern etched his face; "I don't have it in me anymore. I feel tired and I'm wondering where my strength has gone." We talked about it and he agreed to see Dr. Primary Care when we got home.

As I had done through the years, I teased, "You're the old one."

He chuckled and said, "Do you always have to remind me of that?" Yet, even through the teasing and his comment, I sensed he was living inside a new and different kind of fatigue and it started to worry me.

After we got home, Jim put off his doctor's appointment. He said he was feeling better. Men! I wanted to clobber him!

A couple weeks later, the finishing touches were being put on the screened porch. I had just prepared lunch when Jim came in, leaned on the countertop and pulled up his shirt. He dropped his eyes. "Look at this." Bewildered, I stared in disbelief. His abdomen was severely bruised.

"Looks like you lost," I chortled, not believing my eyes. I sensed his nervous tone, and cut the jokes. "What happened? Does it hurt?" I was genuinely concerned.

He claimed he had seen the bruises in the mirror in the morning, but for whatever reason didn't want to show me then, possibly because he wasn't ready to share with me what he was going to reveal next. He took my hand. "Come here." He moved us toward the bedroom and laid on the bed.

"What in the world is going on?" I asked.

"Feel this." While slightly raising his trunk, he took my hand and placed it on his abdomen. "When did you discover this?" I asked.

He answered with a question, "What do you think it is?"

"My guess would be a hernia."

He paused long and hard as he expelled air from his puffed cheeks. "That's what I was thinking."

I was not sure that was all it was. A lot of minor issues had seemed to trouble him since we left Wisconsin. Bouts of diarrhea, tiredness, complaining his strength was dwindling, and now the bruises and possible hernia conjured worry. Jim had even called me into the bathroom one morning to look at his foamy pee. It seemed he always had a logical explanation to dismiss these issues.

Diarrhea was from something he ate. The tiredness was from working on the porch, the bruises from something he bumped into, the foamy pee because he waited so long and it hit the toilet hard. And on it went.

We made our way back to the kitchen. I didn't wait for Jim to do it. Immediately, I called Dr. Primary Care. The earliest he could get in was July 28th.

※

In the meantime, we had eye appointments and a wedding to get ready for.

Our insurance had changed, so we saw a new ophthalmologist. It was not his advanced age that concerned me—he seemed quick, sharp, and in charge—but the old equipment and surroundings of his office. However, his examination was extremely thorough. He almost seemed hesitant to deliver the news. "Mr. Malicki, I believe you have glaucoma. I'll need to do a few more tests."

"Glaucoma?" we said together. The tests were arranged for a few days later and the diagnosis was confirmed. The doctor prescribed Jim eye drops and an appointment was made for a month out.

Kate Moody, who I had watched grow into a beautiful young woman, was getting married. I knew the wedding would be elegant and we both needed something new to wear.

"I hate this crap," Jim said, while struggling through the racks of suits and then searching for matching accessories. He hated shopping for clothes and would only shop for a suit at Men's Warehouse. Why? He liked George Zimmer in the commercials.

The nuptials were classically beautiful, and the reception, designed to be a memorable experience for the guests as well as the newlyweds, boasted fine food and music. There would be no kitchen twirling and dancing that night. We set out to the dance floor, hell-bent on an evening of energetic dancing (as least I did), and the seductive, romantic magic that only a slow dance with Jim can bring. However, Jim tired easily when we took to the floor for something more upbeat. We said our goodbyes earlier than normal. Jim blamed the heat for his exhaustion. I didn't know then, but it was the first of the lasts. We would never dance again. Not even a twirl in the kitchen was to pass through our future, only in my dreams.

New bruises came and went, including raccoon-looking eyes, which we still thought was from rubbing during the night. When Jim came home from the mall and told me he couldn't do all nine rotations and have to rest because of upper abdominal pain, we thought it was the hernia. Every day the pain grew a speck, thereby diminishing his distance.

Even though I had already purchased the ticket for my flight, I told Jim I wouldn't go to Wisconsin to visit Mom, not until he saw the doctor and he said everything was okay.

℘

Medical Visit One, July 28th, 2006

Finally, Jim got to see his primary care doctor. My flight to Milwaukee was the next day, and I was anxious thinking I'd probably have to cancel, but when Jim advanced toward me from the doctor's examining area, he was beaming. "I'm okay." And that's exactly what he emphasized. "I'm okay. It's a ventral hernia. If it gets worse, I can see a surgeon, but for now everything's okay. You can go to Milwaukee in peace, I'm okay."

"Hmmm? And your walking? What about the bruises?"

Jim had never worried about his health, but he didn't abuse it either. Healthwise, unless the heart/stroke gene kicked him, he thought he'd be strong at least until his 80s. After all, when we discussed old age, which was rare, he'd tease that he would be taking care of me. "I'm the healthy one," he'd say. We'd both laugh and I'd say, "But you're the old one, time will tell." So, when "the healthy one" heard he had a hernia and nothing more serious, his major anxiety was relieved and he was thrilled; his euphoria at the news preempted any further questioning. He went from a head of chaos to one of calm with the hernia diagnosis. I didn't get it, and knew when I got back from Milwaukee, I'd have to encourage him to get back to the doctor.

Dumbfounded, I asked, "And what about your lack of energy?" I pushed hard.

"I didn't ask that question!"

"What?!"

"I'll be fine. At least it's not a tumor or something."

Unanswered questions left me hanging in disbelief.

My questioning annoyed him. "It will be okay," he repeated in a firm and direct voice. A bit bewildered by his attitude, I decided to let it go, for now at least.

Although it didn't at all feel right, I went to Milwaukee as planned. We agreed to talk twice a day; in the morning after Jim's walk, and in the evening before bed.

26
SEARCHING
AUGUST 2006–DECEMBER 2006

Disease can be messy, complicated and complex, and a variety of symptoms started to penetrate Jim's body. The recent presentation of a hernia, tiredness, bruises, foamy pee, wheezing, and walking problems hung heavy the whole time I was gone. Jim had been a bedrock of good health, yet the tendrils of an unknown intruder lurking in his body worried me.

I arrived on July 29th ready for mom-daughter activities and to have fun with family and friends, but I was uncomfortable. I should have trusted my instincts and stayed home! Every morning, like a tape recorder, I asked, "How did your walk go?" Jim would answer, "Pretty good, but I still can't get back to all my laps." He did not share with me that his laps were decreasing daily.

Finally, at the end of the first week I asked him to be truthful and tell me how many laps he was doing. "I can't make a lap without stopping to rest," he responded. The answer set my head spinning.

"What? Did I hear right? Call Dr. Primary Care today and get in as soon as possible after I get back," I demanded: This time I'd be going into the examining room with him.

I was exceptionally anxious and excited to see Jim when I arrived home on August 12th. I missed him and had become increasingly worried about his inability to walk without pain. Throngs of people were being herded through security, opposite the aisle where those who had disembarked were headed in the opposite direction. Through the pack, standing against the edge of a bathroom alcove, I noticed a bearded man waving me toward him. It took several hard stares before I realized it was Jim. As excited as I was to see him, I thought to myself, *Ohhh nooo, he's grown a beard. He knows I hate beards.*

I managed to steer my way toward him. He grinned heartily. "Like it?" he said as he rubbed his fingers through the red, gray and brown mess on his chin.

"Noooo! Not at all! You know I hate beards!"

"Admit it, you like it," he said as he leaned over for a kiss.

The hug and the kiss were exactly what I needed, but I couldn't help myself. I teased, "If you want a bigger, better kiss, you'll have to get rid of that."

As we started down the corridor, I gazed up at the direction signs for baggage claim. "This way," I directed, then noticed Jim was not next to me. He was several steps behind.

"You'll have to slow down; I can't keep up. I need a place to stop and rest." We found a bench and sat for several minutes. I was horrified and freakishly scared. It didn't seem the man sitting next to me could be Jim. It wasn't only the beard; it was that he had no stamina for walking. He had to stop. Between baggage claim and the car, we made two more rest stops.

Medical Visit Two, August 15th, 2006

The clinic note impression reads: "Mr. Malicki is a 62-year-old man, who presents today with exertional epigastric pain, dyspnea on exertion and diaphoresis." (In other words: Upper middle abdominal pain with labored breathing and sweating upon exertion).

Jim was a fanatic about being on time and arrived everywhere he went at least fifteen minutes prior to the specified time. Early onset old man style walking and additional rest added a minimum of fifteen minutes to arriving on time for an appointment. Consequently, we left the house so early that we usually ended up sitting in the lobby for a half hour or more before his appointed time! It drove me crazy! However, I didn't say anything, as he was anxious enough.

We approached the examining room together and took our seats. The doctor, a fill-in for his regular primary care physician, had obviously read his file and was up to speed regarding the hernia.

During the next few minutes she listened, examined, and concluded an EKG was necessary. Her flicker of uneasiness had not been lost on me. She took a breath, and with undisguised concern she pronounced, "I think it's possible you may be having a cardiac event. Immediately, when you leave here you need to go to the emergency room for evaluation. I'll call ahead." The urgency in her voice left no room for second guessing.

Totally taken aback, for support I leaned into the chair and watched as Jim stared at her wide-eyed. His shoulders drew back in frightened question. Palms up and out, he threw it out there. "Am I having a heart attack?"

She sensed our fear and responded quietly. "A thorough evaluation will be made in the emergency room." There was no time for any further discussion about his condition. We were headed to the hospital.

I was petrified. Jim's family history was chock full of heart attacks, strokes, and open-heart surgeries. His brother had heart surgery, his mother died two weeks post-heart surgery, and his dad suffered numerous strokes. Afraid Jim might follow in his family's footsteps, when he turned 50 I started to keep an aspirin beside the bed, one in my wallet, and one in the glovebox. I encouraged him to carry one as well. He started taking Lipitor when his cholesterol got too high.

Medical Visit Three, August 15th, 2006

Rattled, I sprinted to the car. Afraid, I couldn't get Jim to the emergency room fast enough, I prayed. *Is he having a heart attack? Is he on the doorstep to heart surgery? What, Lord? Please let him be okay.*

In the space of the few minutes it took to get the car, Jim's face and bearing had withered considerably. Between that and his pained gait as he walked from the lobby, his outward identity was that of a much older man. His shallow voice was toneless. "Well, I guess it's my turn."

Once again, I dropped Jim off, parked the car, and sprinted back to his side. "Well, let's get in there," I urged. He paused a few seconds. "Come on," I urged again.

"Oh, God, I hope I don't have to go through what my mother and brother went through. I'm dreading this." Jim told the receptionist why he was there.

A wheelchair was ready. "We've been waiting for you."

Quicker than quick, he was escorted to an examining room. They moved so fast he lost track of me. He hollered out, "Hon, are you there?"

"Yes, I'm right behind you."

Efficiency was on parade. Every individual that passed in and out of his room was tasked with their own set of questions and activities designed to ascertain if Jim was having a cardiac event. He was hooked up to a monitor, blood pressure, pulse, and temperature were taken, and blood was drawn to test his cardiac enzymes. When the tests came back the cardiologist ordered a stress test.

A nurse entered and explained the risks and benefits of stress testing. When she presented the authorization form for Jim to sign, I kind of felt like he was pretending this wasn't happening. Once again, he paused, and signed only after I urged him to do so. The nurse walked away with the paperwork, and he was swiftly whisked to the inner sanctum of the hospital.

Anxiety wouldn't let me sit still. My nerves drove me outside to get some fresh air and to call the kids. I called Sherry first. You know how kids put their hands to their ears, close their eyes and go *"la la la"* so that they don't hear something they think might be gross like their mom and dad had to have sex to have them. That's almost how Sherry reacts when she hears about illness of those she loves. If she doesn't hear about it, it doesn't exist, and if it doesn't exist, she won't have to worry about that individual. Her first reaction was that I was being "overdramatic and jumping to conclusions." "It will be fine," she said, which left me feeling a bit scolded. I was with her dad every day, and I was scared to death because I now suspected something much more serious than a hernia.

Doug expressed concern and asked that I call him as soon as I knew anything.

I drew in a deep breath, let it out slowly, and walked back in. I looked around the room as I waited for Jim. The space was devoid of anything friendly; the windowless walls, icy-cold air filling the space between those walls, sterile equipment, and voices and inanimate sounds on the other side of the door were displeasing. *"Come on."* I paced waiting in that small space. *He should be done by now.*

Finally, a sigh of relief. Jim was back in the room. "How did you do?"

He answered. His voice carrying a weary and fearful intensity. "I'm wiped out and scared."

"I know, I know, I love you." I nodded plausibly as if I really knew how he was feeling, which I didn't! He was stretched out laying still. I pulled my chair next to him. I would describe us as uncharacteristically quiet and tremulous while waiting for the results. I felt Jim's fingers tighten on mine when the doctor walked through the door.

Due to Jim's shortness of breath and upper epigastric discomfort, the stress test was limited. It suggested a small defect consistent with an inadequate blood supply to the heart muscle. Dr. Cardiologist recommended that Jim be admitted for medical therapy and cardiac catheterization. Frankly, I was relieved he'd be staying. With his family's history, I wanted him probed and prodded further so that nothing would be overlooked.

It was late when I got home. A new, daily ritual commenced that day. From then on, fervent mutterings and sometimes long and deep ramblings to God about Jim's health interrupted and ended my every day. I had always thanked God for our good health and good life, but my prayers took a turn that night. Clumsy and inarticulate, I dispatched God to help the doctors quickly find the answers to Jim's problems, and to sweep them away. I was growing more fearful by the day.

So, Lord, this has been some day, a very scary day. Lord, is this something more than a hernia problem? Is his heart in danger? He has so many different things going on with his body, I don't know how or if they tie in with a heart problem or hernia, but then again, I'm no doctor. What a long day it's been, Lord. Sitting in the hospital and waiting for procedures and answers is so draining, but thank you, Lord, for the doctor today who sent us to the ER and all the modern equipment to find out what's wrong with my Jim...

...Lord, please let the tests tomorrow reveal if there is a problem, and if so, that there is an easy fix and he'll be on his way. And, if there is a heart problem, what about the hernia? Does he have two problems? Please calm my fears! We need you and love you, Lord, I trust you will take good care of my Jim. Goodnight.

A good night it was not! In bed I tossed and turned, out of bed I paced and prayed. My heart was at the hospital. In the morning I rushed through my routine and arrived at the hospital early.

"Hey, honey, you're here early," Jim said with a smile. We kissed, and what a kiss it was. *Hmmm?* I thought. For all that was about to be going on, he seemed in a good mood. I think it was a show, as he tried to alleviate the anxiety in both of us. I accepted that. Certainly, on the outside he appeared less anxious than I was.

"I had a good night. If you're going to have a heart problem, the hospital is the place to be," he chortled languidly.

Surprise and delight! One of the kids from the Hood who was now a nurse, was assigned to Jim. It was such a comfort to both of us that he'd be there while the procedure was taking place, but when it was time to shave the hair from the site where the catheter was to be placed, it got a bit awkward. The Hood kid and Jim did their best to allay embarrassment for both. They bantered about a bit of humor that had nothing to do with what was taking place. It remained professional, but I believe they were both uncomfortable. When I called Doug prior to Jim's catheterization, he couldn't believe what I was telling him. "Oh my God, are you kidding me?" he laughed. He couldn't believe of all the nurses on staff, his good friend was the one chosen to play a part in Jim's procedure and who would have to, of all things, shave his dad.

A corner of his mouth twitched up as he signed off on the procedure. Without his glasses he squinted and looked at me straight on. "I love you, honey. I'm afraid the next time I see you it might be after heart surgery."

"I'll be here praying the whole time. Love you too, soooo much."

Once again, he was snatched away from me to the hospital's inner sanctum. Immediately unglued, all I could do was pray to make my plea to God.

Dear, Lord, please take care of my Jim. Let him be okay and that we get good news. I repeated this over and over again.

When the door opened it startled me. They were rolling Jim back to the room. Confused, I wondered what was going on. *Is the test done already, does he need surgery?*

EXAM NOTE:
Coronary arteries, Normal

EXAM NOTE CONCLUSION:
Valvular Heart Disease, Moderate Mitral Regurgitation, No Evidence of Atherosclerotic Coronary Artery Disease, Normal Left Ventricular Function.

That was it! No artery surgery! We left the hospital with instructions to make an appointment for an echocardiogram to take a closer look at his heart valves and to start Toprol, a high blood pressure medication.

During the drive home, Jim was unusually quiet. I pushed my thoughts to driving on the busy road when I heard him release a heavy breath. "I don't have clogged arteries. That makes me feel like I won the lottery."

Ready to make a turn, I almost forgot I was driving. I didn't voice it, but I was stunned. My head was asking, *You feel like you won the lottery? But what about mitral valve regurgitation, the hernia and all the other issues?!* Simply put, he was on his way home, just where he wanted to be.

We made the echo appointment for August 22nd.

Medical Visit Four, August 20th, 2006

It was about 5:00 on Sunday when we decided to relax in the screened room. We sat in our favorite chairs in a place where our yard and heaven came together. While the blue jays screeched their harsh trill, we watched the sun penetrate through the leaves. I was amused, and Jim completely annoyed, at "those damn squirrels" who cleverly jumped from nails purposely placed in a post to keep them out of the bird feeder. We had agreed not to talk hernias and hearts. Easily, it was the most beautiful hour we had spent in a long time.

Dinner was ready at 6:00. Afterward, we settled in to watch some TV. The beautiful evening did not at all prepare us for what was to happen next.

Jim got up to head to the bathroom. He pushed forward out of the recliner, took a few steps, and bam hit the hardwood floor. To say my heart fell down right there next to him is an understatement. Panicked, I thought it was his heart. "Oh my God, what's happened? Are you okay?" Splayed out on the floor, he tried pulling himself up. He finally settled in against the wall, where we both took a few seconds to gather our wits.

"I'm fine, I'm fine." He was harsh in his insistence. Due to everything that had been going on, he knew I was going to say, "I need to get you to the hospital," but he didn't want any part of hearing it.

I paused to calm myself down and to search for the right words. In a mild tone, I said, "You need to be checked out. Nobody loses it and crashes to the floor without a reason. What if it's your heart?"

He eyed me hard. "I'm fine, and will be fine! I'm not going to the hospital. End of discussion." I wouldn't let up. We argued; then I decided to call Sherry. I thought maybe he would listen to her and George.

Defiantly, Jim carried on in the background. "I'm fine! I'm not going to the hospital." Over his voice I recounted, with as much clarity as I could muster, what happened.

Both: "He needs to get to the hospital, now!" Murmuring something under his breath, he tried to edge away from me, but he did snatch the phone when I pushed it toward him.

"Here, listen to them. It only makes sense to check this out."

We barely said a word on our drive to the hospital. I could tell he was agitated and nervous about what would happen next. And, my thoughts repeated, *Dear God, what is happening now to my Jim? Did they miss something with his heart? Please, let him be okay, please, Lord!*

The recent catheterization triaged him to the top. With proficient swiftness, monitors were pressed into action, while a salvo of questions were uttered in quick succession.

"Are you experiencing any pain?"

"Only when I walk," Jim responded.

"Are you feeling any pressure or fullness in your chest or abdominal area?"

"Yes. In recent weeks I always have a full feeling."

"Where? Your stomach?" He was not in a good mood and nodded warily.

"Have you been dizzy or lightheaded?"

"No."

"What did you have to eat and drink in the last several hours?"

"We had salmon, asparagus, and a salad."

"When you fell, did you pass out?"

"I don't know. It happened so fast. I got up, and the next thing I knew I was on the floor."

We waited well over an hour for the results of a CTA of the thorax. "Apparently, you were not following instructions for using Toprol," the doctor commented. Toprol was the blood pressure drug Jim had started three or four days prior.

"Didn't anyone tell you that you shouldn't get up quickly, until you get used to the drug?"

"No," we responded together.

Well, now at least we knew we couldn't rely on the doctor or pharmacist to list every possible side effect. I looked at every single instruction sheet that came with medication from then on out.

‽

In the meantime, the grass needed mowing, a task I thankfully never had to do. Mr. "Grass Perfection" was too particular and loved every second he sat on the mower. Silly me, I suggested we hire someone until we figured out why he couldn't walk without all the pain. He breathed hard and seemed to be looking at the ceiling for an answer. "I can still do it," he said a bit sternly.

Journeying to reach the shed at the top of the hill, an acre or so in the back, was too much of a rough climb.

"All I have to do is get to the mower," he asserted. I watched as he drove his truck up hill to the shed. He made it and was able to get on the lawn tractor. I stayed alert, moving from window to window to see how he was doing. Adamant to prove he could handle it, he navigated around the yard bent on perfection, which he did accomplish with the grass, except he was not able to trim. For all his effort, the yard remained shabby around the edges. Unfortunately, that was another last. We hired a landscaper who did a good job.

Medical Visit Five, August 22nd, 2006

It was echocardiogram day. Jim's thrill over "winning the lottery" had spent itself out. He pursed his lips, as he tried to remain positive. Once again, I prayed, *Dear God, please let my Jim be okay.*

"From a cardiac standpoint, you are stable," the doctor reported. "You have mitral valve regurgitation. For now we will watch it. Come back in three months for another echo, and then we'll assess if surgery is needed."

Astonished it hadn't been addressed, I asked, "But what about his walking and abdominal pain?"

"I don't know," the cardiologist answered apologetically. I scratched my head in astonishment.

We were still at square one with regards to his walking and pain. We made another appointment with his primary care doctor. Whatever was happening, no one could figure it out, so there was no stopping it from getting worse.

Medical Visit Six, August 31st, 2006

We realized the doctor probably wouldn't have an answer, but we were there, in his lobby, hoping he'd come up with something. "Jim," the nurse called out. He rose slowly and took a few seconds to catch his breath. Finally erect, deliberately and methodically, he made his way back to the examining room.

"I wonder if this could be intestinal angina," the doctor thought out loud. He ordered a CTA of the abdomen to look at Jim's vascular supply. The doctor said if the CTA is normal and Jim continued to have abdominal pain, he'd suggest he see a surgeon for the hernia.

Medical Visit Seven, September 5th, 2006

An abdomen CT angiogram was performed for intestinal angina.

> **CLINIC NOTE:**
> Impression showed everything was "normal," except for an enlarged irregular prostate gland. "This may be due to prostatitis although prostate cancer cannot be excluded."

I was surprised when I read the clinic notes regarding the CTA. I don't ever remember the word "cancer" being used. I feel certain we would have looked into this further had we known that "cancer cannot be excluded." In retrospect, with everything else that occurred later, it was probably good we didn't hear that word.

We continued, with tireless determination, to search for a diagnosis. Even though he could barely walk from the lobby to the doctor's office, we couldn't get Jim a handicap designation because he didn't have a diagnosis, and I have to say that got my goat. It still does. I continuously had to remind myself not to judge every time I saw someone park in a handicap spot that walked or ran from their car without apparent difficulties. *Dear God, please don't let me judge. Who knows, they may have something that's not evident and need that handicap sticker. It's not mine to decide!*

Medical Visit Eight, September 13th, 2006
Another doctor, and still no answers.

> **CLINIC NOTE:**
> *"...since June he began experiencing cramping lower abdominal pain that was severe enough to take his breath away and was associated with a bloating sensation. When he would stop walking for a few minutes this would resolve. Since June this has progressed to the point that he is not able to walk at all without experiencing pain and bloating. He reports having two to three bowel movements a day which at times increases upwards to four to five movements a day..."*
>
> **IMPRESSION:**
> "Patient has diastasis recti which is a weakness in the linea alba between the two rectus muscles without any defect in the fascia, this is not a true hernia, and is a variant of

normal. His abdominal symptomatology sounds reminiscent of irritable bowel syndrome."

CONCLUSION:
A colonoscopy consultation was scheduled for September 26th.

༄

My dear, compassionate friend, Michelle, has a keen sense for recognizing when one is troubled. She knew we were struggling for a diagnosis and arranged for the ladies of the Hood to get together for lunch to better fill them in, cheer me up, and lend support, and that they did!

Holding back tears, I explained Jim's vague, non-specific symptoms. Layer upon layer they'd appear. There was no knowing when diarrhea, bruising, tiredness, raccoon eyes (we later learned was periorbital purpura), or foamy pee would come or leave, but it was the exercise induced pain, shortness of breath, and now wheezing that were my main concerns and always there. We lived in fear about what the highly regarded doctors could not figure out. My feeling at the time was that they looked at the logics of the symptoms, especially the abdominal pain on exertion, but not beyond that. "It's like we've hit a wall," I cried.

༄

Car guys might disagree with me, but there is an overabundance, in my estimation, of car shows in the fall in Middle Tennessee. Jim was intent on going to the show in the mall parking lot. The pain versus benefit, when measured against the pain, was not apparent to me, but I was not about to tangle with him and break his spirit. *Dear God, we are going to need your help. How in the world are we going to accomplish this*? I asked.

Jim could still drive. However, in order to get him as close to the door or event as possible, I started doing most of it. It was a long walk back to Jim from where I had parked and I rushed, so as not to keep him waiting. "Rush" was becoming my middle name.

Walk, stop, rest, walk, stop, rest. An unnatural walk, each step was sized up, measured and weighed before he moved. My heart ached for him. Incredibly, he made it to the center of the crowd. There would be no roaming, so there he stood. He cajoled with friends, talked cars and shrugged off questions about his health. A deep tenderness overtook my heart that day as I watched him. *Geez, I love that man,* I thought. Tears stoked my concern, and the measure of my feelings in that moment threw me off balance. I prayed right there in the center of the crowd. *Dear God, please help us to find out what is wrong with my Jim so he can get better.*

It didn't take long until he started to wither.

"My stomach is acting up again; I need to use the bathroom."

Dear Jesus, how do we manage this? I asked. He'd had a small bout of diarrhea in the morning, but he thought that was over with. *Oh, God, please let us make it to the bathroom on time.* The struggle was fierce. We barely made it to the inside of the Sears store on time, where I held my breath until he opened the door to the men's room.

Fortunately for us, the patio furniture on display near the bathroom became a respite. *Thank you, God.* Relief. We sat for about ten minutes which permitted Jim to rest and to feel confident his stomach was okay. It was to be another last. There were no more car shows or events of this type in Jim's future.

∽

Sunday Mass, then lunch was something we looked forward to. During this stretch of time it became a driving force to get us out of the house. I would drop Jim off at the handicap door and park the car. We arrived extremely early so we were guaranteed the last pew. Unfortunately, four days after a beautiful September Sunday, clumsy me caused it to become another last. The last time we went to church together.

Medical Visit Nine, September 26th, 2006

Jim met with an APRN at the Gastroenterology Clinic. It interests me that in reading the notes of that visit, it is recorded: The patient "denies abdominal pain," though the assessment was for abdominal pain, which was Jim's primary complaint.

> **GASTROENTEROLOGIST RECOMMENDATION:**
> *Perform a full colonoscopy for evaluation of abdominal pain.*

Risks and complications were discussed with the patient. An appointment was made.

ಬ

September 28th started as a good day. No doctor's appointments, no places to go, and nice weather.

"There's a branch down in the middle of the front yard," Jim complained. I didn't doubt him, but I had to have a look for myself. It laid under a black walnut tree, sticking out like a sore thumb. Given how hard it had become for Jim to take care of yard chores, the branch taunted his declining mood. "I'll deal with it later," he croaked, as he turned away.

We had lunch, and afterward I encouraged him to head to his garage and forget about the tree for a while, that we would deal with it later.

My intention was to spare him the frustration and pain and do it myself. After he drove to his garage, I scurried to the front yard. *Hmmmn, this is bigger than I thought,* I brooded. Yet confidence graced the air. Resolute, my plan was to drag it as far as I could, rest, and drag it some more.

I sized up the situation and weighed my dragging options. Because it branched out in a number of directions, I grabbed it at the point it broke off the tree and hoisted it over my shoulder as best I could. *Dang, this thing is hard to move,* I whined to myself. I tried another tack. Hardly a burly lumberman, I put it down, faced the end where it broke, and walked backwards uphill. Its branches grabbed and stuck to the grass at times, but I managed to make progress. *If I can get it to the driveway, maybe I can tie it to the hitch and drag it to the backyard tree line.*

I tugged and made a bit of progress. I told myself, *Only a few more pulls, Marie, and you're there. Work with me, you stupid branch; we can do this.* I yanked with all my might and it stuck throwing me off balance. I lost grip, and down I went, elbow-first on the blacktop.

"Oh my God, son of a bitch I screamed!"

Somewhat stunned, I struggled to get up and rushed into the house to take a look at it in the mirror. I told myself, *Maybe it's not as bad as it feels*, but the pain was simply terrible. Telling Jim would be dreadful, but I needed to get to the emergency room.

I put ice in a gallon baggie, held it to my elbow with a towel, and ran to the garage. Deep in thought, facing into the engine compartment of the Chevelle, Jim didn't hear me come in. "I think I broke my elbow," I panted.

The words swung his gaze my way. "What!? He wore a thoughtful expression as he stared in disbelief at the towel and ice bag. Like a kid who knows she did something she should not have undertaken herself, I told him I fell on the driveway and hit my elbow square on. "What were you doing? How did you do that?"

"I'll tell you on the way to the hospital."

Needless to say, when he saw the branch at the edge of the driveway, he put two and two together. Consternation edged his face. "Hon, I told you we'd figure out a way to get rid of it, together."

"I was trying to help," I said, as I put up my good hand to signal an end to the conversation. The dear heart said no more.

We arrived at the hospital. The parking lot was full. I cursed the fact Jim couldn't get a handicap placard. "Go home and I'll call you when I'm done. There is no sense in you walking this distance," I implored. He just wouldn't have it. Uphill all the way, Jim labored hard, stopping to rest every few steps. My fear was that we'd get through the door and Jim would need immediate medical care as well. I felt sick inside for his having to do this.

Questions were forthcoming as I was attended to. "Can you raise your arm, bend your elbow, palm up, palm down? How did this happen? Did anyone try to hurt you?" After a cursory exam I was taken down the hall for an X-ray.

A break was confirmed. My arm was put into a splint and an appointment made to see a doctor at the orthopedic clinic. My despair over taking on that stupid branch overrode the supreme confidence I had when I schemed to keep Jim from tackling the project. Ugh! Instead of making Jim's life easier, I made it harder for both of us. Between September 28th and November 28th, five more doctor's appointments were added to our agenda, solely for the care of my elbow.

∞

About a week later, Jim and I were scheduled for a fun visit with a friend and her mother, who were visiting from Knoxville. Our plan was to meet at Merridee's in Franklin. I salivated thinking about their chicken salad on oat bread, and I was excited to watch my friend pleasure in the scrumptiousness of Merridee's chocolate pie, her favorite. Before we left, however, I had the dilemma of my hair; more specifically, how to curl it.

I was able to blow dry my thin, scraggly hair into a semi-foundation for styling. Handling the blow dryer with the opposite hand was tricky, yet I did it. However, I was utterly helpless with the curling iron. I asked Jim to help me. Even though my request for help was exceedingly sweet, the simultaneous shake of his head and roll of his eyes said, "Are you kidding me? I think you've created a problem for yourself," he teased and smiled back at me. "I know nothing about your curling iron. I'd help you, but you know I can't do that," he smiled again.

"Sure, you can," I cajoled. "You have a whole garage full of tools! Let's practice with it before I heat it up."

So we did. After a short lesson in curling 101, with emphasis placed on where to touch and not to touch, I plugged it in on its lowest setting and prayed neither of us would get burned.

A few close calls later and we were done. My hair didn't look as good as usual, but better than blown dry scraggly. I praised him as best I could for taking on the challenge. He critiqued the final result and robustly whooped, "Now you know why I wasn't a hairdresser. When we get to Franklin, stay far to the side of me so we can make believe we don't know each other," he laughed.

"Ha ha, funny!"

It was a great time. Friendship and Merridee's lived up to our expectations. It was also another last. Jim was never again able to go to Merridee's, or hang around in downtown Franklin, as we occasionally liked to do.

꼬

It was October 3rd, and a busy day it was. A full cast was put on my arm. Then something I didn't expect to hear while I was there: "I'd advise you not to drive. Auto insurance companies may not pay if something happens while wearing the cast."

It was also the day that Nancy Moody and Lucy Battle met us in the parking lot of the orthopedic clinic and filled the back end of our Saturn with coolers full of food so I wouldn't have to cook while my elbow healed. The blessings we received that day from these families extended throughout Jim's illness and beyond. Exchanging full and empty coolers became the norm. From the orthopedic clinic we headed a few miles away for Jim's appointment.

Medical Visit Ten, October 3rd, 2006

DR. PRIMARY CARE CAME UP WITH THE FOLLOWING:

1. We will schedule pulmonary function testing.

2. We will set him up to see Dr. Sports Medicine.

3. I have left a message with Dr. Gastroenterology about doing an upper endoscopy as well as the colonoscopy.

4. If all of the above is negative, I suggest that we may make copies of all his workups and he might want to get a second opinion at either the Mayo Clinic, Cleveland Clinic, etc.

Medical Visit Eleven, October 4th, 2006

PULMONARY FUNCTION TESTING:
Negative

Medical Visit Twelve, October 10th, 2006

It was colonoscopy day. My plan was for Jim to drive us there, and for me to drive home. Based on my orthopedic doctor's comments, Jim wouldn't hear of it.

"Geez, it will only be to get you home when things are done. I can pull the sling up and have my hand on the steering wheel."

He nixed the idea—"Lately, fate hasn't been too kind. It would be our luck something would happen"—so, our dear friend, Mark, drove us to the clinic.

As he puked in the recovery room, Jim's weary words, which I couldn't understand, choked in his throat. The forceful expulsion made me think he was about to turn inside out. Distressed, we waited it out and Jim was finally cleared to leave.

However, we weren't far from the hospital when Jim knew he was going to be sick again. I watched from the back seat as he licked his lips, squirmed, and pulled at the seat belt. "Stop, Mark! I'm going to be sick!" Mark was probably close to being sick himself with Jim's repeated episodes of nausea. The poor guy, he got a whole lot more than he bargained for when he offered to drive that day.

PROCEDURE FINDINGS:
Normal, except for the finding of a small ulcer which was of no consequence at the time.

Medical Visit Thirteen, October 11th, 2006

Jim was examined by a sports medicine doctor.

DOCTOR ADVICE:
"Have surgery to take care of hernia."

Medical Visit Fourteen, October 26th, 2006

We visited with a general surgeon.

> **SURGEON RECOMMENDATION:**
> "I recommend he see a plastic surgeon for abdominal wall reconstruction. I think reconstructive techniques used by a plastic surgeon might be more helpful."

Medical Visit Fifteen, November 6th, 2006

We visited with a plastic surgeon who was upfront.

> **RECOMMENDATION:**
> *"Do a tummy tuck to tighten the weakened and separated muscles, but I can't guarantee that it will completely solve the hernia problem (diastasis recti)."*

The letter to the insurance company requesting approval for the surgery stated in part: *"The consensus is that he has a symptomatic diastasis recti. The surgeon has recommended that he see a plastic surgeon for surgical correction of this."*

I was skeptical. *Would this surgery solve his problems? The hernia maybe,* I answered myself. *But what about all the other things that would come and go, and that frankly, Jim brushed off? The bruising? The diarrhea? Why did his pee sometimes take on the appearance of beer foam? A strong skepticism and uneasiness sludged in the pit of my gut.*

∽

While waiting for the approval of the tummy tuck, we visited the ophthalmologist to check on Jim's glaucoma. We learned the pressure had gotten considerably worse and Jim was prescribed new drops. We then went to get our flu shots. My elbow continued to heal, and prior to Thanksgiving the cast came off. Whoopee!

☙

Ahhh, Thanksgiving, my favorite holiday. It's about getting warm and cuddly, rejoicing in family love, and best of all, no presents are required. So, I was incredibly excited when I heard my sister and husband would be coming to visit. Suggestions were bandied about; going to a movie won out.

We had stopped going to movies because the distance getting into the theater did not seem achievable. When it was suggested that we see a movie, my inner voice was telling me, *There's no way Jim can handle this.* But I guess Jim was more fearful of the lack of normalcy his days were taking on than he was of trying to walk into the theater.

Before I finished my thought, he wholeheartedly gave the thumbs up. "Let's go." I was surprised and not surprised.

John dropped us off at the entrance. Denise got the tickets. Jim struggled to make it inside. His steely will to resist the intense pain at the sucker punches thrown to his abdomen, made it possible for him to reach and benefit from a rest on the nearest bench. He crept up to the next bench, and finally into the theater. It was incredible to me the look of pain that spread across his face during this journey. He mumbled something and gave me a sideways glance.

"What is it?" I asked.

"*Phooff,*" he breathed out, "I didn't think I'd make it, but I did." His wan smile said it all.

I don't remember the movie. I only remember the entire time I was seated next to him, I thought how he'd have to go through this when the movie ended. Over and over I repeated, *Dear, God, please let him make it back to the car when this is over. Please relieve his pain.*

☙

A couple days later we were back to see the eye doctor. He was keeping close tabs on Jim's glaucoma, and expressing increasing concern over its progression. We scheduled another follow-up appointment for January. We arrived home and there was another concern.

"*Harrumph,*" Jim sounded.
"What's the matter, hon?" I inquired.
"Take a look at my ankles and feet."
"When did this start?"
"A few days ago, but not as bad as today."
I immediately phoned our primary care physician for an appointment.

Medical Visit Sixteen, December 2nd, 2006

Jim was still ambulatory, but it took increasing willpower to walk through the abdominal pain and ankle and feet swelling. As the days passed without a clear answer to what was going on, our imaginations were running wild as we scoured the Internet for an answer to Jim's symptoms. We wanted someone, akin to the fictional Dr. House, to compress all the data and give us a diagnosis. Whatever it was, we'd deal with it. By the sixteenth visit we knew there was a lot more going on than a hernia.

> **CLINIC NOTE IMPRESSION:**
> Sinus tachycardia of uncertain etiology
> Peripheral edema
> Exercise induced abdominal pain
>
> **PLAN:**
> Dr. Cardiology was paged for a repeat echocardiogram. A urinalysis, TSH, sed rate and chest X-ray to work up the peripheral edema were ordered. The chest X-ray did indicate a right pleural effusion and right middle lobe pneumonia or atelectasis.

Medical Visit Seventeen, December 5th, 2006

Anxiety drenched the air the morning of December 5th. We were headed to the hospital for an echocardiogram, but first we had to drop off the 24-hour urine storage container that we had on ice in a cooler.

That done, we crossed the hall and entered Dr. Cardiologist's office.

> **ECHOCARDIOGRAM ASSESSMENT:**
> "From a cardiac standpoint, I feel the patient has had deterioration in his cardiac status with progressive mitral regurgitation, tricuspid regurgitation and right ventricular dilation. I suspect that his pulmonary hypertension has also progressed. Based on these findings, I feel that he should be considered a surgical candidate for mitral valve repair or replacement and tricuspid repair. I have contacted Dr. Surgeon who will see the patient in the near future."

Once again, our sensibilities were derailed. Now we were headed back across the hall for some blood work.

We sat there waiting, both our heads full of questions that we were too stunned to ask when we were told he'd have to have surgery.

"Well, at least now we have a diagnosis I started out, whispering. "Hopefully, fixing your valves will take care of all this."

I didn't say more to Jim, but I spoke with weary disgust at myself for not asking the questions that were now coming to mind. I usually had a list of questions, but I certainly was not prepared for ones like, *Does this mean his pain will go away with repaired or replaced valves? Or is it the hernia causing the pain like Dr. Sports Medicine said, and this is a separate problem?*

Petrified concern etched Jim's face. "It's my heart we're talking about. God, I can't believe this is happening."

He asked the same questions I had run over in my head. "Is that why I have the pain when I walk? What about the hernia? Will that still cause pain or was it my heart all along?"

"I don't know," I said softly. My feelings and brain were going in many directions. I wondered if the inability to walk without abdominal pain and the diagnosis of a ventral hernia, later known as diastasis recti, were miscues that muddled a quicker heart valve diagnosis.

※

I believe it was the next day we received a call from Dr. Primary Care. Jim didn't want to talk to him on the phone, so I took the message. The urine test determined he had something called monoclonal gammopathy of undetermined significance, or MGUS. Dr. Primary Care was frank. "This has to do with the blood that's beyond my scope of knowledge. I am making a referral to a hematologist."

Based on the little information Dr. Primary Care provided, we did a quick search for monoclonal gammopathy. The surgery was our main concern and the abnormal protein being produced in Jim's body, could end up being fairly benign, or so we thought. *One thing at a time,* we told ourselves.

Medical Visit Eighteen, December 8th, 2006

Jim was referred to a highly respected thoracic surgeon. We were assured his credentials regarding valve surgery were first rate. As with any surgeon, time is of the essence during a visit. We were happy to hear Jim's surgery would be minimally invasive, which meant they would not have to separate Jim at the breastbone. The surgeon didn't dissect the hows and whys in overloaded medical speak, but he gave us enough to understand what Jim could expect, and did it in a respectful way. We felt good about him.

Medical Visit Nineteen, December 21st, 2006

We pulled into the parking lot and we were caught off balance. The sign on the outside indicated it was a cancer center. We checked the address; we were at the right place. Bewildered and a bit alarmed, we talked about it. We knew hematology had to do with all things blood, and people have different blood cancers, yet the word "cancer" on the building sent a chill through us.

Dr. Hematologist was thorough and kind and gentle in her ways. She noted Jim had something called "free light chains" in his urine and abnormal protein, and that palpebral ecchymoses (eye bruising) were classic signs of amyloidosis. Neither of us had ever heard of amyloidosis; I asked her to spell it.

"It is a rare disease. A tissue biopsy will be necessary to confirm the diagnosis. If it's okay, I'll get in touch with your surgeon to see if an endomyocardial biopsy can be performed during your heart valve surgery." She was thorough and used fairly plain language in her discourse explaining the disease. Although I was wrong, the words "plasma" and "bone marrow" channeled my brain to leukemia and cancer. What I finally did take away was that a protein build-up can occur in various tissues or organs that can make them malfunction. Basically, they gunk up areas where they land. She noted that although it wasn't a cancer, in some ways it was treated like cancer. Chemotherapy was typically used, and in some cases when the patient was healthy enough, a stem cell transplant would sometimes put the disease in remission.

The plan was for Jim to visit with the hematologist on January 18th to follow-up with the results of the biopsy. Blood tests and urine were also completed.

When we got into the car, I pulled out the piece of paper that read amyloidosis. *"Dear Lord, what are we in for?"*

I looked it up when we got home. After reading the first article I decided to not go any further. The article I clicked on made amyloidosis seem cold and vicious in its stats and prognosis. The words, as I recall them, noted that the median survival rate of amyloidosis with cardiac involvement was approximately one year. My throat quickened. I gasped for air while my eyes started to glaze over. I closed the computer. It was so still in the house, I wondered what Jim was doing. I was glad he didn't see this, and I decided I wouldn't tell him. I stared blankly at the wall for a long time. One day, one step at a time I finally convinced myself. Let's get through the surgery first and wait for the biopsy before taking this on and jumping to conclusions.

༄

Doug's refreshing holiday spirit was welcome, but it was hard to sustain the mood. Christmas didn't hold the power needed to lift the heavy, gray veil that had been hanging over us for the last six months. The progression of Jim's disease seemed to have reached a tipping point. Grisly pain shuddered through him as he walked to the bathroom or bedroom, and even with the addition of Lasix, his ankles and feet were swollen most of the time. His appetite and consequential bowel movements were distressing.

Peace on earth ignored our house. We spent Christmas night in the exhaustive, agitated darkness of our living room. The on again, off again abdominal pains were all-encompassing and merciless, and he had an urgency to use the bathroom often. Finally, it seemed to settle down a little. He whispered, "It's not so bad right now, I want to lay down."

He laid down; I covered him and went back to the recliner. Supine on the couch, it didn't last long. He croaked, "I can't lay here." I swiveled my head from its "trying to sleep" position on the recliner to where Jim was once again writhing. Anxious, I moved to the couch and gripped my left arm under his right to steady him as he fought to thwart off his bodily discomfort. In spite of my "helpful" efforts, comfort eluded him. While he strangled a pillow seeking relief, I rubbed his back. Countless times over the course of that dreadful night I prayed comfort be brought to him.

It was sometime in the wee hours of the morning when his aggrieved, aching abdomen seemed to settle down. I cast my eyes to his beleaguered face. He was pathetically worn out and appeared broken-down and dreadfully old. I didn't care; I was thankful he felt some relief and we had made it through without having to go to the hospital on Christmas. *Thank you, dear God. We made it!* Whether it was food poisoning, or whatever, we never did find out. Doug and I felt fine; we had Christmas Eve leftovers. Doug and I had thought it strange that on Christmas Day Jim opted for a frozen dinner; maybe it was that. Finally, by mid-morning on the 26th, he started to feel much better, although we were wiped out.

Medical Visit Twenty, December 29th, 2006

December 29th was the last medical visit before Jim's heart surgery, scheduled for Wednesday, January 3rd. Doug was with us, and we were grateful for his steadying influence. We kept telling ourselves the surgery was going to take care of his problems, and that the cardiac biopsy would be negative for amyloidosis. At least, that was our prayer.

The preoperative evaluation and history and physical report on December 29th commented as follows:

THE DIAGNOSES:
Mitral valve disorders
Tricuspid valve disorders, spec as
Nonrheumatic
Procedure(s):
Replacement, mitral valve
Replacement, tricuspid valve
With cardiopulmonary

When we met with the surgeon prior to Christmas, a woman who represented a pharmaceutical company was given time in the surgeon's office to speak to us. "Mr. Malicki, we're doing a drug trial with heart surgery patients on a promising drug for post-surgery blood pressure."

I wish I could remember the details, but I do not. I didn't at all feel comfortable with Jim's participation, but he insisted he wanted to do it. His preoperative evaluation and history and physical report also lists "Study Drug (for BP)" among his medications. I didn't think it was wise, so our disagreement created a bit of friction between us from the time we met with the surgeon until the day Jim signed the papers at the preoperative evaluation. I still wonder today if the drug had anything to do with the outcome. I'll never know.

The day was tiresome for all of us, especially Jim. He listened thoughtfully and persistently gnawed at his lower lip as he tried to digest the details and calm the commotion in his head. His efforts to appear upbeat were betrayed by the look on his face. The full realization that the risks associated with this surgery certainly had fully settled in.

We went home, I prepared supper, and the three of us settled in to watch the news while we had a drink to calm our nerves. The Manhattan he made for himself, and which he barely took a couple sips from, would be another last.

PART FIVE
TWELVE WEEKS

*Hard times will always
reveal true friends.*

~Anonymous

27
A HEART LIKE WOOD

January 2007 arrived—there was background buzz in the world that ordinarily I'd have been interested in. With all the noise in my head regarding Jim, however, I barely acknowledged the news of the day. Nancy Pelosi became the first woman Speaker of the House in U.S. history, the Apple iPhone was unveiled, and J.K. Rowling completed the seventh Harry Potter novel. What did any of it matter? Jim was sick.

☙

Surgery is always a risky event, but for Jim, having this kind of surgery was like an invitation to his own hanging. Yet, there were moments when he tried to make light of it. On a cellular level, he was a car guy, and he once chuckled, "Like an old car, my valves need to be repaired." As for myself, I tried to rest comfortable in prayer, knowing God was listening and our prayers would be answered. In fact, I felt sure of it.

"Surgery will be fine, the valves will be fixed, there will be no amyloid; nothing to worry about." I didn't know our lives were about to reset. On the cusp of being sucked into a vortex, as a couple, we'd never be able to escape.

We lived 45 miles from the hospital. Jim, who seemed to have an anxiety disorder about being on time, insisted we stay at the Holiday Inn the night before surgery. The kids were with us. To use up a little time after we arrived and get our minds off things, it was suggested we go down to the lounge for a snack. Jim sniggered, "I'm buying," as if we all didn't know that already.

My most repeated phrase was heard again. "Are you sure you can make it?" I felt sure this would be the death of him before surgery, but once again he was insistent for a bit of normalcy. He made it. We had some snacks, except for Jim, whose diet was water. Small talk was all we could muster.

When we got back to the room, we turned to the task of completing Jim's anti-infection wash, which we would also have to do in the morning.

He wasn't a jammies guy, but we bought him new pajamas, and washed them to keep the sheets from touching his skin. He took his shower; I applied the cleanser and dried him, following the guidelines for each cloth.

We sat on the edge of the bed ready to say good night. We held hands and softly prayed the Our Father. So as not to disturb each other's sleep, we got a room with two beds. Feeling tomorrow's looming presence and our need for sleep, Jim turned toward me and slid his arm around my waist. A simplistic, loving kiss passed between our lips. "I love you," we repeated to each other.

I could tell he was drifting toward sleep, but it didn't take long before he was fully awake. The angst and silence weighed in on me. I wanted to go to Jim's bed and hold him, or be held. I whispered, "I can't sleep; can I join you?"

"Please," he responded.

I snuggled into him. The chaste smell of his pajamas was at my nose, and I remember thinking how strange it was to hold Jim while he was wearing pajamas. I held my arm around him until the alarm announced it was time to get up, an alarm we didn't need. The foreboding amazement that we were only a couple hours from Jim's surgery overwhelmed me. *Is this real?* I asked myself.

The second anti-infection wash was completed; we dressed and hurried off to the hospital. Doug was driving. The dead-dark winter morning played tricks on the eyes. A one-way street turned us around and we were headed in the wrong direction. We all sensed something was wrong. One look at the compass told us we had to find the one-way street headed the other way. Jim was nervous and almost hysterical. "Doug, what are you doing?" He couldn't resist saying, "This is exactly why, when you have to be somewhere, you leave some extra time." We arrived before 5:30.

Jim's name was called. He provided the required information, then like a gaggle, we all followed a lady out the door. Jim and I headed up the elevator to the surgery center; the kids were guided to the lobby where I would join them later for the wait.

An aide, who seemed a bit flush and hurried, took the lead to the surgery prep area. I couldn't believe there were no wheelchairs available, which meant Jim would have to walk. He struggled mightily to keep up with the aide and no matter what I said to him he moved with purpose at his own pace, that of a thirty-year-old with a long-legged gait. *Idiot*, I said to myself. *Jim will be dead before surgery.*

I went to Jim's side. I didn't care what time the surgery was scheduled for, or if they were behind schedule. I said, "Let's rest for a few seconds."

"We don't have time," Jim responded, but we stopped. Jim's breathing was difficult and he leaned on me as he grappled with the pain. The long-legged guy finally realized we were not immediately behind him and came back to figure out why we weren't on his heels.

Duh, I thought, but I said in the nicest voice I could muster, "I told you he couldn't keep up."

I was once again directed to a waiting room, where I sat alone while Jim was prepped for surgery. The distress of getting Jim this far, and what he was facing, gave me that "curdled milk swirling in the gut" feeling. I found the nearest bathroom and hurried in. Dreadful diarrhea! I rushed back and forth to the bathroom. It didn't seem to take too long until they called me back to see Jim one final time before he was wheeled to the operating room. I saw him lying on the gurney. *Plop*, my heart squished into the mess at the bottom of my curdled stomach. I had a few loving, encouraging things I wanted to say, but my stomach would not allow it. My kiss was a quick peck on the cheek. I sprinted double-time back to the bathroom calling out, "I love you, honey." Another two seconds and I would not have made it on time!

Finally, my stomach had settled enough that I could get away from the bathroom. I joined the kids in the main lobby of the hospital. There was a desk in the corner of the floor where we were told the surgeon would meet us with

Jim's post-surgery results. In the meantime, we could follow Jim's status on the surgical patient status screen and make small talk while we waited. It's amazing how it mesmerized us: pre-op, surgery, then recovery.

Soon, it was our turn to head to the corner. The surgeon's summary: "The surgery was successful. The valves did not need to be replaced; they were repaired." Off-handedly, as if preoccupied with his thoughts, Dr. Surgeon commented that he had never seen a heart like Jim's. "Its texture seems woody. In all the surgeries I've done, I don't recall seeing a heart like this. You can see him in about an hour when he is taken from recovery to CVICU. In the meantime, he's doing well. Go get yourselves some lunch."

We thanked him and went for pizza. "Wood*y*" stuck in my head. I didn't feel completely relieved. That he could repair the valves was great, but "woody?" *Woody? What is that all about I thought. Is there another hurdle ahead of us*?

We quickly ate and dashed back to the hospital. We pushed on the double doors to CVICU. What the heck? They wouldn't open. More than anxious, I knocked until someone exited and we walked through. By this time my heart was beating like a jackhammer, and my stomach, again, was tenuous at best.

The nurse asked, "What took you so long?" We looked at each other and wondered what she meant, as it was a bit under an hour we had been gone, and besides that we were locked out!

"He's in there and doing well," she said, pointing. I stepped in and immediately, before anything else, noticed his left arm. *What the heck*, I thought. *Why is his arm jumping like that*? The involuntary and uncontrollable movement initially made me think he was cold and shivering, but it was only his left arm and he was uncommunicative.

I didn't expect him to speak with all the tubes connected to all the post-operative equipment used after heart surgery, but what I did expect was some eye movement and response to my hand squeezing. "Hon," I repeated over and over.

"Dad," the kids repeated, but there was no response. Zip, nada, none! To me, he seemed comatose.

My panic escalated with each question. "Why is his arm doing that? How come he doesn't seem to realize we are here? What's going on? Is this right? I was under the impression he'd be at least a little responsive."

The nurse's swift response to Jim's arm movement and general condition brought in a call for help. She rapidly perused the monitors, checked the connections to all the post-surgery wires and tubes, then hunched over and put her face in his: "Jim, Jim, squeeze my hand!" There was no response. She pinched his feet. There was no response. Others arrived. We stepped wide to give them the space needed to work. Although well-trained and excellent medical professionals, I watched as the CVICU staff were visibly perplexed. Someone commented, "Maybe it's a stroke, or a seizure."

Dr. Surgeon had been contacted and entered Jim's room. I was struck by the intensity as he signaled one of the staff to fill him in. Although Jim was pinched, poked, and flashlights waved across his eyes, Dr. Surgeon was unable to elicit a response. Concern was etched across his face. "Let's get an EEG and CT head done."

Fear drove me to prayer. My new watchwords: *Please take care of Jim* and *I'm afraid* pummeled from the depth of my heart as I witnessed the whirlwind of activity at Jim's bedside. The realization there was no conclusive analysis that could provide an answer seemed surreal. *Oh my, dear Jesus, what is happening to my Jim? I'm sooo afraid. Please, please let this pass from him and make him well.*

The people who typically work in the shadows swept into Jim's room. A din of voices, another flurry of activity. This time it was to remove Jim from CVICU life-sustaining support to manual and portable devices for transportation to the lower level. They were preoccupied, but their work was sober and respectful.

I told everyone I was going with. Before they rolled him out, I took his hand and bent to his ear. I didn't know if he could hear, but told him, "I love you. I will be right here with you." Responsible for their respective pieces of equipment, the mobile staff monitored Jim as he was rolled down the hall. Someone hollered, "Run down there and get that elevator ready." When we arrived, there was no waiting. Picture a freight elevator; that's what it looked like. It accommodated the hospital bed and everyone else who packed in there. Except for the hollow sound as the elevator moved down the shaft, it was a quiet ride. My fear gauge was approaching critical.

I went beyond weeping. I paced the hall and punched the air with both fists. *Damn, damn, damn, son-of-a bitch!* I sobbed uncontrollably and prayed and begged God over and over: *Dear God, if Jim is going to die today, please don't let him die in that room on a cold, hard table. If it's his time, please, don't let him be afraid. Don't let him be afraid to die.*

Jim did not die in that room. *Thank you, Lord.*

Dr. Surgeon stayed with the CVICU crew to the latest hours of the day. I had admired him for his intellectual scope, but my respect for him heightened to a new level as he genuinely worked so hard on Jim's behalf.

However, before he left, he delivered news that was measured and difficult for him to say. "I'm sorry, I believe there's a possibility Mr. Malicki may not survive. We'll monitor for any changes and continue testing to determine what's happened."

Dread and fear burdened my thinking. *What do I do now? What do I specifically need to do now for Jim, his comfort? Is this real? Do I have to decide where his body goes if he dies? The kids and I need to talk. Oh my God! This can't be happening. Is this me? Is this my Jim's life I'm considering here?*

Harken back to Catholic grade school teachings: I don't know if I understand the church's teachings regarding the Last Rites, but I couldn't take a chance with Jim's soul, and it's what he would have wanted. Maybe the hospital could get a priest for me. I left Jim's side. The nurse was gentle and told me she would get in touch with a hospital chaplain regarding my request.

Doug decided he needed to get some air and make sense of his own emotions. It was either late at night or early in the morning. I looked out. The normally busy sidewalks were empty except for Doug and the cellular signal between New York and Tennessee that brought comforting words from his high school friend, Subir.

It was several hours before the priest arrived: "In the name of the Father, and of the Son, and of the Holy Spirit …"

I thought the deathbed ritual seemed profoundly unearthly, which I guess it was. The kids and I tottered in disbelief as we watched the priest step back out to the hall after Jim's anointing. I thought, absolutely, Jim's guardian angel must be here somewhere. I looked around but couldn't find him.

We were in a sad, sad stupor—talking about a funeral.

Somewhere along the way it became Thursday, the fourth. There had been no improvement, but he held his own. I decided to take a small break.

I headed to the lobby and there they were: the Hood. It was incredible to see so many of them there all at once. They had dropped everything to come and fill us with their love and support. Michelle was the first to come forward and hug me. The hug line did not break until every single one of them approached and wished us well. My heart was breaking and they were there to help hold it fast. To this day I tear up when I think about the love in the room that day. What had started as a neighborhood of people coming together from differing parts of the country to work at Saturn turned into an assemblage of friends bonded as Tennessee family.

"You need something to eat. Come on sit down," someone urged. I hadn't noticed when I walked into the room, but what bore resemblance to a church potluck was set up on the counter and side of the room. What they put together was incredible.

It was then I heard Sherry talking to George, still in Illinois. "Mom and Doug have all their peeps here. I have no peeps." George was on his way.

28
UNINTENDED CONSEQUENCES

Wednesday blurred into Thursday, then Friday. We learned that the cardiac tissue biopsy was positive for amyloidosis. Once again, my heart dropped and my equilibrium shifted off balance. *Oh my dear, God, no.* "Woody" once again came to mind. I felt so uncertain about our fate.

On Friday a tour-de-force of physicians popped in and out of Jim's room, yet they had not come up with a diagnosis. However, one did order another MRI. Later that day, a neurosurgeon we had not met called us to a conference room in neuro-intensive care. He had reviewed the results of the MRI and continuous EER monitoring.

I was terrified about what we would learn next. *Dear, Lord, please, the layers of bad news need to stop*!

Dr. Neurosurgeon spoke with a cultivated, practiced voice when he delivered the news. Generally, he was a nice man, though the preponderance of his words made me feel as if he physically struck me and I was ready to take a dive. Although he was the messenger and an okay guy, my backlash energy wanted to reach across the room and break his kneecaps. To me the news was that fierce.

"Mr. Malicki has suffered a cerebrovascular accident, a profound right brain stroke, a side effect of surgery."

At the news, our collective breaths sucked the air right out of the room. My head went into a spin while my heart pitted in disbelief. I had witnessed my father-in-law's strokes. It was as if his brain untethered itself from parts of his body. Paralysis and dysphagia that required a feeding tube immediately came to mind. How would my honey be able to recover from valve surgery, amyloidosis and now a "profound" stroke, an "accident" and "side effect of surgery," all the unintended and never imagined consequences of surgery?

Dr. Neurosurgeon talked on. "Because the stroke is profound, recovery, if there is to be any (*If there is to be any? I thought. Are you f'n kidding me!?*), will be long and hard. But don't lose hope. The brain is resilient. Every stroke is different."

I couldn't take in any more. The uneasy creep of nausea that would stay with me for months and months started to build. My head and heart were perfectly broken.

29
DEATH BACKS AWAY

Death backed away. For several days Jim remained in a Limbo of sorts, and there were times I felt I was at his wake. I couldn't help but mourn what happened to his body. Hypnotized by the rhythms of the monitors and the regimen of the hospital staff, I stayed vigilant in my watch.

On January 8th, he had an upper endoscopy and a nasoenteric feeding tube was placed.

On January 9th, he was weaned from sedation, but remained intubated and it was time for movement and a neuro chair. Designed for postural control and correct body positioning, it arrived later that day.

His body was a weight that needed the assist of a patient lift. These devastating words to God crossed my mind. *Oh, God, will he ever walk again? Please, please let him recover from all this. I know you're the only one who can perform miracles. I pray you consider Jim worthy of a miracle.*

I felt my prayer was sort of answered. A new liveliness switched on. Jim tried to understand his surroundings and his own body, and I was presented with a gift. As he caught sight of me, an amiable smile lit new life into the room. He started "speaking" with right hand motion and gestures. He was able to keep his eyes open for stretches of time, but his vision was still unable to track past midline to the left.

Therapists, both physical and occupational, made their initial visits. Cognitive and visual perceptual deficits affecting functional performance and all activities of daily living (ADLs) were assessed. Determination: "Patient currently will require max for all bed mobility, functional transfers and ADLs."

It was now January 11th. Cher, George, and Doug were still with us. The doctors decided it was time to take Jim off the ventilator. "He's coming around nicely, better than expected. It's time he was extubated."

The doctors assured me he could be re-intubated if necessary, and the consensus was he would do fine. However, Jim's living will referred to life-sustaining treatments. He did not want any prolonged use of machines or medications if the burdens of treatment outweighed the expected benefits. Due to this, I had a decision to make. Should he be re-intubated if the doctors were wrong and he was unable to breathe on his own? I felt sure he had started to make progress and decided to re-intubate if necessary. The decision did not sit well with one of the family, who discerned that I was going against Jim's wishes. I fully understood, but my decision was made. Words were said, tears were shed, and one of us had to take a walk.

Extubation was seamless, but his mouth, throat, and tongue were dry and he had a forehead that, to him, seemed to be on fire. Doug and George held an all-night vigil. By morning, a batch of used, moistened sponges on a stick overflowed the trash, and the guys were worn out placing cold washcloths on his forehead. I was told his right arm was ever diligent as he signaled demands for a cold cloth to be placed on his forehead, only to want it off a minute later, and 30 seconds later back on. There was no fever. Finally, tired George, in a propulsion of kindly words, conveyed to Jim, enough is enough. There would be no more cold wash cloths on his forehead, and that ended it!

It was at this point that sore and barely audible words were spoken that were hard to decipher. We learned his swallowing was delayed. Consequently, speech therapy was initiated. When they arrived, he was sitting on the edge of the bed with assistance, another accomplishment since being extubated.

30
MAKING HEADWAY

Strong and supportive is how I would describe our family, especially during those first twelve days of January. The emotional creatures we are, we shared fears, prayers, hugs, hand-holding, and quiet moments required to refocus and shore each other up. However, separation was inevitable. Jim was making headway, and the kids had to get back to work. I knew we'd all remain strong and supportive and be there for each other, but it was to be support at a distance, a separation like none our family had faced before. The "we had a great time" and "looking forward to next spring, or Christmas" was notably absent. "We'll try to make it back soon" took on a whole new meaning.

While Cher squirmed as she tried to hide her sadness and vulnerability, my dear son-in-law, George, took charge of the moment. His eloquent expressions of love and caring brought us all through the "see you later, goodbye" moments intact. His exact words to Jim have been lost with time, but the force of love and encouragement displayed in an uplifting tone and the squeeze of Jim's hand was enormous. The smile and thumbs up Jim projected as we departed his room that evening was encouragement for us all. Misty-eyed we returned home for a late supper and a good night's rest.

Well, I didn't get a good night's rest, and wouldn't you know it, when Sherry and George left, there were major snow and ice storm warnings throughout the Midwest. *Dear, Jesus, please get them home safely.* When I got the call that they were safe and sound in their home, I uttered out loud, *Thank you, dear Jesus.*

Later in the day, Jim was transferred out of CVICU to the "heart" floor. By this time, Jim's speaking consisted of a few sputtered, quiet spoken words. If you leaned in with earnest focus, his words were distinguishable and made sense.

My sister, Denise, arrived on January 14th. Before Doug picked her up at the airport, we stopped at the hospital. Although Jim seemed hungover from his sleeping pill, he smiled. I tried to greet each day with hope, yet I donned a suit of armor before I entered the hospital to shield myself from the unpredictability of what I might hear or see. Doug helped to clean Jim up, and removed 12 days of beard growth from his face. When he was done, his face appeared markedly thinner. Jim looked like his dad.

His spunk returned. He hated the bedpan and worked with what strength he had to throw it off the bed. He was edgy and rapidly became unmanageable as he tried to get up to go to the bathroom. Barely audible, but clearly frustrated he stated: "Doug, Doug, feet" as he pointed to have Doug stand him up. A formidable commotion developed between the three of us as Doug and I tried to calm him. I needed to call for help!

A thoughtful and helpful nurse responded. She asked us to wait and came back with something called a "Steady Eddie" and a young man to help her. Jim was placed on the seat of the mobile device. It had a front bar and handle bars. He was rolled to the bathroom and positioned over the toilet. His demeanor was mean as he struggled for dignity while using the bathroom. Empathetic as she was, the nurse stayed close, but faced out the doorway to give Jim privacy while on the Steady Eddie.

The next time he pushed harder for bathroom privileges. I figured out he despised the Steady Eddie almost as much as the bedpan. He wanted to sit on the toilet with no device and the door closed. Jim needed assistance so that he would not fall over while sitting on the edge of the bed or a chair without arms. He needed to be tucked in or held. I agreed to stay with Jim while he used the bathroom. The whole time we were in there he wrestled the Steady Eddie and would not listen to reason. He used the strength on his right side to push his body out and under the front bar. Even though I did everything I could to keep him on the seat, alarmingly he slid and ended up half-stuck between the bar and the floor. Frightened and angry with him, I screamed "help" several times. Two individuals ran in and wrestled him back into the chair. The whole incident was followed by what I describe as the first of my "nursing home" speeches. I despised doing it and didn't want to scare him, but I was panicked and afraid. He didn't fully comprehend that if he hurt himself and didn't cooperate, they may not accept him for in-house therapy. Too often I had to iterate that due to stroke difficulties, there was no way I could take care of him on my own, not in his current state.

Doug left to pick up Denise. It wasn't long until my beautiful sister arrived. I can't measure in words the amount of support she gave me.

◈

Monday, January 15th, 2007, was my first full day journal entry. I have included different entries throughout the next chapters.

I got up that day at 4:45 to see Doug off. Before he left, I was already looking forward to him coming back on the 26th. My dear friend, Beth, arrived to pick him up and take him to the airport. What a huge blessing that was. I then received separate early morning calls from Sherry and George. In quiet moments, the kids were constantly on my mind. I knew having their dad so sick was on their minds, and I prayed his condition didn't affect their days.

More importantly, on that day, Jim was assessed by a representative of the in-house rehab hospital I was hopeful he would be transferred to. The plan was to take the morning's therapy evaluation, talk to Jim's nurse, and to evaluate his total medical condition to ascertain if Blue Cross Blue Shield would approve his transfer. I thought that had been taken care of, and we would wait for the physical transfer. So suddenly, I was once again scared, thinking, *What next and what if they don't give him a chance?* A note I made to myself. *"I have to build an alliance for Jim's care. In his own way he is working so hard to be 'normal.'"*

A second evaluator visited later in the day. We talked a great deal. Although it was a bit hard to hear Jim's answers, I listened and he was able to answer them all. A sampling:

Q. "What year is it?"

A. "2007."

Q. "What is the date of your birth?"

A. *"April 14th, 1944."*

Q. "What city is this hospital in?"

A. *He named the city.*

Unnerved, I gulped hard when Jim was asked what city the hospital was in. I thought he might say, "Rota, Spain." Every day I drilled Jim about the date, his birthday, what hospital he was in, the city, and so forth, to prepare him for his daily "debriefing." That particular day he asked me, "How did we get to Spain?" Now I was confused! "Spain?" He glanced at the rooftops out the window and was adamant he was at the Navy base in Rota. I wore myself out trying to convince him otherwise, but when the evaluator asked, he answered correctly. Astounded, I wondered if he had been playing with me, but immediately dismissed that. Unfortunately, the next day, and until he was moved to the rehab hospital, we had to go through the whole Rota routine again. After a couple days of this, I came to believe it was the sleeping pill hangover that caused morning confusion. Afternoon evaluations were so much better.

We finally got to the last question:

Q. "What is our president's name?"

A. *"Asshole." His answer came through clear and without hesitation.*

I laughed out loud. It was the funniest moment in weeks. To say he didn't like George Bush is an understatement; it was an impolite truth he might not have muttered otherwise, as he never talked politics with outsiders. The evaluator, staid and with no sense of humor, gave him an astonished look; it was the second-best laugh I had had in weeks. When he left, I thanked him profusely and prayed Jim's tongue and my laugh didn't dig us into a hole.

I was in the bank parking lot when my phone rang. A nurse was on the other end and told me Jim was suffering from malnutrition. "He requires long-term support for feeding. He needs a PEG tube, and we need your permission to do this." I was taken aback. Malnutrition? After a somewhat lengthy discourse, I granted permission for the procedure.

Before Denise and I arrived at the hospital, the tube had been placed and his last drainage tube removed as well.

Mark and Michelle brought us a wonderful basket of food. It was sooo good. It was not the first nor the last time they brought food. Everyone in the Hood, and the Moodys and the Battles made sure I had homemade food every single day, or something from Merridee's! When one cooler was emptied, a full one was there to take its place. These exceptional, loving people accompanied us on our journey, provided food, rides back and forth to the hospital every single day, and love, encouragement, and sustenance each step of the way!

~

On the morning of the eighteenth, Jim was snoring away when physical therapy arrived. "Hon, you have to wake up," I said as I gently placed my hands on him to shake him out of his sleep stupor. He was not happy to wake up! Ornery and agitated, he refused therapy and wanted nothing to do with any of us. The nurse said he was that way most of the night. I remember thinking, *I wish they wouldn't give him so much sleeping medication because then he doesn't do well when physical therapy comes in.* The foul air continued with anyone he came in contact with, but mostly me. I knew this wasn't the "real" Jim, so I gave him slack, but it was nerve fraying. When I'd had enough, I delivered a withering critique that I thought I might regret. I spewed that to love and cherish in sickness and health didn't mean I had to listen to what he was dishing out to me and everyone else. I told him I was hurting, the kids were hurting, and so was everyone else that loved him, and he needed to give us a break. *Phfoof!* I did get through and rattled his cage a bit. The air drained from him, and I felt guilty, but only a little. As the day went on, his cloudy mood seemed to dissipate. Maybe it was the back rubs!

Denise and I spent many hours rubbing Jim's back that afternoon and evening. It seemed to provide him great relief and relaxed his tension, but was physically exhausting for both of us. His insistence on taking off his sweat pants, only to put them back on again immediately, didn't help either. Over and over again I did this, until frustrated and ready to collapse from the weight of the day, I told him, "Sorry, I can't do this anymore today."

Before I went home, I got the word that if he stayed healthy, he'd go to the rehab hospital early the next week. I told him I loved him and we kissed. As I was making my exit, he said, "Love you. Sorry to make you sad."

"Love you too," I repeated over my shoulder while heading toward Denise, who was waiting in the hall.

On January 20th, Mark and Michelle stayed with me all day. Such beautiful people. Jim was so restless trying to get out of the Steady Eddie. Mark helped as best he could. We both realized if Jim got hurt he wouldn't be able to go to rehab, and we were all determined to get him there.

It seemed it was a day of talking, then preaching, then pleading, all in order to keep him settled and his mood up. A deluge of emotion was spent that day, then this.

31
SPIRITUAL PLANE

In my journal that night, I noted it as "Jim's Story." Even if I hadn't, I think I would remember it as if he told it to me yesterday. Here goes:

It was late evening when Jim's demeanor took on an urgency that didn't involve the bathroom. I had to lean in close to hear what he was trying to tell me as he sobbed and wiped his eyes with a paper towel. He was about to burst. With the tears still welling in his eyes, he indicated he wanted my hand. I took his hand, he settled down and spoke. "Never be afraid to die. Tell the kids never to be afraid to die. It's okay to die."

It was in that emotional and touching moment I realized the fear of dying held no power over him. He went on to tell me, almost verbatim, what happened that night they took him down for the scan. He told me about the commotion in his room, and how it comforted him to hear the words I whispered to him, and for holding his hand as we journeyed down to the exam room.

I was aghast, as I thought everyone believed he was comatose at the time, or maybe I just thought that. He then went on to tell me, "It was so cold in there. I couldn't wait to leave."

Still clenching my hand, he told me something that startled me. He articulated that for some time, he watched from above as they readied him for the test and put him in the machine. Fearful that they were going to lose him, their pleading words, over and over were, "Jim, stay with us. Jim, stay with us." As they were pleading with him to stay, he said he found himself entering the most magnificent light. "It was powerful and I wanted to go to the light. It was peace and beauty and love, nothing like I've seen before. There were people all around. I could see my guardian angel. He was on the side. Then I saw your Grandma Jablonski in the front. Your grandma told me, 'Jim, it's not your time. Go be with those you love. When it's your time, we'll all be here waiting for you.'"

On many levels I think you can imagine my amazement. For Jim to transcend and catch a glimpse of another realm was something that movies are made of. Jim put together sentences, not just words, and never lost his train of thought or deep soulful emotion as he told me this most astonishing story. These were Jim's first full sentences since the stroke.

Like everyone else, I had heard stories, seen movies, and read books about this type of phenomenon, but hearing it from Jim took my breath away. For a long time, we continued to hold hands. I sobbed in astonishment and could not leave his side. *Thank you, dear God, that he was able to share this and that he did not die in that cold room. Thank you, dear God, that he's in your hands and will not be afraid to die. Thank you!*

Over the course of time, I have dwelled on his story for hours. Maybe our minds do play tricks on us when we're in that twilight of departing, and some might call it a drug induced dream, but I choose to embrace his words as a definitive answer to the prayers spoken to God in the hallway while I waited for Jim to leave the exam room.

Jim certainly did not want to die, but when the time would come he would not be afraid. In an attempt to live life, he continued his struggle every day to overcome his disabilities.

32
HARD ROAD

Time thrummed to the beat of a different drummer at the rehab hospital. Considerably faster, and the rhythm repeated itself the 65 days Jim was a patient there. Whether it was the removal of the fecal pouch upon his arrival, therapy, or whatever else they did there, except for weekends, time seemed to march along at considerable speed. However, for Jim, who was making progress no matter how deliberate the pace and exertion, the progress seemed slow.

It also became a life of directives: Take this medication, up this way, down this way; go to the left, look left; eat here; practice reading; try to walk; try not to slide out of the wheel chair; try to stand; try to balance; reach for this, and on and on it went.

After the pouch removal, Jim was put into "briefs" or adult diapers. The awkwardness and self-consciousness of wearing them and the indwelling catheter he had when he arrived at rehab, were difficult for him. He repeated over and over, "Like a baby." At times, dismissive facial expressions and poor decision-making and reasoning invaded his psyche as well. Although his dignity had been injured by wearing briefs, he said something to a friend he never would have said pre-stroke. She had stopped by to drop off some food and to visit. He interrupted the conversation and took it to a whole different place with this: "I felt like a baby." He continued and echoed to our friend a comment the nurse who removed the pouch made: "A baby wouldn't have so much hair on his butt."

I about choked and took on his embarrassment and apologized profusely to our friend, who, in the end, completely understood. Then, in frustration, I scolded him which in all manner wasn't right. I expected the pre-stroke Jim, and that day it wasn't to be. To this day I feel terrible about my whole reaction. It was then I fully realized he had been broken in two, not only his body had been victimized by the stroke, but his cognitive and social skills had been enfeebled more than I thought. *Dear Jesus, he has so much to overcome, please let my Jim recover. Jesus heals.*

Later that day, as I thought about how at times his brain seemed a jumble and his concentration somewhat fractured, I wondered if some of his mental process difficulties were the result of the eighteen medications he took every day, which not only soured his innards, but made him extremely groggy and "out of it," sometimes for much of the day.

Even though Jim's dad had a series of strokes and I thought I knew a bit about them, I became acutely aware that I truly had no feel for the magnitude of their repercussions. I initially thought it was all about paralysis, maybe speech or eating disorders, but it was so much more. The cognitive losses were almost as difficult to wrap my head around as the physical. Jim's concentration and attention span were pretty much zilch immediately post-stroke. He couldn't get to the left with his vision or even realize there was a left side. Later, when he was able to eat, I turned his plate so he would eat food on the left, and of all things, he was sometimes rude! This was hard for me to accept, because he had never been rude before. Yet, the old Jim, his love for us and sense of humor, revealed itself at unexpected times. The complexity of the stroke was beyond my realm of understanding.

By the end of the second morning, we had met all the therapists and Jim's neurosurgeon. I was impressed with the caliber of his team and the reputation and standing of his neurosurgeon. That same morning, he got his first ice chips, ginger ale, and apple sauce. He brushed his teeth for the first time in three weeks, but gagged, and a woman from speech grilled him with many of the same questions put to him during his "entrance exam." I was certain he was in good hands. The current focus would be on swallowing, speaking, sitting, balance, and areas of cognition in an endeavor to rewire his brain.

Shock! I stood paralyzed in the hall as I watched the therapist wheel Jim to the neuro gym! There was no way one could have prepared me to see Jim pushed in a wheelchair. *A wheelchair, that's a wheelchair.* My head couldn't wrap around it. And his shoulders, there was something different about the set of his shoulders. What has happened to his body? All those weeks in the hospital when he was in a bed or a chair it seemed "normal" for someone sick, but to see him wheeled away struck me with a harshness that was jarring. Why? I don't know, because I certainly knew he couldn't walk.

The neuro gym was busy and noisy. Everything was so emotional about that day. All those people working so hard, and to think Jim would have to do the same. I cried on and off all day. When I pushed Jim back to his room, I sobbed so noisily people stopped to ask if I was okay. I could only shake my head. I became consumed with praying. I talked to God, Jesus, Lord—you name it—most of any given day.

~ JOURNAL ~

"Dear Lord, this has probably been one of my more emotional days. Give us strength and courage. Dear Jesus, please heal my Jim. Jesus heals, Jesus heals."

On day three in rehab, Jim got a shower. It had been three and a half weeks since he showered in the hotel prior to his surgery. Two nurse assistants put him on a gurney-type thing with a hole at the bottom so the water would run away from the body. A long hose with a shower head was used to spray and rinse. I did the washing, they did the rinsing, and I can still see his red, sore butt from when he had the pouch on. It was my initiation as an active participant in his physical rehab.

Little things that made me smile were a part of my days as well. That evening after the shower, I told Jim, "I think I lost my pen."

Wrapped in a cute smile, his response was, "I have one."

My face stretched in surprise. "Where?"

He grinned and said, "In my truck." I shook my head and smiled. I could tell he was happy that he made me smile. All the way home I thanked God for that little bit of Jim that popped through, and that he was finally able to be showered.

※

Jim's therapy schedule shaped our days. A typical schedule hung on his bulletin board every day.

>   Breakfast—6:45
>   Speech Therapy Group—8:45
>   Physical Therapy/Occupational Therapy—10:15
>   Speech Therapy—11:00
>   Lunch—11:30
>   Physical Therapy Auto Ambulator—1:45
>   Physical Therapy/Occupational Therapy—2:30
>   Dinner—4:45

Most mornings when I arrived, Jim was in therapy. He might be in a wooden box, his body held upright to learn balance, or placing pegs into holes on a board, being taught how to maneuver the wheelchair, or a myriad of other therapies undertaken to rehabilitate his body and cognitive abilities.

One morning I walked in on a mini-brouhaha between Jim and his therapists, who he teasingly called the "Torture Twins." He argued: "Scooch is not a word!"

"Sure, it is," they teased back.

He wouldn't relent. Begrudgingly, after a lot of coaxing, he complied and moved sideways on the mat.

It was funny. Throughout the whole nine and a half weeks he was an in-patient there, out of the clear blue, he'd assert to me that "scooch" is not a word.

Other days, I would get there before occupational therapy and oftentimes find him helplessly slouched in his wheelchair. He always tried to get out of the chair or the bed by himself. A strap across his lap helped to keep him sitting up, somewhat. He seemed to wiggle so he'd end up half in and half out. The bed was alarmed and it drove him crazy!

After I straightened him in the chair, we took it upon ourselves to tidy up. I wheeled him to the sink, where we started with the teeth. My diligent effort to teach him to use his right hand with assist from his left side to put the toothpaste on the brush was exasperating, but we kept at it. Only when I reminded him that he had a left side did he brush his teeth on that side. It was the same with shaving.

The bathroom issues continued. He wanted his privacy and sometimes a minor fracas would occur. One morning I came in and Jim announced, "I fell off the toilet." The staff had informed me of this before I even got to his room. There was no one to blame. He struggled and it was pure accident.

☙

Weekends tended to be cheerless. It was not only the gray of winter—fewer people worked the weekends and there was little therapy. This made for long days. One Sunday was particularly long. Jim appointed me "It" for urinal duty. I spent my day "on call," with the urinal strategically situated for quick serviceability. In all honesty, I couldn't wait to go home. I was ready to go crazy hearing, "Hurry, I need it now."

A Sunday morning in late February:

~ JOURNAL ~

> I cried in the shower this morning and prayed with all my heart, "Please don't let Jim suffer because of my sins. I know God that things don't work that way, but I am so sad and somehow for a minute I thought maybe you were punishing me through him, yet I know God, you don't work that way."

I got to the rehab hospital and it was chaos from the get-go. He wanted to pee and for me to get the bottle before I even took my jacket off. I thought that afterward, I would get him shaved, teeth brushed, etc., but he thought he had to keep peeing.

That the urinal be at Jim's beck and call (sometimes at less than two-minute intervals) and in position, was a paranoia painstakingly elaborated to the point that he got irritated when I did not anticipate he had to go. When he did have an accident, it was because I didn't anticipate his need for the urinal in a timely manner.

The phrase "you need to" never sat well with me, and pre-stroke Jim would never say it. So, in combination with the word "anticipate," it drove me bonkers. I loved him, felt terrible for him, and gave him a lot of leeway, but by dinner I had had it! I murmured into his ear a strong, "Do not say 'you need to anticipate' again." I walked out of the room. I was worn out and needed a breather. I carried tears in my eyes the rest of the day. For weeks he continued to use "anticipate" for many of his needs.

One day in speech therapy he stopped paying attention to the therapist, held out his hand toward me and said, "You didn't anticipate."

"What?" I said.

"I need a Kleenex. You need to 'anticipate' these things." *Arghh, now I need to "anticipate" his need for Kleenex.* I handed him the Kleenex without saying a word. There were differences in his thought process and personality that bewildered me at times. This was one of those times.

∞

It was a cold and gloomy Sunday. We were going stir crazy and decided to roam the halls. We strolled most, if not all the hallways in the hospital, and parked ourselves at the windows overlooking a brown courtyard. The dark gray sky seemed to carry anxiety and gave up no clue that spring was around the corner.

As we stood there, Jim asked to be straightened in his chair. "Hon," he said in my ear as I bent over, "Why do you think this happened to me?" I knew he wasn't asking, "Why me?" He wanted to know why he got what he did, and its purpose in his life and ours.

Emotion welled in his eyes as he shifted his gaze upwards. I took his shaky hand as he sought an explanation for his health problems.

As Jim spoke, he couldn't reiterate enough his love for our family. What a sight we must have been there in the hall as we slobbered our tears. The raw rhythm of life and its reflections had caught up with us that afternoon.

Among other things, Jim talked about Doug and his wish for Doug to find a wife, and soon. "Someone like you," he told me. He further said, "Maybe God gave me this so Doug could meet one of these nice therapists or a nurse. At least something good would come of this. I worry I'll never meet who he marries or see my grandchild if he doesn't hurry up."

My words were: "Someday he will find a nice wife, and we'll rejoice with a grandchild." My prayer was, *Dear Jesus, with Jim's health I have doubts, but you're in charge, please let his dream be fulfilled.*

∞

Jim received many gifts and cards, too many to mention during his time in rehab. The most appreciated was the Marine Corps blanket mentioned earlier.

Then there was Blessed Francis Xavier Seelos. "Who is that?" you might ask. That was my question exactly when someone brought in a piece of mail addressed to Jim at the rehab hospital. The envelope's contents included a brochure with directions to Seelos' shrine located at St. Mary's Assumption Church in New Orleans. A small biographical booklet told his story: He was called to a life of holiness as a Redemptorist priest and was beatified by His Holiness, Pope John Paul II, on April 9th, 2000, but the most intriguing item in the envelope was a relic of Seelos'. The relic is encased in a quarter size pendant. It bears resemblance to a piece of stone. However, growing up in the Catholic Church I've wondered if it's a piece of Seelos' bone.

For whatever reason, Jim took it as a sign of something important and accorded it special treatment. I was perplexed. He had me place it under his pillow every day before I left the hospital. He was always spiritual, but it seemed strange to me. It managed to stay with him throughout his hospital stay. The relic now sits in a drawer with miscellaneous "Jim" items. I wonder about it at times. Maybe someday I'll make it to Seelos' shrine.

∞

It took me less than a minute when I met Michelle to realize she had a special heart, an inner self that was well developed and always said what needed to be said.

Besides coordinating the back-and-forth rides for me, and all the food she prepared, on a Sunday evening in rehab, she surprised us with an elegant dinner you can only imagine eating at the finest of restaurants. Mark and Michelle carried boxes into the dining room that included food, an antique tablecloth, fine china, silverware, cloth napkins, and flowers for the centerpiece. It was a startling expression of love and caring. Sadly, Jim was in one of his rude moods. He wouldn't eat, and I had to hurry through dinner. That evening, when all was said and done, I cried for the wonderfulness of our friends, and that Jim's cognitive change prevented him from enjoying something so special.

※

Visits from the guys picked up his spirits tremendously. Most days one or the other was there to visit in that time before I left for the day. Mark, Paul, Don, and Jim brought him immense joy, and "guy talk," typically about cars. They teased constantly. Somewhere along the way, Mark became the "old goat" and Jim the "old fart."

※

Within the tight corners of his room and areas surrounding it, from mid-January through much of March, it seemed we were living in another realm. We had virtually no privacy; a curtain provided the only barrier between Jim and me and his roommate and others. The Zamboni-like machine to clean the floors, the cleaning agent, and occasional urine smells until Jim's clothes or sheets that were soiled could get cleaned, were part of the realm. And, I'll never forget the electric stapler noise coming from the desk down the hall that almost drove Jim insane.

※

Signs of spring started to punctuate the air and sky, and with them, Jim's spirit awakened when we were able to get outside. The flowers and birds were a tonic as the filtered sun rays spun through the new leaves. He became ambulatory with the guidance of an individual with a gait belt and a walker, while I followed close behind with the wheelchair. However, he was never completely on his own; he needed help to go from the bedroom to the bathroom, or even halfway to the bathroom. His left hand was able to squeeze mine when I asked, yet he couldn't do anything with it, but that was still progress. Although his handwriting was squiggly, he learned to write again, but staying to the left of the page when he tried reading, or doing such things as crosswords remained problematic. His focus to the left never fully returned.

ಸಿ

The sunlight on our faces felt good that spring day, but as much as I wanted to rejoice in it, the shadow on the sidewalk of a man in a wheelchair and a woman pushing him, was one of doubt and fear. He still had the rigors of amyloidosis to deal with, and although he had come a long way, he would continue to need help with most daily activities, including toileting. And, sad to say, I already felt I had been over-taxed with regards to his paranoia about the pee bottle. *One thing, maybe he will like the food better at home.*

~ JOURNAL ~

Jim complains about the food every day. Today he said, "The next time they ask me about the food and how much I ate, I'm going to wag my tail."

ಸಿ

As a consequence of my Catholic upbringing, my prayers became rote and petitional. Similar wording is found throughout my journal. A bit from my journal two days before "we" were released from in-patient rehab:

~ JOURNAL ~

Dear Lord, we are ending this stage of Jim's recovery. Please... (Here I go again, begging, I wish I wouldn't beg!) What I am asking for is a complete recovery for Jim, amyloidosis and all health issues. Please don't let the amyloidosis get in the way of his recovery. You have given us so many pocket-sized miracles that have added up to a lot during these long weeks. You're an amazing and wonderful, God.

Also, Jesus, bless the people, the caretakers, doctors, therapists who do their good work. They are amazing. I wish I had the aptitude and empathy they express in their daily lives.

Our friends too; oh my gosh, Lord, thank you for all those wonderful people. Please, Lord, give me the strength, courage, patience, knowledge as we move forward through this journey.

"Do you want to take one last look?" I asked as I pushed Jim from the neuro gym. Dispassionate, he simply responded, "No."

෨

Discharge day was not the sunny day I had hoped for, but at least Sherry and George had come to help. My plan was to arrive early in order to give Jim a leisurely shower. A big day was planned and I wanted him to feel refreshed and relaxed. The weather was uncooperative. The sky, dense with low hanging gray clouds, pounded sheets of rain against the windshield. The pavement seemed to disappear in the clouds and rain. At times, traffic slowed to a stop.

I didn't give up on the shower. About the time he was naked and I was able to get him on the shower chair, a "Billy code" was broadcast over the intercom. I had no idea what it was and ignored it. My shoes were off, the shower head placed in a trajectory so I wouldn't get wet, and the water was warm. I rolled him in.

It turns out the "Billy code" was a call over the PA system to available hospital personnel to line the exit hallway to congratulate Jim's efforts and wish him well as he moved on. I have to say they were patient. The resounding display of well wishes and cheers and handshakes as I pushed him past all those wonderful people was spectacular. "Good luck, Jim," "Congratulations," and "Hang in there, Jim," were heard all the way to the door. Words could not express my love for the rehab "family," and how congenially acquainted we had all come to be in Jim's care.

※

When we got home, we ate a quick lunch and headed to Dr. Hematologist. Once again, she was very thorough explaining amyloidosis. Sherry, and George in particular, had a lot of questions. Due to Jim's health, a stem cell transplant was nixed. Her recommendation was a regimen of chemo to be taken orally and steroids. Jim didn't have any hesitation saying he would do the chemo.

While I put his belongings away that we brought home from the rehab hospital, George and Sherry made supper while Jim rested in his recliner.

~ JOURNAL ~

I'm already worrying about tonight. I'll have to do the urinal. I pray he can get that under control and that someday he'll once again be able to walk to the bathroom himself.

Dear Jesus, thank you for the miracles that brought Jim home today and that the kids are with us. Please continue to bless us with your grace and miracles. Help us to focus one day at a time. Thank you for being my support in this. I love you, thank you for everything. Love, Marie

George worked so hard trimming bushes, while Sherry and I went to get the handicap tags for the cars, and then we went to the mall. I tried on clothes. I am down to a size two. Where did my weight go?

At 12th & MARQUETTE

∞

The next day:

~ JOURNAL ~

Hi Lord, WOW, sleeping is a hard, hard thing. I feel I want to be next to Jim so that he doesn't "swim" after using the urinal, but boy, I'm questioning my strength for this without getting sleep. In the morning I cried and complained. I am now embarrassed in front of you, Lord, about that. I am so sorry for what it did to you and Jim. As a result, Jim was depressed today and only ate a little bit of chicken soup. So now I need your help dealing with Jim's depression.

When the kids went home, the goodbye tore me up inside. I swallowed hard, and told myself, *Breathe deep!*

PART SIX
BETWEEN THIS PLACE AND THE NEXT

There are things we don't want to happen
But have to accept,
Things we don't want to know
But have to learn,
And people we can't live without
But have to let go.

~"J.J." Quotes from *Criminal Minds*, Season 6, Episode 2

33
FACE-OFF – AMYLOIDOSIS

AMYLOIDOSIS: DEFINITION IN PART FROM THE AMYLOIDOSIS FOUNDATION—AL amyloidosis is caused by a bone marrow disorder. The bone marrow produces cells in the blood system, including plasma cells. These plasma cells are the part of the immune system that make antibodies for fighting infections.

In AL patients, these plasma cells don't form properly. Abnormal misfolding results in cells that run amok and form amyloid.

These misfolded amyloid proteins can be deposited in and around tissues, nerves and organs. As the amyloid builds up in an organ, nerve, or tissue, it gradually causes damage and affects their function. It often affects more than one organ and can be systemic.

There are different types of amyloidosis, including familial. I thank God Jim's was not from some gnarled family DNA that could be passed down to the kids.

AMYLOIDOSIS: (MY DEFINITION)
AL Amyloidosis is a loathsome, pernicious and well disguised saboteur that masquerades itself and makes it hard to diagnose.

Symptoms Jim experienced, although not all at once:
- Heart murmur, valves (eventual valve repair)
- Foamy urine (like a frothy head on a beer)
- General weakness

- Muscle loss
- Fatigue
- Palpebral purpura (bruising of the eyelid)
- Abdominal pain which caused him to stop walking
- General bruising

34
PATIENT AND CAREGIVER

Twenty-four/seven caregiving was grueling. When I mulled it over, I realized we were squarely in the thick of our pledge to take care of each other "in sickness and in health." I laughed to myself. Somehow, "for richer" had passed us by. Like all couples, we knew that in all probability, one of us would have to take care of the other, but for me, at the age of 58, it all seemed too soon. Recently retired, we headed full steam into planning a trip to Italy in the summer of 2007. We had talked about it for years, yet with Jim so ill and now back home, it seemed like we landed on an alien planet instead.

Fatigue was my accomplice. Every day I opened my eyes I said, *Can I do this day?* I'd answer myself, *Buck up, Marie, you can do this.* My mantra, *Take it one minute at a time, Marie, don't think too much ahead, one minute at a time.*

Particularly trying were those times I felt unqualified with regards to Jim's emotional health and the way his stroke calibrated encounters with the world around him.

Humongous planning was required to make our overloaded "work day" flow. The rhythms and routines of our pre-stroke life were lost to the disease.

೧

Ahhh, to sleep uninterrupted. Nights were fitful and restless. We needed a new mattress. The involuntary movements of Jim's left arm rippled through to me, which interrupted sleep for both of us. Additionally, he woke me often—for something to drink, to use the bathroom, to help him move to the other side, or when he had to use the urinal. The issues were identifiable and we worked to solve them.

Jim's sister, Evelyn, desperately wanted to help and offered to pay for a new mattress. "Get the best you can find," she encouraged. Her generosity purchased an adjustable, split-king Sleep Number bed. We were almost giddy. The push of a button enabled more comfort, and because it was the split version, I no longer felt the effects of the involuntary movements of Jim's left arm. After the giddiness had subdued, we elevated our heads and laid a long time talking. I took Jim's right hand. He hadn't lost his touch, and held my left hand with a delicacy that had pleasured me in so many ways. The bed was worth that very moment in time.

The hematologist-oncologist suggested we try external Texas catheters at night. The use of the word "Texas" made us both laugh. We knew nothing about these things. I felt weird and stupidly shy when I asked for them in a half-laughing voice. We grappled to figure out which were the easiest to put on and take off. There were wide band, narrow band, self-adhesive, watertight adhesive seals and pop-on, to name a few. Then there was the size thing: a whole other issue! The blasted things! None of them were easy to use especially on a patient who had not been circumcised. One time, it took 45 minutes to get it on right, and sometimes as long to take it off when glue was involved, sometimes at inopportune moments, it fell off.

One evening as I wrestled it on, Jim's comedic personality shone through his recent stoicism. "Keep your nose to the grindstone," he coaxed, a dopey grin on his face.

Haughty in my attitude, I replied, "Errr, you better be careful, mister. Looks like I'm the one in control here."

"Touché."

છ∞

Not enough sleep and always in a rush. One morning Jim woke me at 5:00 to use the bathroom. I sat him up on the edge of the bed, secured his gait belt, moved the wheel chair in place and hung the catheter bag on the side of the chair. "Hurry," he urged.

"I'm doing the best I can," I responded.

I guided his movement with the gait belt, but in our rush, got sloppy. Whoosh, an explosion of errors! He toppled forward, and I screamed, fell back and hit the dresser and wall on my descent to the floor. Jim dropped full anchor on top of me. Rattled, I tried to get a handle on our situation. Jim's terrified voice asked, "Are you okay? I'm sorry, honey!"

Tears spilled as I steadily wiggled my way out. I didn't want to hurt him or disrupt the catheter bag. *Breathe in, breathe out,* I said to myself as I moved my body free. *Now what,* I thought? *How do I get him up off the floor?*

Gently, this way and that, I tried to shift his body weight so he might be able to help me get him up. Utter defeat! Exasperated, I called our neighbor.

Our neighbor had so generously offered his services when Jim returned home from rehab. "Call anytime you need help," he said. I don't think he could have ever imagined it would be to save us so early in the morning, and in our bedroom. It was a curious scene: Jim on the floor in a T-shirt, Depends wrapped around his bottom with the catheter tube dangling and me, flush with tears in my citrus fruit printed pajamas. It would be a rude awakening for anyone.

My shoulders, back, chest, and upper left arm ached, while the riot of bruises turned every shade of blue, green and yellow.

༄

A hurried breakfast, then a sponge bath in the kitchen started each day. We could not manage the logistics of getting Jim in a safe position to get him into either shower. When we tried, we thought we'd both end on the floor. Sad for Jim, his last real shower was the day we took him home from the rehab hospital. It's weird, but many mornings as I bathed him, the non-sexual intimacy and conversation seemed to uncover another layer of love.

༄

Although I had prayed that amyloidosis and Jim could come to some truce, it didn't happen. Chemo was scheduled and it was time to pick up Jim's meds. Afterward, we stopped at Mark and Michelle's so I could give Michelle a special gold angel I asked Evelyn's jeweler to make. We had so many wonderful angels help us and watch over us during our journey, but I would say Michelle was the archangel. With deepest admiration and love, I gave her the exquisite gift. Her determination and commitment interceded to bring tranquility to our days. I can never thank her enough.

A mosaic of thirty-six pills each day for four days, then on the fifth day I'd take him for a Neulasta shot.

By the time we got home a quiet riot was roaring through my head. I was in unchartered and scary territory. I knew I needed to quiet the disorder to get everything straight. My attention was focused on a plan for flawless dispensation of all those pills. I decided to lay sticky note paper across the kitchen divide. On each sticky I carefully noted the name, color and size of pill, with directives; time to take, and what to take with them (food or not, no milk, etc.), all the time wondering if all this effort would pay dividends. *God, I pray I have this right. It feels like I am going to poison him.*

Jim asked, "Is the venom ready?"

"Ready," was all I could say.

~ JOURNAL ~

I pray you grace Jim with good health and give us life to old age together. To all the sick, please bless them, bless the caregivers, give them a break once in a while. Please bless all mankind with an understanding, love and compassion for one another. Love you, Lord. Marie

---

Time was scarce. Out-patient therapy started the day after Jim's first chemo dose. Three days a week of therapy at a clinic 23 miles away, and doctor's appointments packed most days to capacity. The calendar snarled back at me, "No more." There were times I felt I was running alongside a moving train.

Jim was a self-proclaimed great driver. At rehab they taught me how to put him in the back seat, and thus I became his chauffer. His view from the back seat apparently made him feel like I was always speeding and reckless. He asked, "When did you learn to drive like George?" He had always criticized our son-in-law's driving. "Do you think you are driving a four-door Corvette?" he hollered from the back seat. Purposely, so he would hear, I made a deep, extra loud groan.

⁂

Jim had his troubles as he came off the steroids. For a day or two his face, neck, and scalp broke out in a rash. His bowel movements became the consistency of peanut butter, too gooey to come out, I thought. Nothing except blood from his hemorrhoids seemed productive. He never had to throw up but felt nauseous. It seemed to me his body was giving up, and I didn't know how to help, except to be a motivational coach and try to meet his needs. At times, the drugs pared away his ability to think straight and his behavior became a bit erratic.

He turned the overhead lights on in the car. I shut them off. He turned them on again. I turned the TV off when we went somewhere. He turned it back on. I turned it off. He turned it on again. I would put his seat belt on. He took it off. I put it on again, he took it off. He motioned for me to take his gait belt off, but he didn't even have it on.

⁂

Doug arrived for Jim's 63rd birthday. The kids gave him a Marine officer's sword. Excited, we took a picture of Jim with his Marine Corps blanket and the sword. An examination of the picture rattled me to the bone. In recent weeks I had been looking at him through the tired slits of my eyes and didn't notice how he changed. The lines in Jim's face were etched with distinguishing features of his dad's, when his dad was in his mid-80s. A terrible sadness and tenderness overwhelmed me. He looked sick and desperate for healing. It didn't help the blanket was laying across his lap, like a picture from an "old folks' home." When George called to sing *Happy Birthday* to him, Jim told him he sings about as good as he drives. We all had a good laugh. With Doug's help we were able to go to Applebee's for dinner.

It was time for Doug to leave. Jim and Doug talked and had a loving goodbye. I took Doug to Mark and Michelle's and they took Doug to the airport. When I arrived home, Jim admonished me, "Shooosh, talk quiet." When I asked why, he said, "Doug is sleeping in the bedroom."

"Honey, Doug left less than an hour ago. I took him to Mark and Michelle's. Remember?"

He remained a perplexed and confused soul all evening.

※

A good friend who noticed my calamitous attitude was plunging to a deep state, encouraged me to focus on moments of gratitude and grace. I took her advice. My first entries included:

~ JOURNAL ~

Hi, Dear Jesus, Jim seems optimistic today. Thank you. This is grace!

Smitty called. They had a great conversation and some laughs. Thank you, again. Grace.

I snuck out from rehab to have lunch with Nancy and Lucy—more grace.

A therapist helped put Jim in the car, more grace.

However, when I included gratitude, I still couldn't control my waves of rote and petitioning prayers that ran through my head and remained in my writing. I was constantly trying to light a fire under the word "hope." "Jesus heals," and words that asked God to restore Jim, were with me all day. It never stopped, but at least I started to realize there were also a lot of moments to be grateful and happy about.

Before bed one day, right after we finished our prayers, Jim asked, "Do you know what I prayed for?"

"That you get better, and soon?"

"No," he replied. "I prayed that you don't say 'ahhhhhh' every time I ask you for something or when I have to pee, and I'm sorry I have to ask you for so much; but when you do that, it reminds me how I am, what you have to do, and that makes me sad."

I hadn't realized I was doing that and prayed that night that I'd be able to end the "ahhhh's." I also prayed, *Lord, could our skunk (that had been living under our deck) find a new home or get hit by a car? He makes me nervous!*

Several days later:

~ JOURNAL ~

I notice I haven't seen the skunk or smelled his odor. Thank you, Lord–gratitude!

35
GO FOR A WALK

Jim had survived the surgery and stroke, but there were times I wondered if he'd survive all the hard work to healing. Yet, even through the ups and downs, he remained optimistic. So much so that despite signposts at therapy that his advances in recent days had been almost nil, he declared, "Hon, will you please bring me that cane?" He pointed to the quad-based cane sitting across the room.

"What are you going to do with that?"

"Go for a walk," he responded.

I was more than nervous, but we needed to work at walking. I silently petitioned Jesus for success and looked around for potential hazards. I set the foot stool on a cushy chair across the room. Jim said, "Get the foot stool out of here; I don't want it around." I complied.

I wound the gait belt around his waist and helped him to stand. "Ready?" I asked. He had his game face on and seemed ready for anything. Carried on an air of confidence, he took a couple of steps forward, but then zigged when he should have zagged. He lost his balance. Whoom! The lurch forward was fast and hard. His full weight crashed onto the cushy chair and slid to the floor. Once again, dread squeezed at my heart. I shrieked, "Are you okay?"

"I think so."

I looked at him splayed on the floor. Once again, I was unable to get him up, so I called on our dear friend, Donald. Without hesitation, he said, "I'll be right there."

"Thank God you decided the chair was a bad place for the foot stool," I commented while waiting for Donald.

"He motioned me to move it."

"Who?"

"My guardian angel."

"It's a good thing," I replied. I thought it appropriate to silently chastise his angel for blinking when he should have kept Jim from falling. *What the hell; where were you,* I thought? *He said you had him move the stool. Why couldn't you have kept him from falling?*

Reflectively, maybe his angel could foresee the fall and sought to mitigate its consequences? I was always baffled about his angel. I'll never understand Jim's intuition or insight with regard to his kindred spirit in the brown suit, who came to reassure and advise him.

36
DELICIOUS DINNER

Nancy Moody called. Nancy Moody and Lucy Battle wanted to bring dinner on Sunday, and asked if they could use my oven. Even though my oven was a disastrous mess, I didn't hesitate with my "yes." The next time we were home for a stretch before Sunday, I made sure to use its self-cleaning feature. It also gave me something to focus on besides Jim's illness. My buffet was worked over, so I chose a tablecloth, napkins, and anything else I needed to make the table look special.

Jim had agreed to the dinner with my former bosses and their wives, but a couple hours before they arrived, he started to fret.

For my benefit he said, "It will be nice to have them," but his voice pulsed with nervousness.

"Hon, what are you worried about?" I asked.

"Nothing."

"I know there is something. Please tell me."

It turns out he had become paranoid he might have to use the bathroom when they were visiting, or that he might have an accident in front of them. He felt disturbed that he continued to need so much of my help. More than anything, he was feeling less assured of himself as a capable man, comparing himself to the successful and healthy men that were coming to visit. My first task beyond tablecloths and napkins was to rev up his self-esteem, to assure him he had importance and that he was not identified by his illness or paralysis. As he considered my words, his eyes crossed mine and some of the tension seemed to dissipate. "If I tell you I need to go to the bathroom, just hurry, okay?"

"Don't worry. I'll be watching and listening for what you need."

Our friends gave us a lot of reason for joy that day. There was the fabulous food, great conversation, and good laughs about everything under the sun, including politics. I deliberately wore a Hillary shirt to cause a bit of fun political hoopla. It worked. To this day, the ever-present care of these wonderful people can make me tear up. The meal: salad, potatoes, salmon, and chocolate pie were scrumptious. Better than that though, was the joy and distraction they brought to our home that, if only temporary, made us forget the everyday struggles of Jim's illness.

37
THANK YOU

By this time, so much kindness, love, and prayers had been expended by so many, we needed to get busy thanking everyone. So, instead of merely thinking about writing a thank you letter, I sat down at a table in an unused room while Jim paced through his therapy in another. Forty-five identical letters were sent out. Unfortunately, I don't have the final version, but I do have a rough draft I scribbled in my journal. Here it is:

> On behalf of myself and Jim, it's time I sit down and thank all of you. God has blessed us every day of this journey with your encouragement, loving prayers and much more. All this gave us the courage, strength and support to push through on the days we felt tearful, depressed and tired (ohhhh-so tired). In addition, we thank you for the following:
>
> Your valuable time, laughs, jokes, cards, gift boxes, phone calls, rides back and forth to the hospital and rehab (what a great gift), moral support, all the great food (how wonderful was that?), the beautiful dinner at in-house rehab with the table set so beautiful, the flowers, chiropractic adjustment, haircuts at the hospital, help with the handicap sidewalk at our home, running to CVS to pick up prescriptions, picking up the picture frame, getting the mail, the daily prayer from Chattanooga, chauffeuring family to and from the airport (sometimes, it seemed in the middle of the night), for taking care of Sherry and George's dogs so they didn't have that concern, for the journal and note cards, for those who used vacation time to be with us when we needed them most, for coming

At 12th & MARQUETTE

to our rescue before dawn, for being there in cardiac step-down when Jim thought he could walk and I needed physical help to keep him from getting hurt, for making the house/deck handicap ready, for getting my car washed, for the mattress, for taking my garbage to the dump, for fixing my tire, for bringing dinner and your wonderful company, for the yard work, for the radio antenna, for picking Jim up off the floor on a Sunday evening, staying all night in CVICU to suction Jim's lungs after the ventilator was removed, for exercising his arm and leg and helping him walk, for listening to me when I rambled and was scared. Last but not least, doctors, nurses, therapists, techs and all hospital staff, and the UAW for great health insurance. We thank you.

Most of you know Jim is about ready to start his second round of chemo/steroids. He did fairly well with the first round, although after getting his Neulasta shot he felt weaker than usual, had a bit of a head and neck rash and was nauseated for about two days. He is also scheduled to have Botox injected in his left arm. He continues in outpatient rehab, and we'll do this until the Blue Cross dollars run out.

Each and every one of you have enriched our world with kindness and compassion. We care deeply for you and your families. May God keep you close, and bless you day-to-day with good health. We love you. Thank you. Marie and Jim

38
CRICKET

Crickets. I freak out when I hear them sing and I absolutely go bonkers when I see them jump! On the few occasions they got in, they inevitably turned up in our bathroom. It was Jim's job to get rid of the dirty, ugly creatures, but as with all his jobs, it had now become mine.

After I got Jim settled, I went into the living room to write in my journal. Not many minutes later I headed to bed, got nice and cozy, and there it was: that high pitched, whiney chirp. Geez! I knew I couldn't sleep unless it was taken care of, so I grabbed a towel. As if made of stone, I stood and watched and listened. Nothing! Where did that thing go? Hesitantly, I inched into the bathroom, whipped the towel around, and still nothing. I closed the door and put the towel at the bottom of the door so it couldn't get into the bedroom.

I fell back to sleep, but not for long. Jim needed to use the bathroom. I pushed him in, listened and looked around. No cricket, so I hurriedly put a small bathroom rug in front of the toilet and tended to Jim. Wouldn't you know it, I heard it again. "Hurry up," I said. I wanted out of that bathroom. As soon as I was ready to wheel him back into the bedroom it hopped and I went on a terror. The small rug was readily handy, so I flung it, and it landed on Jim's head. "What are you doing?"

"I've got to get that thing."

"Don't kill me in the meantime," he chuckled.

There it was again! "Careful," Jim hollered. I flung the rug with everything I had. Victory! It squarely landed on top of that obnoxious, dirty thing. My prayer was it would suffocate under there. Satisfied that is what would happen, I left the rug on the cricket overnight. I'd deal with its dead body in the morning.

Two more times that night we got up. I carefully wheeled Jim past the rug and smugly thought, "I got you buddy."

It grossed me out to think I'd have to lift that rug and dispose of it. Ambivalent, I gently lifted the rug. To my astonishment, it was not there. "What the heck?"

Fearful cricket hater I am, an inordinate amount of my precious time was spent hunting that repulsive thing down. It was to no avail. Dead or alive, I never saw it again.

39
NOSTALGIA

Several days later, while waiting for Jim at rehab and fantasizing about getting some good sleep, a beautiful song floated to my ears, a praise to the divine. It was coming from down the hall. It wove itself to the center of my core. The melancholy mood contorted my face as I desperately struggled to hold back tears. "Praise to the Lord" swept me back to St. Adalbert's, where nostalgia settled on a vision of a young couple. They stood at the altar vowing to love each other "until death do us part," powerful optics that caught me completely off guard, tore at my heart and set the tears flowing.

40
CHEMO ROUND TWO

~ JOURNAL ~

Lord, I sure do love Jim. Every day I love him more. I would give anything to have him be his old self. I hate that he is the way he is now. I keep thinking about how he must feel inside. Sometimes it still seems as if this is a dream and I'll wake up and everything will be fine.

Lasix 40 today and Flomax. He had to pee so much, but I think he needs to get that swelling down in his legs. He'd be able to walk so much better without the edema. Again, not himself. He was picky, tired and generally spaced out. When I asked him what I should write in here about him he said, "Put in there that I'm grumpy." Jim took a one-and-a-half-hour nap and complained about not getting air and the pressure on his chest.

The next day at rehab, Jim seemed puny and worn out. Therapy was not good. As for myself, I was feeling numb and overwhelmed.

"Hurry, I have to pee," Jim cried out. I got him into the bathroom, but before I could get him in place, he started to pee. He moaned, "I'm useless. I wish I wasn't around." While we were in there, I noticed his face, neck and scalp were breaking out again.

He endured all manner of grief that day. The night wasn't any better. He needed in and out of the bed the entire night. Our energy had been zapped; by morning I was too tired to bathe him. It was the first time he would miss his bath since we got home from rehab. Jim, who always worried that he would stink, could have cared less.

The following day, I thought Jim was going to die. He didn't pee and he wouldn't drink. He refused his medicine. I had to plead with him to take it, and he was delusional. I put him to bed and he told me to read Job. I tried, but between his delusional talking and my worry, my eyes blurred in tears.

Doug arrived the next day and Jim was better. I noticed the swelling in both his legs was down. Doug took over so I could do some much-needed shopping. He helped Jim with the urinal, put him in bed, and helped him back to the wheelchair. *God, thank you for our wonderful son,* I thought. One of my stops was Lowe's. Without Jim there it felt soooo wrong. Sadness overwhelmed me. When we had embarked on all those projects together, Lowe's was the happy place. It wasn't that day.

At the end of the day, I thanked God that I had Doug there to help me get Jim ready for bed. When Jim was settled, Doug and I made ourselves a drink and relaxed a bit before calling it a day.

Calling it a day didn't last long. We thought Jim was fine when we put him in bed, but he wasn't. Once again, he started to hallucinate, he was sweating profusely, and he was extremely uncomfortable.

~ JOURNAL ~

"Dear Jesus, I still don't know what to make of all this. Even after all these weeks and months it's foreign. It still doesn't seem possible that this is happening to my dear Jim. And Doug's compassion, where did he get all that? He's amazingly full of love, gentleness and care. He did so much for us both today. He saved our day."

Sadly, the next morning came too fast and it was time for Doug to leave. We were all emotional. Jim had always been a family loving man. When Doug left, it seemed his heart exploded. His love and deep respect for Doug could not have been greater.

He felt the pain as he watched him leave, but yet, a little later in the day, he said, "Is Doug using the pressure washer? I hear the pressure washer. What's Doug doing in the front? Don't flush the toilet too much so Doug doesn't hear it." He also kept telling me about the quarter size circles that floated around the room.

41
UROLOGY DISASTER

Jim and I discussed the peeing issue over and over. We hated the thought of seeing another doctor, but thought maybe there was a pill or something he could easily take to alleviate the problem.

What an ugly, absolute disaster and ruinous experience it was at the urologist's office.

The doctor assured us he worked with stroke victims. I asked him if he knew what amyloidosis was. Without hesitation he answered, "Yes." There was a bit more discussion. Based upon our description of the problem, the doctor recommended Jim have a urodynamics test. I was hesitant, but to my surprise Jim agreed with the doctor's recommendation. The following is from my journal following the test.

~ JOURNAL ~

Angry! More surgery?! I believe the doctor is nuts! Surgery–isn't there a pill or simple in-office procedure or something else? Jim will die with more surgery. Urological tests. Horrible! No one to help Jim get on the table. They stood back and looked at us almost with horror as I struggled to help him. There was no offer to help, and when I did ask for help, the two people in the room timidly held back. I feel terrible and am angry that he has the pain from the urology tests and the lingering burning. It's 9:40 p.m. and he hasn't peed since he had the test.

Jim couldn't get comfortable and decided to try to sleep on the recliner, so I "slept" on the couch. I encouraged him not to worry about soiling his brief that there were plenty in the closet and I would change it when needed.

I am angry, Lord. Not at you. As a matter of fact, I don't know who or what I'm angry at, but it's burning inside me. I'm so pissed that Jim has to continue to have pain. It's one issue after the other! We're supposed to go to therapy tomorrow. I doubt we make it unless we get some decent sleep.

Lord, there is so much to do to take care of Jim and no time. With cooking, washing clothes, taking him to the bathroom, bathing him, and everything else, the day is gone. Hardly any time to even pick up the supplies I need for him. "Overwhelmed" is the word for today. I'm operating in a fatigue and I'm feeling an annoyance and disdain for all the work, and I hate and loathe myself for feeling annoyed! I long for peace and health and sleep! DONE! Going to the couch to try to sleep!!

The following day:

~ JOURNAL ~

Terrible pain from urodynamic tests:

1) Call doctor?

2) Wait to see if pain subsides?

3) Take Lasix this morning?

4) Jim refuses.

5) Nauseated.

6) 10:00 to drug store to pick up anti-burning med.

Second day following urodynamic test:

~ JOURNAL ~

Bad day, but we made it. Jim insisted that John, my brother-in-law, was sitting on the green chair in the living room and talking to him, and that he was able to walk from the recliner to the bed. He insisted he wasn't dreaming.

Peeing, peeing. He peed all over everything right after I washed him. I had to change socks, shoes, everything.

I got Jim ready for therapy. Because he had several loose bowel movements earlier in the day, I asked him if he had to poop. Answer, "no." I got him into the wheelchair, rolled him out back and around to the garage, and guess what, he had to go back in to poop. We never made it to therapy. Too much pee and poop all day.

We used 22 briefs within 24 hours. Constant. Constant.

Several days later:

~ JOURNAL ~

Hi, Lord. I am worried about Jim's color today. I don't believe he slept a wink last night and this morning he is already confused about things. I'm concerned about his forgetfulness and cognitive abilities. He's so in and out of reality. When I put him on the toilet he said, "Close the door so nobody sees." Of course, there was no one else in the house.

I said, "Who would see?"

He answered, "Sherry or your mom."

Another thing, Lord, if I say, "Are you okay?" one more time, I think he will want to kill me. It's a habit, something that started in the hospital. Lord, I can't stop. If I hear him grunt or move or fart, or anything at all, I say, "Are you okay?"

42
HALLWAY LIFE

Much of the time when I sat by myself in the hall at out-patient rehab, I tended to muck around in angst. The question that circuited my brain every day was the same. Was the decision to transition from in-house rehab to home the right decision? Were we wrong to go home? Maybe he should have gone to a nursing home that provided therapy. If he was in a nursing home, I still would have been there every day, and he may have gotten more therapy, and I would not have been so run down. I could have hired someone to watch over him at night. On the other hand, going to a nursing home would have been devastating to his psyche, and to mine as well. I would have felt I let him down. I second guessed myself the whole time Jim was sick.

On the days we waited in the hall for the therapists to be ready, we saw many of the same people almost every day. A beautiful little girl in rehab named Liv said upon seeing her mom, "Good to see you," and gave her mom a hug. Mrs. Poplin never failed to say, "How y'all doin'?" If she saw me alone, she'd say, "How ya doin' girl?" Then there was Mr. David, a man on a mobilized wheelchair who scooted anywhere he wanted to go, and believe me, I was on guard because he sometimes forgot the rules of the road. Another woman in her wheelchair seemed to be set in a permanent position by the door, waiting for her sister. She often asked me for her "nerve" medicine. One day as we waited, Jim saw an older, heavyset woman dressed in a compilation of prints. When she smiled, you realized she had no teeth. After she passed, he started to grin. I asked him what was so funny. He said, "I think that was Miss Tennessee 1922." I couldn't help but laugh myself. The moment was gleeful. His words and sense of humor presented a breath of fresh air that cut through the angst. My pre-stroke Jim had shone through.

43
MOM AND MIKE

My mom and brother, Mike, came to help out. Our moods picked up considerably. Mine, because I got to see family and get some help, and Jim's because the further away he got from his last day of steroids, the more his mood improved.

Mike stayed with Jim at therapy while Mom and I took a break to go to lunch. He also worked his butt off in the yard, or I should say, they worked their butts off. Mom amazed me as she hauled brush uphill to the tree line. At 85 she had a lot of energy!

Mom and I headed to Walmart. While we shopped, Jim asked Mike to call me to come home so he could use the bathroom. Mike asserted himself and said there was no sense in sitting uncomfortable for the two hours I'd be gone. Jim gave in. Although both were distressed and uneasy, the job got done. Not easy for either of them.

I'd be remiss if I didn't mention the miracle of the loaves and fishes occurring at our house. That's exactly what it seemed like when our refrigerator went from almost nothing to almost full when Nancy and Lucy brought us ham, ham salad, soup, and casseroles. It was all so amazing. Not having to worry about dinner and lunch made our time with Mom and Mike so pleasurable.

When it came time for them to leave, I had no way to thank them. Thanks, hugs, and kisses didn't cut it. Their help was immeasurable. My saving grace? Sherry and her friend Penny would arrive within a week.

During the time Mom and Mike were with us I came within a breath of tangling into a therapist. Due to my respect for them, however, I thought better of it. She did a good job with Jim, but what she asked me to do almost made me blow my top. I bolted upright and into a defensive posture when she stated,

"You need to provide us some support. Jim needs to do his homework," she added. Some of the homework consisted of workbook sheets and recall exercises to help Jim's cognition. I was the first one who wanted him to get better, but how in the world did they think I could squeeze all that in? For all their training, I felt they had no clue how exhausted I was, and what it was like to be a full-time caregiver of someone with Jim's impairments. It rubbed me the wrong way. It seemed to insinuate I wasn't already doing enough. It took great emotional energy and self-talk to convince myself I would not feel guilty if we didn't get it all done.

~ JOURNAL ~

Thank you, Lord, for Mom and Mike, and for Jim's good therapy today. I also thank you for the laugh today when Jim was trying to put his shirt on for the night. He ended up with his head in one of the arm holes and his right arm in the head part. I asked him, "Are you a turtle?" He laughed and asked, "Do I look like one?" I replied, "Yes." We started to laugh uncontrollably. It felt good to share a laugh.

∞

The next day:

~ JOURNAL ~

What happened to Jim's happy mood from last night? He has been so grouchy, and of all things, flowers, hoses, and sprinkler stuff irritate him. He told me flowers are a waste!

Lord, when he is better will I be able to live a "Marie" life? It's hard not being able to do things I love. If not, then what? I love him with my whole being, but on days like today when he expects so much and is sooo grouchy, I almost can't stand it, and want to pass the baton to someone else for a bit. And, today he's been throwing the "Well at least you can walk," thing at me. I cried. Then I felt guilty. Why, I didn't do anything wrong? Then he felt guilty for what he said and couldn't stop apologizing. I cried some more. Not good. We're a mess. Good night!

44
LEGACY

"Shoosh! Quiet!" After Mom and Mike left, Jim would barely tolerate any noise. He scarcely tolerated me talking to him. I can't say for sure, but I think it may have been a combination of sensory issues and deep thinking. The silence wore heavy. There were times I noticed his eyes pinching at the corners.

I wish I knew what was on his mind, I thought. I wondered if the light was too bright, or maybe it was his thoughts.

About two days before Sherry and Penny arrived, Jim said he wanted to tell me something. He asked me to move in closer. I grabbed a kitchen chair and slid it next to the recliner.

His eyes glimmered with moisture. "I love you, hon," he started. "I've been thinking I'm not so nice sometimes. I'm sorry. I worry about you and all you have to do, but I think this part is almost done."

Oh, God, I thought as my stomach took a turn. *What's he getting at?* Anxiety bound me at my seams.

Uncertainty had been our foe. At this stage of Jim's illness, however, our future reality was coming into clear focus. When he started to talk, I realized he used the quiet time to bring forth memories. He formulated what he wanted to say to me. His words were simple and pure. I didn't speak much; I mostly listened to all the good and even the not so good, such as our divorce. "We wasted three years," he said.

"Yes, but we did fix what was broken," I said.

"I love the kids with my whole heart. We did good, didn't we? I'm so happy to be their dad. I love those kids." He couldn't say it enough.

He commented on Sherry and George's happiness. "I'm happy she has George. He's a man who will always take care of her, and besides, he knows how to do things." We both chuckled at that.

"And Doug. I hope he finds a wife soon. Someone like you," he said.

As if etching it into his memory, he studied my face for a bit. Quietly and with deep emotion he told me, "Hon, I have great love for you. Always did, even way back when things weren't so good. My whole life I've loved you more than anything. Did I pass the test?"

"The test? If you're wondering if you were a good husband, well, there were a few moments," I said as I rolled my eyes and chuckled out loud. Changing to a serious tone, I told him he exceeded all expectations. "You gave me everything you promised and more."

"And, hon, I feel the same about being your wife. I hope I didn't let you down. Forty years, I am thankful for each and every one of them."

He continued. "I'm not giving up yet, but I've been thinking about when I die. For my funeral, do whatever makes you feel okay. Remember to play 'I'll Remember You.'"

Tears formed at the mention of the song.

He went on for another minute or so until his face dimmed a bit with remorse. "I wish I could have provided you more financial security for when I'm not here and you need help. I feel good there will be my pension and insurance for you, and equity in the house. I just wish there was more."

I started to weep. *My gosh, how I love this man.* I thought, *He is telling me good-bye. I don't want our life together to end!*

The rest of the evening was quiet, but with regards to matters of faith, I was in turmoil.

~ JOURNAL ~

After all the prayers I've said, Lord, and everyone else has said, is he going to die? Today I think he would need an actual miracle to heal. Matters of faith–Holy Spirit–devil–Job–St. Jude–healing–forgiveness and hope. Do I have real faith? Why do I keep praying for Jim to be healed if

I don't have real faith? I'm back to the destiny question. If God created us for a purpose, and then our purpose is fulfilled, did he set the actual date of death? If so, then why pray for a cure and try to change the date? I've heard so many stories about people who've said they are healed by the power of prayer. The way Jim is now, I have a feeling all the prayers will have been for naught. Sorry for my doubts, just exhausted, Lord. Good night.

Our talk earlier was not the end of our intimacy that day. Held in the bounds of our bed that evening, our hands met and our fingers entwined. It didn't seem possible, but our love had elevated to a higher level. I could feel it! Love swirled around, and around, as if to explode in an intense rapture that would shatter the ceiling as it rose to the stars.

I sighed with elation about our love. An old man sighed back at me. I thought how his body, in part, had been reduced to an almost toddler-like existence; the bowels, the bladder, feeding him early on after the stroke, bathing, dressing, walking and everything else, but on this day, God granted him the ability to communicate his thoughts with me. *Dear, Lord, what a blessing!*

45
SHERRY AND PENNY

I hurried to the door when Sherry and Penny pulled in. Jim's left eye showed purpura, and he had aged more and more rapidly since she last saw him. "Leave your shock outside. Your dad does not look good."

It was incredible. From the moment the girls arrived, my life got easier. Peanut butter chicken never tasted so good, and Jim's Father's Day held some relaxation time for me, with a glass of wine with the girls followed by beef tips over noodles. Yum! It felt like Mother's Day! Their activities over the course of the week were centered on making Jim happy and comfortable, and making my life easier.

Toward the end of the week, I had dinner with the Hood ladies. It felt good to get out, but my mind was on Jim that evening. I was barely able to participate in conversation and was able to only muster a half-hearted nod with my dear friends who desperately tried to cheer me up. I couldn't get over how he had looked in the morning. *Not right. Weird,* I thought.

When I got him ready for bed I asked, "What's wrong?"

He said, "I am trying to breathe." I also noticed his elephant size ankles. I suggested we go to the hospital. He refused.

The next day Sherry and Penny left. It would be the last time Sherry and Jim would have so much fun bantering about music and history. Jim was so incredibly sad she left. Once again, I marveled at the great compassion and love of my children, and Penny as well. That evening I wrote in my journal.

~ JOURNAL ~

Hi, dear Jesus, I'm very nervous. I know if I have faith, I shouldn't be nervous. Jim seems so sluggish and his breathing is heavy, and his legs are so swollen. I pray that you please grant us a miracle. I feel, Lord, that I've been in mourning. I miss the cognitive parts of Jim that have left. I also miss our everyday life activities, Jim working on projects, sitting in the screened room, our conversations together, going on vacation and everything else.

And, I still wonder "why?" Again not "why Jim" or "why me," but "why, for what reason does he have to suffer?"

I have a stomachache.

Thanks again for listening to me, Lord. Love you! Marie

&

Nights were more troubled and strenuous. Bathroom and comfort issues escalated, and dreaded thoughts hammered at my anxiety as I wondered if he was dying right next to me. I once again urged him to consider going to the hospital, but he refused. "When I'm ready to go to the hospital, I'll tell you. Come and hold my hand."

&

It was Doug's birthday and I had life and death on my mind all day—Doug's actual birth, and Jim's deteriorating condition. Dr. Primary Care was on the agenda for the next day. It couldn't come fast enough. Yet, on that particular day, Jim endeavored to remain upbeat.

"That looks good," he said, smiling, as he watched a cooking show. "When I'm better and walking, I'm going to start to cook. I'm going to make a biscuit and egg dish."

I almost choked on my laugh. He never cooked, except to use the grill. I reminded him of that. His smile flattened a bit. "I guess I'll need your help," he quipped, "at least in the beginning."

❧

I started the morning pleading to God that Dr. Primary Care would realize the extent of Jim's swelling and wheezing and put him in the hospital. Instead, he said, "The fluid retention and wheezing are likely the result of heart failure. I'm going to increase his Lasix and he needs to see Dr. Cardiologist."

When he told me he'd merely increase his Lasix and we had to wait to see the cardiologist, I started to cry. Drained mentally, physically, and emotionally, I felt like we were once again put on delay. I thought, *Doesn't he realize this is Jim's life we are talking about*. We don't have much time to get this straightened out. I could barely breathe.

Noting my distress, Dr. Primary Care advised, "You need to see me so we can talk." Although he was a good doctor, all I could think about was Jim and I wanted the doctor to shut up and go away if he couldn't help Jim. At that point I couldn't even talk, not to Jim, not to the doctor, or God. No one could help. No one could give me a reason why Jim had to suffer. Distraught, I felt alone, and I felt angry.

❧

Blood, blood, hemorrhoids! Wet farts! That's how the next day proceeded. Finally, it was time to get Jim ready for the night, but before I did that I asked him if he wanted to go to the hospital. "No."

"Are you sure?"

"I'm sure."

It made no sense to aggravate him and keep asking, so I got him ready. I took him to the bathroom, put a new Depends on, hooked up the catheter, put a clean undershirt on and got my pajamas on as well. Jim's sister called. She was upset and nervous, and became more nervous when I told her I had to hang up because Jim called from the bedroom.

"Hon, would you put my socks, shoes, and pants on? I want to breathe. It's time to go to the hospital."

Hastily, I put his socks and pants on. Underneath it all, I was hysterical and shakiness took over. I knew I needed help. I called Beth and Don. They responded immediately.

Cardizem was prescribed. They determined there was fluid on the right lung, his heart was enlarged, and they said he had something called atrial fibrillation. The decision was made to admit Jim to the critical care unit. Beth and Don left for home.

We said a few prayers from the Marine Corps prayer book as we waited for them to move him and I wrote in my journal.

~ JOURNAL ~

They did an X-ray, CT scan and EKG. Will any of these tests give us any "good" news? It's very cold in this room. I'm glad I thought to bring a sweatshirt. I have a blanket on my feet and they are still cold.

Lord, I hate to beg, but could you please grant Jim a miracle? I think that's the only way out of this mess.

A new day has crept up on us. It's 1:49 a.m. and the nurse told us they will be moving Jim to room 342. He wants me to stay with him. "Honey, I'll stay with you until you are settled," I said.

The clock read 3:58 a.m. when I pulled into the driveway. I went to bed and although I thought I could not do it, I pushed out of bed at 7:45, got ready, and headed to the hospital. When I arrived, Michelle was there. A true blessing.

Jim looked much better than I expected and seemed comfortable. However, the nurse informed us that the thoracentesis to remove the fluid from around his lungs was postponed. His blood pressure was too low, 61/54, and the procedure risked a blood pressure drop. A parade of doctors came by: a cardiologist, someone sitting in for Dr. Primary Care, and Dr. Oncologist/Hematologist.

When I left for home that evening, I was thankful for his care and wondered what the next day would bring.

※

Although I thought I slept fairly well, I woke up feeling exhausted and worn out. The weird sensation I was trying to overcome as I drove to the hospital told me something was happening, to buck up, and be prepared for the day.

I arrived at the hospital at about 10:00 and went straight to Jim's room. All hell seemed to be breaking loose. His blood pressure dropped to 54/49, his heart rate went to 169, and he started to take on a bit of a bluish cast. The doctor told us he was in end-stage heart failure and they were not equipped to handle Jim's heart needs due to the amyloidosis and stroke. An ambulance was being dispatched for conveyance to the hospital where he had his valve surgery.

I called the kids and told them, "I think your dad is dying."

They both said, "I'm on my way."

46
BACK TO CVICU

Jim was more or less stabilized and comfortably situated in the ambulance, along with two paramedics and a nurse who worked together as a well-rehearsed team. I was not comfortable, however, as I buckled myself in the passenger seat. I was a basket case, panicked and very jittery, as I listened to the EMTs consider the most expeditious route.

We headed out to the interstate. The ambulance hurtled up the left lane, lights flashing and sirens blaring. Drivers didn't seem to know what to do when they realized we were behind or coming up alongside them. Some moved to the far right, some cut off other drivers while trying to do so, and some didn't seem to hear or see us at all. I prayed, *Oh, please God, please don't let us have an accident.*

We exited the interstate at the center of downtown. Not two minutes after my plea to God to spare us from an accident, the EMT in the back shouted out, "There is someone coming up on us fast! Brace yourselves! We're going to get hit!"

BOOM! The screech of tires and the crunch of metal on metal is something no one wants to experience, especially when you're in an ambulance and your beloved may be dying. I screamed back to Jim, "Are you okay?" He was asking me the same question, as were the EMTs. The force of impact threw one of the EMTs from one side of the ambulance to the other. He flew over Jim and hit his body on the other side of the ambulance. My glasses and Bluetooth were projectiles found after a search of the cab. My seat belt restricted movement forward and anchored my lap and shoulders in place. I don't remember how I was freed from its clutches. When I was able, I tried the door's handle. I couldn't leave. My door had taken the brunt of the impact; the front of an old Cadillac had its nose-end smashed square into my door. It was impossible to get out that way. I looked down at its inhabitant. He was on his phone and glanced up. I'll never forget his face. I gave him a look I hope he never forgets.

Another ambulance was dispatched. The hot sun pressed down on us as the ambulance was positioned in the middle of the road on the sweltering asphalt. For some reason I decided to call Nancy. When we connected, an unintelligible rapid fire "bah-bah-bah-bah-bah" was all that came from my mouth. I completely unraveled, and hung up.

While we waited, a man who seemed to appear out of nowhere told me he had it all on tape. Too shaken to respond, I later learned it was on the evening news.

"You fly pretty good for a big guy. The last thing I saw going over me were your shoes!" I was a complete basket case and Jim was being a comedian! With great concern, the nurse continued to attend to Jim and followed him into the second ambulance.

The police escorted us to the hospital. When we arrived, I felt light-headed and shaky in the literal sense. I wanted to get my vitals checked. As they whisked Jim to CVICU, I said to him, "I love you. I'll see you in a little bit." I was put into a wheelchair, told to put my head down between my knees, and away we went.

All I wanted was to be sure I wasn't in shock and my vitals checked out okay. The doctor quizzed me about what happened. I told him that although I was restrained, I felt like my body had been thrown around. "Please hurry, I need to get to my husband. He may be dying." He checked me over and said all seemed fine. With that, I was on my way to Jim's room.

Jim offered up a smile when he saw me. My heart leapt with joy. We were happy to see each other in one piece, and the anxiety generated in the hubbub earlier had started to die down.

How important were all the monitor numbers and lines? I had a vague idea, but mainly I watched for sudden changes. Based on this, I thought Jim seemed okay, but I needed to know. Out in the hallway I searched for a nurse. No one was nearby. Forced to wait for someone to come by or pop in, I soothed myself, taking comfort in the numbers on the screen that seemed fairly "normal." I was finally able to catch a nurse. I learned that in addition to all his regular medication, he was now on milrinone, norepinephrine, heparin and 5% dextrose. He had converted from atrial fibrillation to sinus rhythm.

Although he was in and out of sinus rhythm, by the time the kids arrived at about 9:00 p.m., Jim was almost jovial. His wit was in top form and he was smiling. Beth, who had visited earlier, said he was "quite the charmer." I almost felt bad that the kids had rushed to get to the hospital, yet earlier in the day the words "end-stage heart failure" and his blue color, to me, indicated that he was dying. The trauma of the day sharply contrasted with the family time we shared that evening. The four of us ended the day with several laughs while watching Jay Leno. On the way home, Doug said, "Dad probably had a good day. He wasn't in the house, or therapy, and something exciting happened."

Hmmm, I thought. *Doug is probably right.*

෪

The next morning, I woke up stiff and sore. Bruises colored my right side, and the tingling on the right side of my head was scary. I debated all day whether I needed to get this all checked out, but never did.

We arrived at 10:45 a.m. Jim had been "dosed up" a bit, and there was something in his mouth that looked very uncomfortable. We learned they were doing something called TEE (transesophageal echocardiography) to look at his heart structure and function.

At 1:00 p.m. they came to do the thoracentesis. Jim was positioned to sit on the edge of the bed. His hospital table with a pillow was set in front of him. A hollow needle was inserted between some lower ribs, and a quart and a half of fluid was extracted. He finally was able to breathe better.

The next day we were informed that Jim seemed to have settled into sinus rhythm. There was talk about weaning him off the milrinone overnight. He would then be transferred to cardiac step-down. Good news, yet I had bad vibes all day long.

I pushed myself to shed the same feeling of dread I had a few days earlier when I drove up Goose Creek to the hospital. The frightful sensation of being off kilter and my head feeling as if it had separated from my body made me think I might black out. It was a calamitous day. *Is another in store? One day at a time, Marie, I told myself. Be restful with the kids.*

When we arrived the next day, the nurse hastily apprised us of Jim's overnight condition. They were not able to take him off the drip that was supporting his blood pressure, which meant he'd spend another day in CVICU. Something else we noticed. His mood had deteriorated, and fast. Even with the kids, he was not responsive. I felt he gave up.

~ JOURNAL ~

Dear Jesus, please heal my Jim. Can we get a miracle? Thank you for our beautiful children who are here trying to cheer him up. Thank you for listening!

Later that day, Paul and Mark stopped by. They made him laugh! Thank you, Lord!

On the way to the hospital the next morning I prayed all the usual prayers. I wondered if it would be the day he'd go to cardiac step-down. I had hoped he'd be in the laughing mood he was with Paul and Mark the previous day, but no. He seemed much worse! I would describe him as flat, devoid of feeling and emotion.

Jim also took a negative posture to potassium and anyone who encouraged him to take it. A sour cringe pinched his face, as the potassium tasted awful. "Potassium face," Sherry teased. He didn't like her teasing. He nailed her hard with a "don't you dare tease me about this" look.

The "Heart Failure Unit" would be Jim's next home. Although his blood pressure spiked during the day and dropped at night, and he still had a propensity to slip in and out of A-Fib, a nurse came to tell us he would soon be moved to the sixth or seventh floor.

Before they headed home, the kids wanted to see Jim laugh. Numerous times Jim and Doug rolled in laughter playing with the toy fart pooter machine. Doug had it hidden in his pocket and let it rip. We all had our laughs, but Jim would not have it, not one bit. He had separated himself from humor.

☙

I jumped up suddenly; the harsh nighttime rings coming from the kitchen set my heart racing. It was 1:50 a.m. The nurse from CVICU identified herself and put Jim on the phone. "Hon, I don't want you to lose me. I'm in room 7013."

"Oh, okay. I'll find you in room 7013 tomorrow. I love you."

"Love you too."

The kids left at 5:15. I got ready and went to the hospital.

☙

Claustrophobia hit as soon as I got off the elevator on the seventh floor. The low ceilings and small rooms had an unfriendly and suffocating feel.

I asked the nurse, "What's going on?"

"His heart rate is low, mostly in the upper 40s, and his blood pressure has been low. They also took him off of Lasix." I wondered why. I thought I'd wait for a doctor to answer that question.

A dietician stopped by. She was concerned because Jim wasn't eating anything, and commented, "Mr. Malicki will have to be on a salt-free diet." Her suggestion was that in my "spare time" I go to Kroger and research food for their salt content. *Yeah right, in my spare time,* I thought. *These people don't have a clue."*

Jim was getting progressively antsy. "Get me to the bathroom," he said. I wasn't able to do that, but in an attempt to preserve some of his dignity, so he wouldn't have to use a bedpan, I called for a bedside commode. He moaned the whole time it took for it to arrive. He was placed on it and sat there for a long time. Eventually he lost the urge and started to complain that his leg was cramping. He settled back into bed with oxygen. My thought was daunting, *How will I ever handle a walker, wheelchair, oxygen and catheter. Will he need to go to a nursing home after-all? Lord, I can hardly stand to think about this. Can I do this? It hurts to pray and think about this!*

As if to tell me, "You need to pray," Jim's minister friend from Saturn stopped by, and then the minister from Michelle's church. Both visits were appreciated and ended in prayer.

Afterward, I prayed on and on like I always did. I thanked Jesus for Sherry and Doug's safe return home and once again asked for that elusive miracle.

∞

When I next saw Jim, he was very agitated. I couldn't understand him. His eyes seemed to be popping out. He scratched and scratched and pulled at his gown unaware I was even talking to him. A nausea pan was on the floor. I found out they gave him Phenergan. Along with everything else, nausea plagued him.

He asked for the pan, then he threw it on the floor. I gave it to him; he didn't want it. I was one more pan throw away from going crazy! In the face of what was happening I bawled. Out loud with raw emotion I called out, *Lord, help him.* Overwrought, I didn't care who heard me.

It was the weekend before the 4th of July and it seemed there was no one to get any answers from. The "teenage" doctors covering over the holiday had little experience and I don't believe ever heard of amyloidosis. My frustration was beyond blowing up. One doctor said they needed to pull more fluids off of Jim, the other one said everything was "balanced." The female teenage doctor told me he would never get use of his leg. I knew she was right, but in the midst of what was going on, her comment was not what I wanted to hear. I let her know it. She started to cry. Then I felt more terrible. I thought, *Oh my gosh! What's wrong with* me? I apologized and so did she. I guess we both learned something that day.

∞

JULY 2nd, 2007

~ JOURNAL ~
I am still sooooooo sore on my right side, bottom of rib cage. Do I need to get this checked out? It's been almost a week now. I'll give it another day or two!

When I arrived at the hospital at 10:45 Jim was not in the room; the bed was stripped. I took a deep breath and sat in the chair next to his bed. *Surely*, I thought, *they would have called me if something was terribly wrong*. I stared at the bare bed. It made me shudder and amplified my fear of Jim dying, of him not being there with me. As hard and completely exhausting as caregiving was, I wasn't ready to set foot on the other side of Jim's life.

Caught off guard in my gloom, a nurse walked in. She wanted to warn me about his condition. She said, "Mr. Malicki could not eat again and he has a lot of nausea. They took him for an ultrasound. He seems to be in a lot of pain and he's swollen. He'll be brought back soon."

Lost in my thoughts, I found myself in the hallway outside his door. It seemed unusually quiet, and the smell was starting to get to me. That recycled air smell that all hospitals seem to have rubbed at my nose, the same smell that made me feel contaminated and wanting to strip when I got home. My clothes went directly into the washer. *Ugh*, I thought, *I could puke smelling this*. I caught a glimpse of him being wheeled back, my heart breaking for him. As he was being helped into the bed I blanched when I saw his swollen left wrist. It was another thing piled on top of everything else! *Fool yourself if you will, Marie, but he is dying. God, am I right, is he dying? Please, please ease his suffering.*

He winced in pain, *ihm, ihm*, and recoiled when I wanted to comfort him. "God, get me something for pain," he cried. I had watched my dad with peritonitis and because Jim couldn't have a bowel movement, I asked if that could be what was causing his pain. They told me they thought it might be a buildup of fluid around the liver and lack of blood flow in it. He finally got a Lortab.

~ JOURNAL ~

Jim asked me for the pan "50" times today and never needed it. He thinks he needs to throw up.

At about 4:00, Jim sniggered and said, "Go and see the sheriff for pain drugs." With that comment, I realized how much he caught when he did all that television watching over the last couple of months.

A few months earlier the sheriff had been arrested for illegally obtaining prescription pain drugs prior to his arrest.

At 4:40 Jim said, "The pain is not so bad right now." Yet he kept going "*ihm, ihm, ihm,*" basically the same sound I made when I was tired.

At 4:49, I recorded in my journal that I thought he was in a lot of pain and prayed, *Dear, Jesus, please ease his suffering!*

The two young doctors came in. He told them the pain keeps getting worse. They talked about morphine, but first decided to take him down for an abdominal X-ray. Results: The enzymes in the liver and pancreas are okay.

~ JOURNAL ~

Tom the "nurse" (a real jerk–who has been bothering me all day) laughed his goofy laugh and complained about someone sending Jose for sandwiches for the "caretaker" meeting. Tom wears red Crocs and has been making all kinds of weird and complaining remarks all day. He gave Jim a dose and a half of the nausea medicine. After Jim dropped the second pill, I went to the desk to ask about getting a replacement. It was then I found out he was only supposed to get one pill to begin with.

For months it was our way of life. Wait, wait, wait for test results. Finally, at 10:50 p.m. they told me Jim's pain is from stool back-up. The doctor seemed nervous. All day I asked, "Are you sure he doesn't have peritonitis?"

Paul and Jewell had been with us all evening. "*Ihm, ihm, ihm,*" continued the whole time. Although the three of us took turns rubbing Jim's back, it seemed he only vaguely knew they were there. He wanted up; he wanted down. He wanted his back rubbed.

Exhausted, we arrived at Paul and Jewell's at 1:00 a.m. I got in my car and headed home. Suddenly, about halfway there, a dreadful feeling of helplessness stormed over me. My heart raced, I couldn't catch a full breath and I became light-headed. Panicky, I stopped on the side of the road to gain control of myself. I recognized it for what it was and finally was able to talk myself through it. Broken and fragile, I made my way home, cursing Jim all the way for having put the dark window tint on my car windows. I had to drive with my windows open to see. Exhausted, I barely got my clothes off and fell into bed.

At 7:30 a.m. on July 3rd I talked to Jim's nurse, who reported that during the night he had two bowel movements and the upper right quadrant pain was gone. When I saw Jim, he said, "Bullshit! I had pain all night." He also threw up three times, mostly liquid. They were planning to take him down for a CT scan and to do blood work. His white blood count went up overnight from 16,000 to 29,000, probably indicative of an infection. *God, please don't let there be anything else!*

When they took Jim down for the scan I decided to go outside for a walk. I needed a place to sit. I had plenty of questions for God and wanted answers. Instead, I called Nancy Moody and started bawling. I felt the weight of the last months crashing down on me. I told her I'm tired of Jim hurting. I also called Sherry. I told her, "Your dad is dying."

Around noon he started asking for ice chips. On and off, I gave him ice chips until 2:00, at which time we both took a little nap.

Three hematologists came in to talk. They felt Jim had amyloid in the liver. It was swollen. A comment from one of the doctors, "I believe amyloid is rampant and there is no reversing the damage that has been done to his organs. The plan is to start chemo in 24 to 36 hours in an effort to contain it."

After they left, I asked Jim what he thought. His eyes were closed the whole time they were with us. I wondered if he had listened. He whispered, "I think that soon, I will be a dead man."

"Do you want more chemo?" I asked.

"Yes. I'll try."

Lord, all this is hard to swallow and comprehend. Jim is honorable and strong. I am so proud of my Jim. He certainly is stronger than I am. Love you, Lord. A miracle would be wonderful!

47
DYING

Patriotism, flags, fireworks, hot dogs, ice cream—America was celebrating. It was the 4th of July. We would not be doing what most people do on the 4th. No parades, no picnic, or fireworks for us. Except that I was grateful for Jim's love and for the kids, I felt we had nothing to celebrate that day.

Before I left for the hospital, I sat for a while with a cup of coffee and gazed out into our backyard piece of heaven. There were ten deer moving about near the tree line. *How peaceful it is back there*, I thought. *Dear Jesus, without a miracle, Jim will not live to see this again.* I got up and walked away.

I arrived at 10:30 and was informed that Jim was going to get frozen plasma. I was unsure why, even after they explained it to me. I couldn't concentrate. I believe it had something to do with his blood being too thin.

A doctor came by and told us Jim was not strong enough for another round of chemo. His white blood count was up to 39,000, and they were wondering if he had an underlying infection.

༄

Physical therapy came by. They moved his legs. He kept his eyes closed the whole time. "*Ihm, ihm, ihm.*"

There was a lot of fluid on the right lung, and left as well, and collapsed on the bottom. His belly was full of fluids. They wanted to get another sample.

I noticed that he peed very little and his legs were terribly swollen.

The pulsing *whoop, whoop, whoop,* of helicopters overhead as they raced to pick up trauma victims and whisk the injured or sick back to the hospital's trauma center was eye opening. So many injured or deathly sick. I wondered,

Are they fireworks accidents? Driving accidents? Boating accidents? Heart attacks? Strokes? The helicopter traffic was almost non-stop. All those families getting bad news. *Lord, spare the helicopter victims and their families from agony.*

It was late when I got home, and it was terribly quiet. Dog tired, I plopped into the recliner. The light was on in the kitchen, but I left it, too tired to get up or move or think. The silence haunted me as I sat numb, unable to even ask God for a miracle. Sometime later, Jim's sister called. She could barely speak and said, "If something happens, can Linda come with me to the funeral?"

ಸಿ

July 5th, 2007

More than harsh is the abuse to the heart when a phone rings at 12:19 a.m. The rings sent a shock wave through me. I buttressed myself against the cupboard. *Lord, please tell me he didn't die alone.*

Jim was back in CVICU. His blood pressure was dropping and was too low. At that moment, it was 55 over 30. "Things are progressively getting worse. We think you might want to get to the hospital." Between my quivers and distress, I called Mark and Michelle, my stabilizing force. They were on their way.

In the six months since Jim's surgery I had prayed for a miracle. By this time, however, I had become cynical of miracles and considered that the miracle, if there was to be one, was that he would still be living when I got there. He was alive, and I thanked God. I learned that although he was unable to put out urine, there was a slight improvement in his vitals.

Mark and Michelle stayed with me until 3:20 a.m. The *"ihm, ihm, ihm"* was louder. I went to talk to him, but he didn't seem to hear. I pushed the recliner closer to his bed and took his huge swollen hand. *Ohhhh his hands I bemoaned. His beautiful, precious hands!* I sat quiet for a while until he seemed to come around a little. I started to speak softly as I expressed my love and thanks for his love for me. Repeating my words from a few weeks earlier, I coursed the highlights of our life together, especially about the kids. I wanted to tell him there was a chance for a miracle, but I didn't. I knew better. When I found myself repeating my words over and over, I grabbed his Marine Corps prayer book and read from it. He seemed to draw comfort from the prayers.

The clock turned 5:00 a.m. Two nurses came in to put a new IV needle in Jim's hand. He kept moaning, "*ihm, ihm, ihm.*" Louder than he spoke in days he said, "Get me out of here."

I whispered, "It's okay."

He said, "No it's not."

When they left, he started to complain about his lips and mouth being dry. They were horribly cracked and blue in color. I offered sips of water and a wet sponge stick. He refused both.

Dear Jesus, please let his suffering end!

6:40 A.M

~ JOURNAL ~

Early morning drives to Wisconsin and Illinois. It's about the time we would get to Lake Barkley. It's always misty there. Together 40 years in August. Married 39 years. We won't make 40. Why does my stomach have to act up now? What time should I call the kids? William is a good nurse. All business.

Later in the day, Jim received Lasix. He peed a little, but it was red and he murmured, "Burn, burn."

A doctor came in to talk. He suggested they do another thoracentesis to relieve pressure in order to make him more comfortable. I agreed; anything to make him more comfortable.

Once again Jim was set at the side of the bed with his head on a pillow on the hospital table. They started the procedure. I bawled the whole time as I cupped his hands. The "*ihm, ihm, ihm's*" got louder. My heart bulged and caught in my throat. They removed two liters from the right and 600cc from the left. Unfortunately, it didn't seem to help much. I once again questioned my decision to let them do this.

Mark and Michelle came later in the day. It was always a relief to get that hug and love they easily extended.

☙

It was getting time for them to leave, but instead of Michelle heading out the door with Mark, she insisted she was going to stay. Before I could ponder her statement, Michelle left the room to look for an extra recliner to be rolled into the room so we both had a place to "sleep." I was gripped in fear and she was determined to help give me rest and peace. I witnessed great love through her actions that night. Although they said Jim could only be minimally aroused, I was up and down, especially when I thought he might be aroused enough to hear me or sense my hand holding his. When I thought he couldn't hear me, I would return to curl into my recliner, tuck my chin into the blanket and pray.

My vantage point from the recliner, gave me a good view to the other side of the room. I searched for a vision of his angel, but as usual, I didn't see him. However, what was as real to me as the angel was to Jim, as if they were in a shadow, was Jesus as he stood and gazed at Jim from the foot of the bed, and Joseph and Mary as they stood by the cabinet. Over and over, my head chanted, *Jesus, Mary, Joseph*; all the while Jim chanted "*ihm, ihm, ihm.*"

☙

Once again, we were at another day. It was July 6th, early morning, and the doctors were on their rounds. There was a din of voices outside his room. I tried to decipher what they were saying. When I saw them laugh, however, I became angry. Even though Jim could no longer communicate or see or hear them, I thought it was distasteful. "How can they laugh when Jim may be dying?" The laughs stopped when they walked into the room. They became serious. One told me his kidneys no longer functioned, another told me his liver was enlarged, and we already knew he had a woody heart, heart valve disease, sepsis, had systemic amyloidosis and suffered from the enormous effects of a stroke, and he had been more and more unresponsive.

"Mr. Malicki's prognosis is extremely poor. His kidneys have already failed, and his other organs are failing quickly. It appears the amyloidosis has won out. The family might want to consider what Mr. Malicki's wishes are for end of life. We'll leave you to your thoughts. If you have any questions, please ask, or you can always speak with Mr. Malicki's nurse."

I dreaded those words. The enormity of them was all before me. I had to steel myself for what I needed to consider. How did we get here so fast? As surreal as it seemed, it was real. I thought and thought and prayed. Eventually, what solace I could take was in our love, so real and strong, and that he was relying on me to carry out his final wishes as outlined in his living will. When I made my decision, to take him off of life support, I called the kids to ask their thoughts. We didn't need to talk long. They both said, "Mom, do what you think is right. We're on our way."

It wasn't long until a hematologist came to speak to me. "Would you consider an autopsy?" he asked. Without a moment's hesitation I told him "No. When he dies there will be no more digging, probing, or poking."

Cher and George were on the road by 7:00, and Doug was able to catch a flight that arrived about 10:00.

Beth stopped by on her way to work with Panera sweets. She had been to Mass to pray for Jim, and I saw her tears as she stopped by his bed.

In the meantime, Mark and Michelle's granddaughter came to pick up Michelle. There were tears in everyone's eyes.

Doug arrived with one of his best friends. I was happy he had that support. Doug then asked if he could have alone time with his dad. Afterward, I once again asked Doug if he was okay with the decision to take him off all medical support. We discussed the various issues and he said, "Okay."

A nurse tried to wake Jim. It was hard. I stared at his lips. They were horribly dry and cracked, they were bleeding and bluish. I wet a sponge and put it to his lips. He did not respond.

I am beside myself! I think, this cannot be happening, not to my Jim. Breathe, breathe! I cry, I shake, then I become numb.

My pulse was pounding in my neck. I couldn't swallow. But it was time. At 12:52, I told the nurse to proceed to comfort care only. I closed my eyes. *Dear Jesus, I pray I am doing the right thing. My dear, dear Jim, I love you with my whole heart.*

Jim's friend stopped by. He stayed for a while, but I had to ask him to leave. I only wanted family there. As time went on, his breathing changed.

It started to take a long time between breaths.

A breath—then wait—I thought he died.
A breath—then wait—I thought he died.
A breath—then wait—I thought he died, and he did.

At 6:20, my dear son-in-law said, "Mom, Dad has died. There will be no more breaths."

48
FUNERALS

No miracle. How could that be? I had desperately prayed for one. In its absence, except for a few moments here or there, I practiced avoidance and denial. My head refused to accept that Jim had died. I held to the thought I'd see him again. We'd kiss and talk about all we had been through together.

I arranged for a memorial service near our Tennessee home, and for what I term his "real" funeral in Wisconsin.

After the arrangements were made, we went to the mall. I had lost nearly 20 pounds and it seemed all of us needed something to wear at the funeral; a tie, shoes, whatever. Because we were shopping, the day didn't feel much different than any other. Jim hated shopping, so it seemed normal he was not with us at the mall.

Jim's body was at the crematorium when the Tennessee memorial took place. We wouldn't get his cremains until the next day right before we would leave for Wisconsin. The memorial service was simple and filled with prayers, beautiful singing by our friend, Darrell, and wonderful words of comfort which generally blew through my ears. I had a hard time listening to people, and I don't remember where my head was through most of it. However, one thing I remember is Elvis singing "I'll Remember You." My mind took me to our kitchen. We were dancing, and it became painful to stifle the tears.

On July 10th, we were on the road. It was our last ride together as a whole family. We packed up our new funeral clothes, death certificates, cremation certificate, and Jim's cremains. The cremains were respectfully placed in the back of my son-in-law's SUV. Still in avoidance mode, when I thought about his cremains in the back of the SUV, I brushed it aside. Too unreal! I couldn't comprehend Jim was traveling with us, relegated to a safe place in the back, away from his usual driver or passenger front row seat.

We met the director at the funeral home my family had used for generations. The arrangements for my honey's funeral were completed.

☙

The day of his funeral dawned brilliant, just like it had on our wedding day thirty-nine years earlier. It was different, however. It was not the beginning of our story together, but the end. Blessings of the celestial spun off the sun-brightened sanctuary and the table where Jim's ashes were placed. A breeze swirled in the air from the open windows, reminding me of our wedding day. As I gazed at the altar of the Blessed Virgin, I thought the prophecy of that day thirty-nine years earlier had been fulfilled.

I greeted many people that day, many who I no longer recognized or whose names I had forgotten. Numerous people from both our high school classes were there, AC Spark Plug, where Jim had worked, as well as family and friends.

When I glanced around at the crowd, I was drawn to a picture of Jim that I had not noticed earlier. I excused myself from the well-wishers. It was a blown-up photo of when Jim was still a band member. Taken aback, I was reminded of how fairytale handsome he was, contrasted to the amyloidosis look that aged him rapidly during the last months of his life. Winnie had dropped it off, and she captioned the picture with the following:

> **At a stop sign, at 7:30 in the morning,**
> **I saw something that only happens in the movies.**
> **Two people met "AND I WAS THAT LITTLE BIRD ON THE WIRE"**
> **and I just couldn't believe my eyes. They looked at each other,**
> **they both had a silly smile, eyes locked, and the rest is history.**
> **I think the Lord had his eye on these two.**

The clock ticked 10:55; the picture heightened my awareness of what was about to take place, and it made my heart race. When the clock ticked 11:00, my heart, his from the first moment we met, was breaking. Utter sadness set in.

This would be the last time we would meet at St. Adalbert's. I had always thought that front pews at funerals are never a good place to be, and that's where I was, saying goodbye to my honey. *Oh, Lord, is this really real?* Protective of myself, I took my head to a different place. I remember thinking about my flowers at home and hoping they would not die while I was gone. I thought about the people who came to pay respect, and repeated *da, da, da, da* in my head to drown out the choir as it sang "Be Not Afraid" and "On Eagles Wings."

I also created an illusion that all would be good, that I'd awaken from this nightmare. As a result, the Mass was a blur. I kept thinking about being home. Delusional as I was, I just knew when I got there I'd awaken from this nightmare and all would be okay. I'd tell Jim about my nightmare and he would hug and kiss me and tell me he would never leave, that this death thing wasn't real.

Doug carried Jim's cremains down the aisle and we followed to the hearse, where they were placed for the ride to Holy Sepulcher Cemetery.

We squeezed into the small chapel for a short prayer vigil. It was when I heard the words, "We ask you to deliver the souls in purgatory..." that I bristled. Purgatory? The place those nuns told us we'd all spend time in when we died? And then Alcatraz came to mind. It was something I couldn't shake for a long, long time.

George knew of Jim's love for the Marine Corps and arranged for military honors. Stoically, I braced myself for the three round volley that would be fired and the inevitable playing of "Taps." Can anyone not shed tears at the playing of "Taps?" The flag detail then folded the flag into its tri-cornered readiness for presentation to me. "On behalf of a grateful nation…"

"Eternal rest grant onto them…" The prayer drilled into me as a kid now seemed absurd. How could it even be insinuated that Jim would not go straight to heaven? He was not the "poor, pitiful soul" the nuns taught us to pray for. Spiritual peace and Jim's ashes were both left at the cemetery. The prayer and the mention of Purgatory were the sparks that fueled an anger for God and the church for years to come. It was extremely exhausting.

෴

Two weeks later I arrived home a "widow." I still hate that word. No matter that during those two weeks I looked at housing in Milwaukee and near my daughter in Illinois, there was a denial that Jim was actually dead. I half expected him to be there and called out to him when I walked into the house. Silence. That's all there was. Silence! There was no one in sight.

I looked out at the yard. He didn't appear from the tree line. Afraid to check it out, I moseyed to his garage. He wasn't there either. Pure brutal grief took over. It was like nothing I had ever experienced. At the top of my lungs, I screamed "Son of a bitch! Son of a bitch! Where are you?" My anger with God was palpable, raw, and edgy. Nausea overcame me every time I thought of Jim and every time I thought of God. There were many, many screams of "Son of a bitch" and too many tears as I prepared myself to move.

Doug spent the holidays with me. There was no tree or decorations. We weren't in the mood, and packing for my move was the priority.

My son-in-law, George, arrived on January 12th. The movers arrived the next day, and there was a dinner with the Hood later in the evening. It had never occurred to me that those simple hellos in 1990 would later hold such an important place in our lives. We had shared life together in work, happiness, sadness, holidays, birthdays, car shows, graduations, weddings, and everything in between, and time with the Hood was especially significant during Jim's last year. I could not have done it without them. Measured by my heart, where I will carry them forever, there was no adequate way for me to express my love and thanks.

The closing on my house was scheduled for the next morning. George and I packed up the few things I had left and headed to the title company. As we pulled out of the driveway, it took everything I had to hold in the tears. I silently prayed Jim would follow me to Illinois.

EPILOGUE

LOVE

There was much I learned. Years away from it, with the luxury of time for deep thought, I've realized my caregiving days were the ones encased in the most profound human love I have experienced. I learned love in a more soulful, in-depth way. My intimacy with Jim was at its very deepest. The kindnesses and expressions of love from family and friends is what carried us through. My prayers were answered in the loving care of these most marvelous people.

FAITH

My faith values were established early in life, and I have been all over the place since then. I was raised to love God, but lost faith in high school. I loved God later in life, then developed great anger toward Him when Jim died. As with all true love relationships, the bond could not be entirely severed. Reconciliation with God brought with it the realization it was Jim's time. Although grief is chronic, I now talk to God about the life I am grateful for, and dwell on the imprint of the happy memories I carry.

CAREGIVING

Caregiving often calls us to lean into love we didn't know possible.

~Tia Walker

There's an astounding number of caregivers in the United States. When I take a walk through a neighborhood, I can't help but wonder which of the houses I'm passing have a full-time caregiver. Most of us are thrown into this undertaking without training, and sometimes suddenly. My days caregiving, were minuscule in comparison to what others go through. I don't know how those who have done it for years manage, as you have to take on so many roles in order to be successful. It is hard work and I felt tested every step of the way.

The caregiver's role as psychologist: Jim's declining health sullied his self-worth. I thought it my job to boost his esteem, to be his cheerleader. It was very draining. I wished I had the abilities of a psychologist.

The caregiver's role as life's transition specialist: We moved from critical care to a regular hospital room, to in-patient rehab, to home and out-patient rehab, and back to the hospital; each a new experience for both of us. Looking back, I wish I had asked more questions about available options for care and had reached further into the system.

The caregiver's role as crisis interventionist: I constantly needed to think ahead about the mechanics of every move we made in order to avoid a crisis that might injure us. A safe transfer from bed to wheelchair, wheelchair to toilet, or any advancement from one place to the next, was a commitment to strategy. I wished I was more muscular and quicker on my feet; someone who thought like his guardian angel.

The caregiver's role as pharmacist: To keep his meds organized and dispensed properly was daunting. Pharmaceutical intellect would have helped.

The caregiver's role as rehab therapist: To learn, encourage and help with exercises, movements and cognitive adeptness was challenging. Physical muscle was needed. Correctly reading and ascertaining Jim's ever-changing cognitive difficulties was arduous.

The caregiver's role as CNA: Toileting, bathing, dressing, feeding, mobility—these activities were all-consuming. CNAs are invaluable and, with an aging population, we will need more of them. It's distressing their pay is so pathetically low. I wished I had had their training.

I couldn't do it all myself; I don't believe any 24/7 caregiver can. The quality of Jim's care depended on the care given to me from those who held us close. Without it, I would not have made it to the other side.

As I gaze through the same window I did when I moved to my condo in Illinois, I notice the ground is covered with a thin layer of snow. My thoughts take me back to the time when I didn't know if I'd ever "feel the depths of hugs again," and if it would ever "feel like home." It took a long time, but hugs and home are real again.

Many of the things of life are still with me. The maroon leather recliner has been moved to my bedroom; the Chevelle resides in my garage, and the Marine Corps blanket still brings me comfort on a cold night.

For years the memories were too fresh to start this book, or to stay with it. Vacant focus held me captive. There are other things. I still limit the music I listen to. Songs and lyrics that used to give me a fuzzy feeling can still bring on a nauseating physiological effect. Some church songs do the same. I tend to avoid them when I can.

No one escapes heartache and deep suffering if you've dared to wholly love. To move forward beyond my loss, to sense the promise of life anew, I needed the encouragement, kindnesses, and most importantly the presence of friends and family. I thank them with all my heart.

And, Jim, if you're reading, OPLLO!

ACKNOWLEDGMENTS

I am eternally grateful to my children, Cheryl and Douglas, son-in-law George, and the newest member of our family, my daughter-in-law Olga. They have urged me on every step of the way. A special thank you goes out to Douglas for employing his sketching abilities in the creation of the cover.

Thanks to Sandra Colbert whose encouragement I could not do without. She read, reread, suggested, and helped me stay the course when I wanted to just set everything aside. Thank you also to JoAnn Ropel, my high school friend, who read the manuscript before edits. Her comments were most helpful.

I also want to thank the members of the In Print Professionals Writers organization, who early on, helped to persuade me to get my story out there.

Finally, my deepest gratitude goes to my beloved Jim. Knowing he would have not only supported, but championed this endeavor was key to bringing this book to fruition. I know he would be proud of me!

Made in the USA
Monee, IL
04 September 2022

12232830R00152